CM Russell

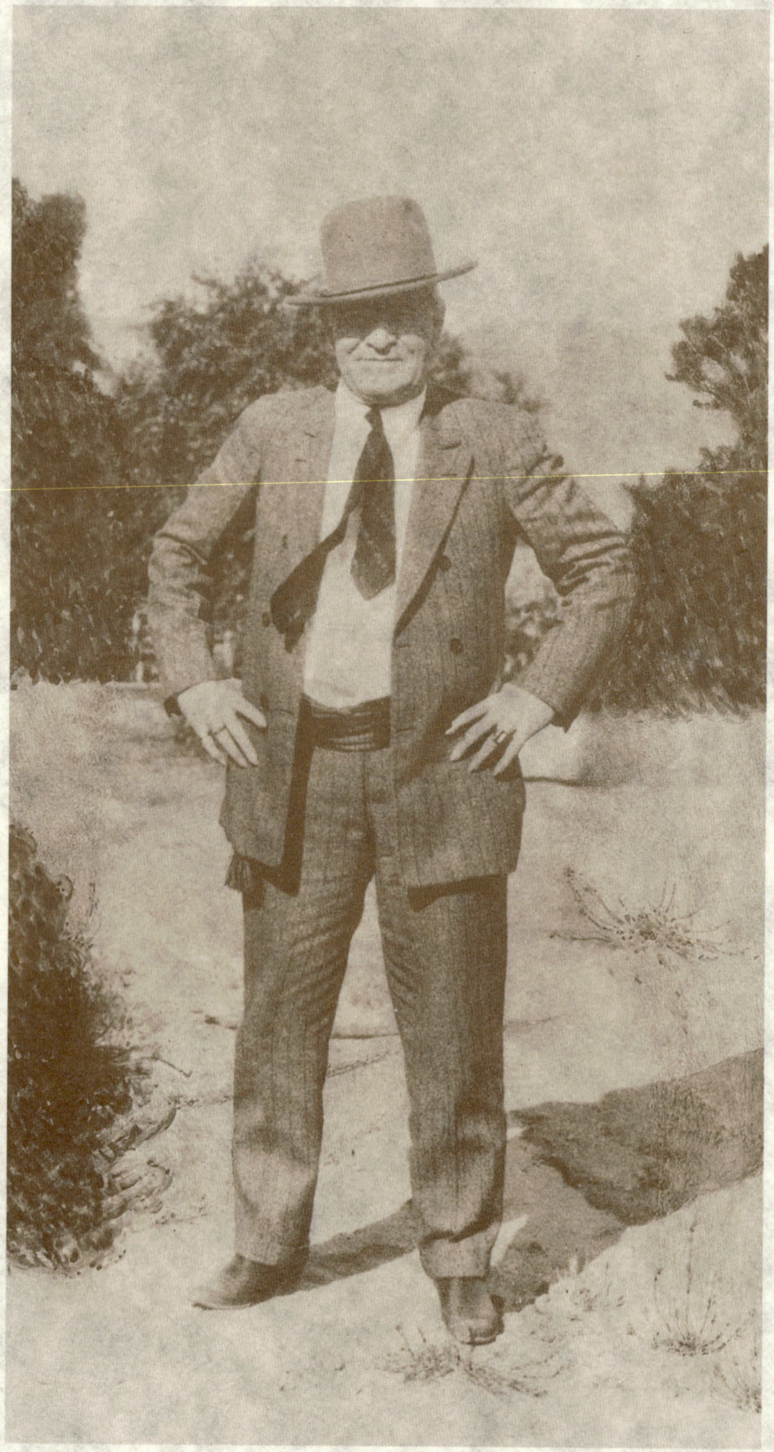

Charles M. Russell

The Artist in His Heyday
1903 - 1926

Gerald Peters Gallery

in association with

Mongerson - Wunderlich

Charles M. Russell: The Artist in His Heyday

August 18 - September 30, 1995
Gerald Peters Gallery
439 Camino del Monte Sol
Santa Fe, New Mexico 87504-0908
Telephone: 505.988.8961
Fax: 505.983.2481

Library of Congress Catalogue Card Number 95-061424
ISBN 0-935037-98-5

Exhibition and catalogue direction: Kellie Keto
Art and photography direction: Dan Morse
Design coordination: Jesse Hansell
Printing by Advanced Litho, Great Falls, Montana
This catalog was printed on Vintage Velvet Remarque a recycled paper.

cover: *At Rope's End,* 1909 (detail)

Contents

Acknowledgements

The realization of this exhibition and accompanying catalogue, Charles M. Russell, The Artist in His Heyday, is due to the cooperation, advice and expertise of numerous individuals. Brian Dippie, Professor of History at the University of Victoria, and Peter Hassrick, Director of the Buffalo Bill Historical Center, brought their considerable knowledge to the project with essays that impart discerning insights into Russell's life, art and philosophies. I am grateful to Rick Stewart for his cutorial guidance and whose comprehensive examination of Russell's sculpture, Charles M. Russell, Sculptor, served as an invaluable resource. From its inception, this has been a collaborative venture with Rudolf Wunderlich, whose connoisseurship and commitment to Russell's art I have benefited from for two decades. Lorne Render, Executive Director of the C.M. Russell Museum, offered me invaluable support in bringing this project to fruition.

This venture would not have been possible without the hard work and dedication of the Gerald Peters Gallery staff. My thanks to Baird Ryan for his assistance in the acquisition of these works; Kellie Keto for her tireless efforts coordinating the program, researching and documenting the collection; and to Dan Morse and Jesse Hansell for their sensitivity to the presentation of Russell's work. With any exhibition of this magnitude, there are innumerable tasks that require careful attention to detail. I would like to express my appreciation to Jodi Aeling for scheduling and loan arrangements, Mark Rivera and Lindsay Smith for preparing and installing the works, and Nina Hockersmith for research assistance.

In addition, there were many institutions that provided documentation and photographs, including the Amon Carter Museum, Buffalo Bill Historical Center, C.M. Russell Museum, Montana Historical Society, Museum of Western Art, Sid Richardson Collection of Western Art, The Snite Museum and Harry N. Abrams, Inc. Ultimately this exhibition was actualized through the generosity of lenders who ensure the appreciation and preservation of Russell's work to the American public.

Gerald Peters

Forward

Charles Russell, affectionately known as "the Cowboy Artist", was so dubbed because he painted the West within him, shaped by his early years on the range. Russell's warm humanism pervaded his art with an interest in the individual rather than the typical, a sentiment that found full expression in the romantic realism that characterized his mature vision. Though often compared with his contemporary Frederic Remington, Russell experienced life on the frontier firsthand. His knowledge and appreciation for ranch life, Indian culture, animal anatomy and behavior set him apart from artists of his generation and inspired works free of artistic convention.

The exhibition focuses on Russell's mature work executed from 1903 - 1926, and includes not only dynamic scenes of action for which he is best known, but also contemplative pictures that symbolize the passing of the frontier. On a technical level, he explored the effects of light and atmosphere, and achieved greater range and freedom in his handling of color. Russell's bronze sculptures demonstrate an equally broad formal range, evolving from the linear realism of his initial works to the more spontaneous surfaces of his later bronzes. His peerless ability to convey motion resulted in a modeling style typical of some of the most avant-garde artists of his generation.

For over two decades, the Gerald Peters Gallery has been committed to collecting and placing some of Russell's most significant works in public and private collections throughout the country. This body of work and accompanying publication was coordinated in association with the Mongerson-Wunderlich Gallery, and is a testament to Russell's considerable versatility as a painter, sculptor, and storyteller. Although for decades he has been celebrated as the preeminent chronicler of the American West, it is perhaps his universal message that looms largest. His devoted friend Will Rogers probably said it best; "He not only left us great living pictures of what our West was, but he left us an example of how to live in friendship with all mankind." His art remains a legacy of his ultimate contribution. I am, as all lovers of the West are, truly indebted to Russell for reminding us of life's greater lessons.

Gerald Peters

Preface

This gathering of works clearly demonstrates the power and genius of Charles M. Russell. The year 1903 has been selected as the departure date for the creation of this collection, as well as the date to denote the "beginning" of Russell's mature period of work. While this may seem like an arbitrary date in the development of his artistic career, an examination of Russell's work prior and after 1903 will confirm a change. Of course, this does not mean there is no additional artistic development or a further maturing of his style and means of expression. To look at the body of Russell's work from 1903 until his death in 1926, one can see a richness and expanse of inventiveness that is clearly developmental and truly remarkable.

Brian Dippie, Peter Hassrick and the publishers have written essays focusing on these 23 years. The authors share information and stories on Russell and his paintings, sculpture and illustrated letters that show the importance of this genuine western artist. Their analyses and opinions explore and explain Russell as a mature artist and they bring an expertise that communicates easily to the reader about Russell and his works. This is great reading combined with great viewing.

There is one other fact that should be considered regarding the year 1903, the "departure" date for this exhibition and the discussion about Russell's mature work. This is the year when Charlie built his log studio, a small 24 x 30 foot red cedar telephone pole building adjacent to his house in Great Falls.

Nancy Russell wrote in Good Medicine:

> "...Charlie said, 'I want a log studio some day, just a cabin like I used to live in.' That year, 1903, the studio was built on the lot adjoinin the house. Charlie did not like the mess of building so he took no more than a mild interest in the preparations. Then one day, a neighbor said, 'What are you doing at your place Russell, building a corral?' That settled it. Charlie just thought the neighbors didn't want the cabin mixed in with the civilized dwellings and felt sure they would get up a petition to prevent our building anything so unsightly as a log house in their midst. But way down in his heart, he wanted that studio. It was the right kind of work-shop for him, but he was worried at what he thought the neighbors would say, so he would have nothing to do with it."

However, after a visit to the log building with his friend Albert Trigg, Charlie said, "'That's going to be a good shack for me. The bunch can come visit, talk and smoke, while I paint.'

> "From that day to the end of his life he loved that telephone pole building more than any other place on earth and never finished a painting anywhere else. The walls were hung with all kinds of things given to him by Indian friends, and his horse jewelry, as he called it, that had been accumulated on the range, was as precious to him as a girl's jewel box to her."

This "shack" became the center of his artistic work, and to a large degree, his life. He would escape there and portray on canvas, in clay and on paper stories of the West. There was, and is, a "magic" where he kept his cowboy gear and Indian collections, where his many and varied friends visited, and where stories were swapped. It undoubtedly gave Russell the personal and famililar surroundings needed to express so deeply and with such skill and knowledge the stories, images and emotions of his west. He could experience through his collections virtually on a daily basis the west he first knew and that had now largely disappeared. In no small way, the log studio with its many associations moved Russell forward as a maturing artist and enriched and expanded his art. The works in this post-1903 exhibition attest to that, and the respective essays reinforce the importance of this adopted son of the West.

Lorne E. Render
Executive Director
C.M. Russell Museum

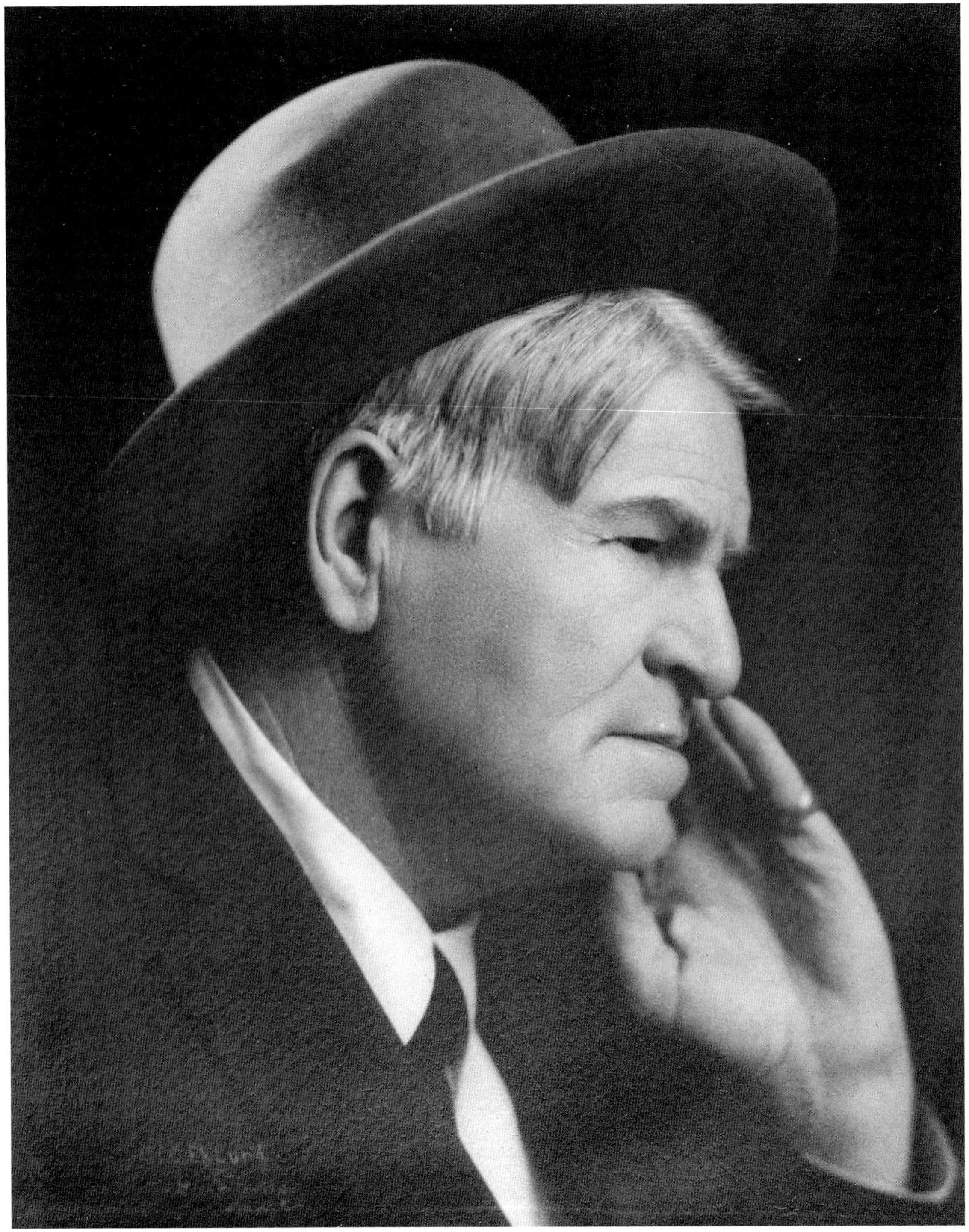

alibris

ORCA KNOWLEDGE SYSTEMS, INC
2 PRESTWICK CT.
NOVATO, CA 94949
UNITED STATES

To: ALIBRIS APEX DC 76670941-41
APEX
800 AVONDALE AVE.
GRANDVIEW HEIGHTS, OH 43212-3473

Shipping Instructions for 3DOXIEST

Print this Packing Slip and enclose inside the front cover of the book.

Please ship this item no later than Fri Aug 14, 2026.

Ship to:

ALIBRIS APEX DC 76670941-41
APEX
800 AVONDALE AVE.
GRANDVIEW HEIGHTS, OH 43212-3473
UNITED STATES

PN #	Item ID	Alibris ID	Media Type	Title / Author	Seller List Price	Order Date
76670941-41	mon0000032958	B083907576	BOOK	Charles M. Russell: the Artist in His Heyday 1903-1926 Gerald Peters	$14.00	Aug, 4 2026

Very good First Edition. Unread. No markings in book. Binding is fine. 197pp. paperback

76670941-41

The West that has Passed

BY PETER H. HASSRICK

He paints the West that has passed from an intimate personal knowledge of it; for he was there in the midst of it all, and he has the tang of its spirit in his blood. He has recorded something of the earlier days in the life of that country, of its people, of their curious ways and occupations, a life that has practically passed; for civilization has come, and before civilization, the elemental passes away, swallowed up in certain conventions that are rightly deemed necessary for the development of a new country.

Arthur Hoeber
The World's Work (1911)

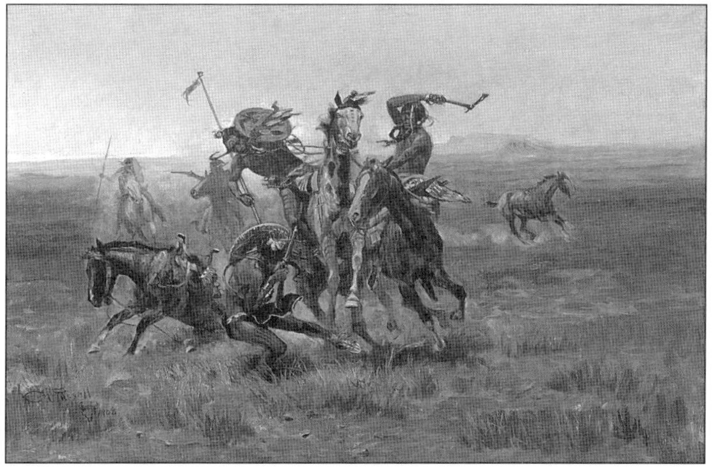

When Blackfeet and Sioux Meet, 1908, oil on canvas, 20.125 x 29.875
Courtesy of Sid Richards Collection of Western Art, Ft. Worth, Texas.

The triumphs of Russell's early artistic life had included his first Saint Louis commission from William Niedringhaus, the World's Fair exposure, and his several one-man shows there in the first years of the century. As the decade ended, Niedringhaus again stepped in, this time to close that chapter. In 1910 he assembled a large group of Russell's oils and watercolors for an exhibition in Saint Louis under the title "Paintings by C. M. Russell," apparently loaning some works from his personal collection and borrowing others from friends and relatives. A good many must have been consigned by the artist, including *Smoke of a .45* and *When Blackfeet and Sioux Meet*. Some had price tags on them. It was a hometown swan song, a bon voyage, for Russell was about to become famous from coast to coast and even internationally.

Certainly he was ready to break out of the mold, if there was one. His financial security appeared sound, since Nancy in 1908 had renegotiated his Brown and Bigelow contract for a guaranteed annual income of three thousand dollars for work used on their calendars. In addition, she had insisted on healthy prices (Charlie considered them outlandish) for his art. In the 1910 exhibition in Saint Louis, for example, *Smoke of a .45* was listed for one thousand dollars and its

Reprinted from Charles M. Russell, by Peter Hassrick.
Published in 1989 by Harry N. Abrams, Inc., New York

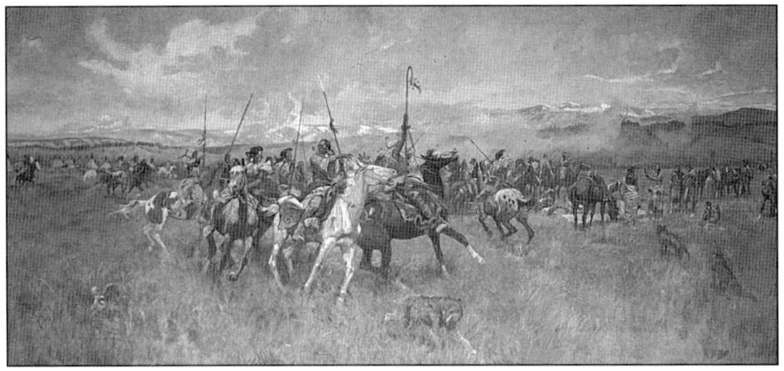

Lewis and Clark Meeting the Flathead Indians at Ross's Hole, 1912, oil on canvas, 12 x 25 inches.
Montana Historical Society, Helena, Montana.

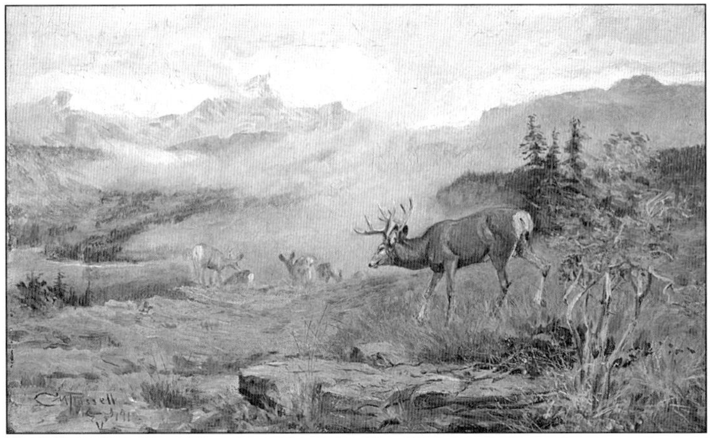

Deer Grazing, 1912, oil on board 22.73, 11 x 17.875 inches.
Buffalo Bill Historical Center, Cody, Wyoming
Gift of William E. Weiss

companion piece, *In Without Knocking* (1908, Amon Carter Museum), for nine hundred dollars. The time was ripe to move ahead. Nancy seems to have led the way, with Charlie working to fill the orders. They were both doing a brilliant job, Nancy marketing and Charlie living up to her every boast and expectation.

Of course the way to keep that momentum going was to produce big work with powerful imagery and universal appeal. Russell complied full force with such paintings as *In the Wake of the Buffalo Runners*. Although he had explored the theme many times before, this latest effort evinced an epic quality, as if Russell were implying more than simple traditional native values. The young woman, surrounded by two generations of family and scanning the horizon for tomorrow's home, evoked a strong message. Perhaps this heroine was the true American Madonna—the leader of her people, the harbinger of peace, and the exemplar of grace. He never took such notions to the extremes embraced by some of his young friends of the Howard Pyle persuasion, who would apply Pre-Rephaelite principles to their western illustrations. But he did overtly exalt the status of Indian women and idealize their place in the scheme of Indian life.

In April, 1911, the Russells returned to New York for the opening of Charlie's first major one-man exhibition at Folsom Galleries. Appropriately titled "The West that Has Passed," it brought him into the limelight as never before. The art critic Arthur Hoeber commented that Russell was still more an illustrator than painter and that his work remained a bit uneven, and Russell heartily agreed with both remarks. But Hoeber also put the Montana artist in his proper place, observing that "he is full of enthusiasm for the country which he paints, and since the death of Frederic Remington [December, 1909], he is almost without a competitor." Hoeber concluded that "among men artistically endowed," Russell was now "the official historian of the West that has passed."

Russell was not one to set himself above others, but he accepted the accolades and, with Nancy's encouragement and hard work, embarked on a spate of exhibitions over the next several years, from Chicago and New York to San Francisco and, internationally, Winnipeg, Calgary, and eventually London. His most immediate successes, however, occurred right at home in Montana. In July, 1911, he was awarded a commission to paint a mural for the wall behind the speaker's station in the Montana State House of Representatives. It had been a tough battle to win the contract, primarily due to competition from more established muralists, specifically John Alexander of New York. But Russell convinced the selection committee that he was the right man for the job.

The task presented substantial challenges for Russell. As he pondered them one day, he wrote to Goodwin: "I got the job of the capital an as the picture is only 25 feet long an 12 wide its got me thinking some... the subject is to be Lewis and Clark meeting the flat heds... this is some jump for me an I am liabel to have to call for help... send for all my New York friends an put them to worke." Russell never lived up to the threat, mostly because he learned, after writing Goodwin, that the painting could be done on canvas rather than with traditional plaster techniques. He was thus able to accomplish the task in his studio, after some modifications in the ceiling were made and after he had traveled to the site of the historic encounter to make color and landscape studies.

A year later, and on schedule, the mural was installed. *Lewis and Clark Meeting the Flathead Indians at Ross' Hole* was the title Russell gave it, and the critics gauged it "his best and most finished product." Subsequent authorities such as Harold McCracken hailed the work as Russell's masterpiece. The artist had used his strongest compositional treatment, the inverted pyramid. True to his conviction that the Indians were the paramount force in early western history, the scene focuses on a swirl of mounted warriors, with the actual greeting of the Anglo explorers quite secondary. The low horizon line gave Russell a chance to concentrate the action as well as to celebrate the beauty of a Montana sky at dusk.

Those enduring the poetic elements of the West became increasingly attractive to Russell as subjects for his art. Certainly he enjoyed recounting the drama and surge of human activity—the cowboy and his steer or the Indian and his buffalo—but the universal, unchanging aspects of nature were also reassuring to him. The human chapters might close and become part of history and remembrance; a mountain park was timeless. Paintings such as *Deer Grazing* and sculptures such as *Buffalo Family* testify to the reverence Russell felt for nature's riches and the skill with which he handled its symbols. The mountains offered humility, autumn colors suggested fulfillment, and the deer taught contentment.

More obviously metaphorical work, such as *His Heart Sleeps*, manifested his dream of continuity. While the burial scaffold cradled in the tree's branches represents loss and quiescence, the buffalo pouring forth from the prairies into the river offer a sense of hope for a future possibly replenished by the resources of

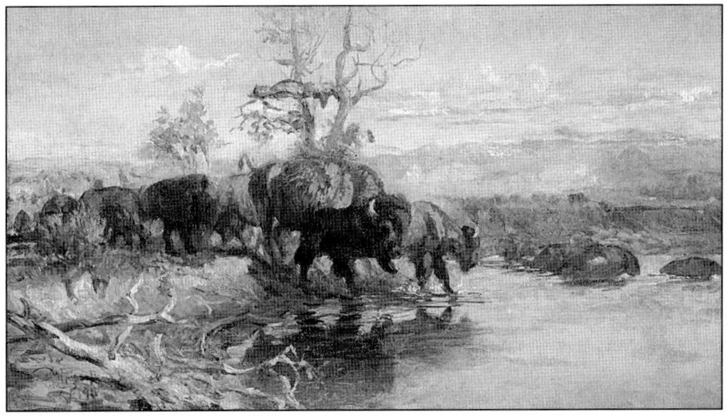

His Heart Sleeps, 1911, oil on canvas, 6.875 x 11.875 inches.
Buffalo Bill Historical Center, Cody, Wyoming
Gift of Charles Ulrick and Josephine Bay Foundation, Inc.

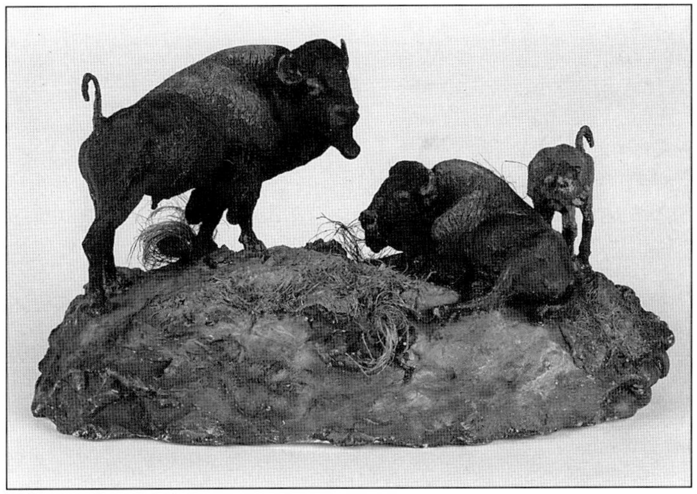

Buffalo Family, 1924, wax model
Buffalo Bill Historical Center, Cody, Wyoming
Gift of Dr. Armand Hammer and Charles Stone Jones

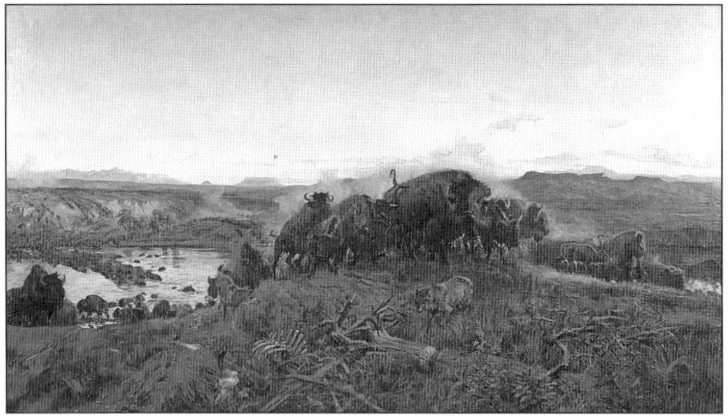

When the Land Belonged to God, 1914
oil on canvas,42.5 x 92 inches
Courtesy of the Montana Historical Society, Helena, Montana

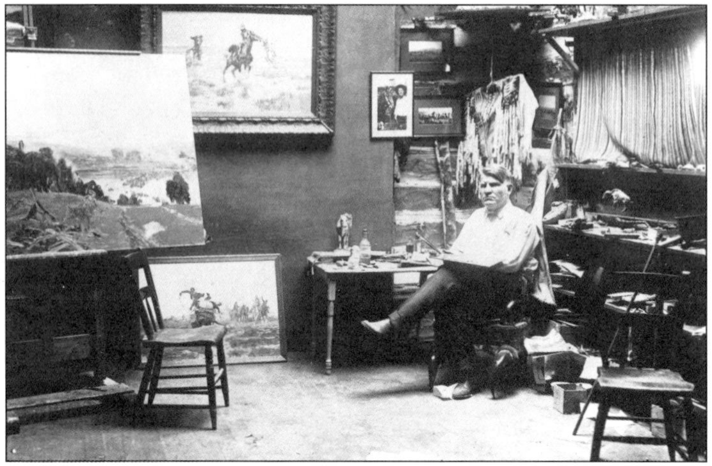

Charlie in his studio, 1914, (photographer unknown).
Courtesy of the C.M. Russell Museum, Great Falls, Montana.

the past. It was all in nature's hands, right where, in Russell's mind, it should have always stayed. His lament was nowhere more clearly stated than in these paintings of wildlife, of nature in her many glories.

When man now intruded on this scene in Russell's art, he was more than likely stepping lightly onto the land, the soles of his shoes soft and the core of his spirit in tune with the elements. In order to achieve such statements, Russell worked hard at selecting empathetic characters to fill his paintings and at harmonizing colors, so that the overall effect might impart a sense of unity. These goals were most fully achieved up to that point in his painting *Carson's Men*. The suffused opalescent glow, the brilliant bands of gold, the voiceless communication of men, and the cushioned silence of the horses' steps in the sand answered Russell's quest for unifying pictorial elements.

A few years later, when Russell was called upon to produce a consummate statement about his beloved West, he chose a subject that left man entirely out of the picture. The Montana Club of Helena had, for a number of years, been collecting representative examples of art related to the state. In 1913 the members commissioned a large piece from Russell, which was delivered in early 1914.

According to Frank Linderman, a friend of Russell's who helped secure the commission, the painting proved to be difficult for the artist. Evidently the central figure, a large buffalo bull, caused most of Russell's anguish. He made pencil and oil, as well as wax studies for the painting. Even so, as Linderman recounted, delivery of the painting was delayed several months because of the problems Russell experienced with that figure. Once the work arrived in Helena, however, and was installed in the club's reading room, all observers agreed that it was Russell's best, even surpassing the mural, according to the members. Russell had been through a struggle, and his dyspeptic expression as he posed next to the finished work is convincing evidence of the battle. Yet he was pleased and gratified and gave the painting the title *When the Land Belonged to God.*

About a month after the men at the Montana Club received their magnificent gift to themselves, the ladies of the Great Falls Women's Club enjoyed a similar, if somewhat more ephemeral, treat in the form of a special afternoon program on art. Mrs. Conner spoke on "How to See Pictures," discoursing on the styles of painters from Cimabue to Whistler. Then Mrs. Hamilton took over, providing an eloquent analysis of Rembrandt's *Night Watch*. The highlight of the program, however, was Nancy Russell's presentation on her husband's life and art. Some of her commentary was especially revealing about the artist and his working methods. She began by observing that "no man can be a painter without imagination. He must live in his picture." Then she explained further:

"In the old days men did not read much but were all good story tellers and many of their lives would have made a romance. Although Mr. Russell is a good story teller he is also a good listener and has a remarkable memory for detail. The stories he heard were history that has never been written and would have been lost had he lacked the ability to put them on canvas. People have said, "Where do you get all your ideas? I should think you would run out of them." With him that is impossible, as his great teacher, Nature, and a few silent men developed and strengthened an already wonderful imagination until now there will be days when he lives in that past that was loved and understood when a boy, and there is no limit to the number of pictures he sees in his world. If he lived hundreds of years he would still be unable to paint them all. . . .'

'Mr. Russell lives in the past as you all know, and when civilization crowds too close and it is not the season to go to the mountains he takes his coat and hat, his tooth brush in his pocket and goes to Mr. Matheson's ranch near Belt, where the Highwood mountains loom up big and the Belt range make wonderful pictures in the evening sun. At this ranch the artist is a boy, he cooks anything fancy brings to mind or at least he tries, from cake to roasting a chicken, which, by the way, he said was pretty good. When the dishes are washed he will, in nice weather, climb a hay stack and from that elevated place imagine that stretch of country back before the white man came, with Indians and their land alive with game. He goes into what his red brothers would call "the Great Silence" where nature teaches her child. When he comes back from one of these visits I have seen him start three big pictures within one week. When laying in a composition as a rule Mr. Russell is very silent, he will sit evening after evening with a pencil and scratch pad, working out an idea and scarcely talk at all."

~

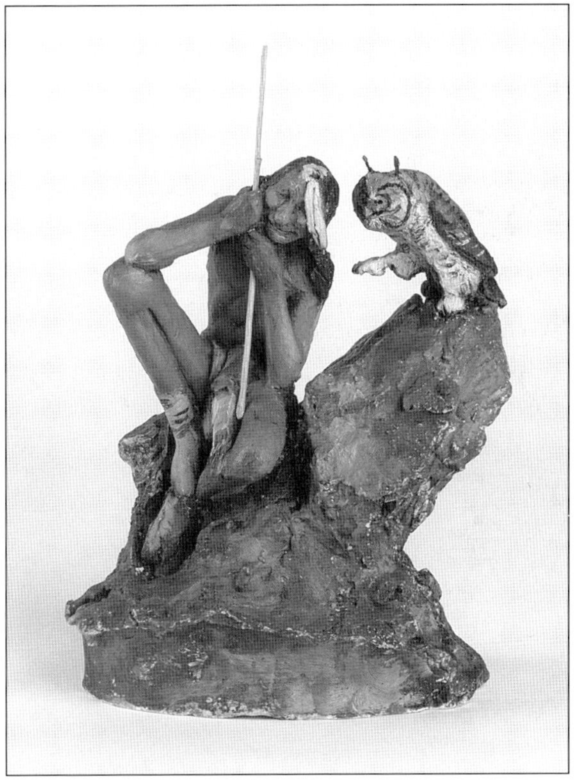

Seated Indian, Owl at Side, date unknown, wax, height 8"
Courtesy Buffalo Bill Historical Center, Cody, WY.
Gift of Dr. Armand Hammer & Charles Stone Jones

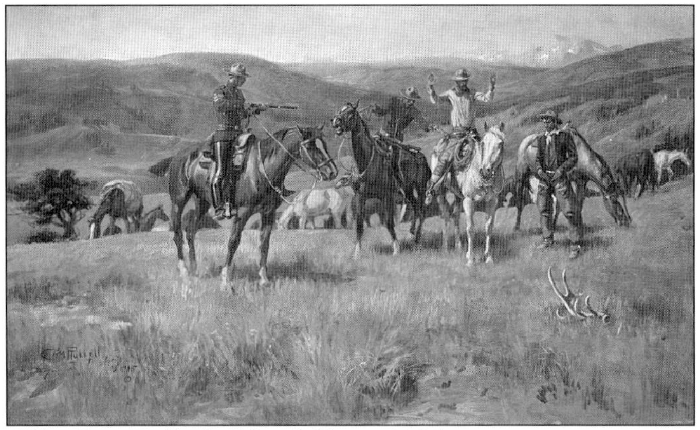

When Law Dulls the Edge of Chance, 1915
oil on canvas, 29.5 x 47.5 inches
Buffalo Bill Historical Center, Cody, WY
Gift of William E. Weiss, Jr.

The pressures on Russell must have been considerable. Not only was he popular at home but he was also in great demand by authors and publishers nationwide. One book alone, Fifteen Thousand Miles by Stage, in 1911, required eighty-five illustrations, including four in color, thirteen black-and-white halftones, and thirty-eight line drawings. The author of the book, Carrie Adell Strahorn, was so persistent that she literally camped out on Russell's doorstep to see that the job was completed to her expectations.

His friend Linderman was more reasonable. When he called on Russell, the artist delivered to the best of his abilities. The illustrations for Linderman, who styled himself an interpreter of Indian lore, are sympathetic and poetic, just as Linderman's tales are. Russell's cover illustration for Linderman's "Indian Why Stories" depicts War Eagle, a solemn and dedicated old warrior who, of an evening and with proper crowd of young listeners, passes down the verbal traditions of his people to the next generation. Russell and Linderman were both raconteurs, both understanding that gesture and expression were critical to laying a plot properly before an eager audience. They were also versed in sign language and Indian symbolism. Russell made annual pilgrimages to the Montana reservations to brush up on his techniques and refresh his imagery. In Russell's illustration these elements are combined with a wash of golden reverie and noble elegance befitting the story's subject.

Russell was somehow able to fulfill requests for illustrations while still performing on an international exhibition circuit. In 1914 "The West that Has Passed" opened at the Dore Galleries in London, and the Russells were there for the champagne. It was all part of Nancy's master plan, which had begun with an exhibition of Charlie's work at the Calgary Stampede in 1912, followed by a show in Winnipeg the next year. These shows brought Russell's work to the attention of an English clientele who in turn had encouraged the sponsors in London. The Britons, according to headlines in the Great Falls papers, were "Enraptured by Russell's Art." They had never seen the likes of such horses and action and were eager for such visualization of the frontier.

Even the Prince of Wales, who later met Russell in Saskatoon, Canada, acquired one of the Montana artist's provocative canvases, *When Law Dulls the Edge of Chance.* Seeing His Majesty's Mounties serving the cause of justice was just too much to resist. Nancy and Charlie must have conspired to produce such appealing subjects for the young prince. At the time of the sale, they actually had three similar subjects from which to choose. Such was their savvy and enterprise.

Russell's exhibition "The West that Has Passed" took many forms over the next several years. As paintings and bronzes were sold by the galleries, new works were substituted, so that at each opening its configuration was different and refreshingly inviting even during a return engagement. When the show was presented for the second time in Chicago, in 1916, there was one particularly exciting oil among the twenty-four paintings and twelve bronzes. Titled *When Shadows Hint Death,* it shows Russell at his best when provoking a dramatic effect. His brilliant narrative capacity may have evolved just as Nancy had described to the Great Falls Women's Club several years earlier. The story was no doubt one Russell had heard around some campfire in the Judith Basin. Its resolution as a pictorial composition was probably achieved of an evening around the dining room table, one of those silent evenings when the artist was transposing the oral traditions of his youth to the pictorial expressions of his mature artistry. The initial sketch merely suggests the finished composition, but it was enough to serve as the genesis for an engaging painting.

Of all the expressions mastered by Russell in the paintings done at the height of his career, the affectionate portrayal of paradox was perhaps dominant. The situations generally involve man, the solo hunter or trapper, faced with the unexpected quirks of nature. The characters in these humorous dramas are presented with an immediate and perplexing decision—whether to confront nature and risk losing everything or to concede, leaving bounty and human needs aside as an admission of nature's victory. The scenes are never resolved in the paintings but rather left to the viewers to place their own morality and values on the determination of destiny. The viewers' conclusions did not really matter to Russell. He had had his chance to raise the question, and much of his own spiritual fiber was rendered just in the asking. Where, for example, is Russell's sympathy in *Whose Meat?(p. 17)* or *Meat's Not Meat Till It's in the Pan*? Is man out of his element or is he challenged, mind and body, to conclude these scenes with a dominant confidence? Those who knew Russell would have bet that he sided with nature. But then, throughout Russell's life, nature had lost, and he had dedicated more than common effort to its lament. Even today, the question is mute and only valid in having been posed.

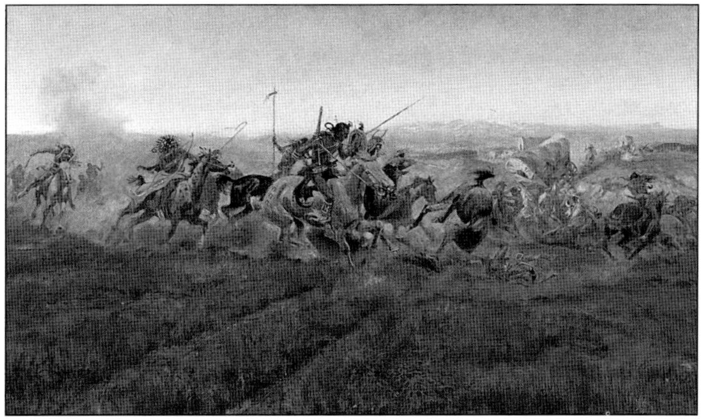

Jumped, 1914, oil on canvas, 30.5 x 48.25 inches.
Amon Carter Museum, Fort Worth, Texas. 1961.157.

Because Russell invited friendships so openly, many came to know him well. Those who were close to him often went out of their way to expound on his virtues. In 1917 his friend Philip Goodwin did so at great length for a writer in Recreation magazine. His comments provide a good understanding of Charlie from a perspective other than Nancy's. Much of it corroborates her story.

> "He has the true old-time plainsman's and trapper's gift at spinning yarns, and his equal as an original camp-fire raconteur will rarely be heard. He is decidedly human, with a very keen sense of humor and daring imagination, is naturally droll, has perfect control of his remarkably striking features, has a pleasingly mellow bass voice, excellent power of description and tells a story as a gambler plays poker."

These are helpful and insightful observations, but the person who really knew Charlie, who through his association provided the most revealing view of the man and the artist, was Joe DeYong. The two met in 1914, and Joe became an apprentice artist and something of a member of the Russell family after 1917. He lived with them and worked at Russell's side in the studio off and on for the last ten years of the artist's life. DeYong never achieved much success in his chosen field of painting. As a sidekick of Charlie's, however, he provided immensely valuable companionship and a fascinating record. Joe was deaf, so the two communicated in sign language, at which they were both known to be proficient, or through an exchange of verbal interrogatories by Joe and scribbled replies from Charlie. Many of these written responses are extant today in the collections of the National Cowboy Hall of Fame and the C. M. Russell Museum. Although one-sided, they speak to the daily activity in Russell's studio and his thoughts on art.

For example, Russell is known to have had two or three canvases in process at any one time. However, only through a note to Joe is his working method on each canvas revealed. "I think its better to work all over your picture—not finish one figer and then another... it rests you." Replies to Joe's questions also reveal Russell's affection for Catlin and Wimar and his true feelings about his New York cronies such as Goodwin or Dunton, who, without models, were "lost" or who got better once they "quit borrow[ing] of Remington." Joe also made notes about Russell's use of color, his inclinations toward pattern, and his choice of compositions. On Russell's color, for example, DeYong summarized: "stubborn, endless-experiment, continually struggling to match the colors available with those effects repeatedly seen in nature."

Russell's painting *Watching for Wagons* must have been the result of such experimentation. The strong golden light raking in from the left highlights the two prominent figures in the strong but lopsided composition. They focus on abstract shapes in the distance. The glaring light and restless pose of the horses and the young warrior animate the scene, portending a future that the older man, static and propped up by his spear, may not live long enough to know or suffer its tragic consequence.

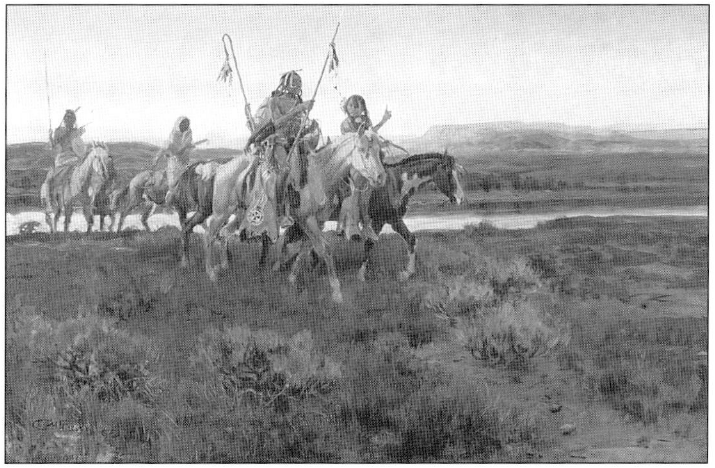

Piegans, 1914
oil on canvas, 24 x 36 inches
Museum of Western Art, Denver, Colorado
Photograph courtesy of James O. Milmoe

On his regular visits to neighboring Indian reservations, Russell usually traveled with Nancy, but occasionally with a friend like Frank Linderman. He often carried a camera and photographed gatherings of Indian leaders and old-timers, drawn to them just as he was to timeworn cowboys. He came away from the reservations inspired to preserve their historic past, tinted only with the fresh color and memories of his recent visit. *Piegans* may have resulted from such a sojourn. It is a splendid record of long-gone days when the language of men and nature was, by common understanding, unspoken—only sign and gesture.

Some of Russell's patrons were not content with quiet reflections of past nobility enshrouded in a Montana dusk. They wanted what the artist was famous for—action, history, and drama—that "D¸sseldorf tableau" menu. Among such patrons was Dr. Philip G. Cole of New York, who commissioned several major pictures, in which he wanted a touch of the Wild West. What better scene than the buffalo hunt of the Grand Duke Alexis and Buffalo Bill, which took place on the Nebraska hills in 1872? The completed painting portrayed Cody as something of a tour guide, pointing out to his guest the best bull and the most advantageous line of attack. The Indians brought along to lend authenticity to the scene performed their task well, providing a vigorous counterbalance to the relatively passive involvement of the great scout.

Although this is a dynamic painting thematically and compositionally, the symbolism figures even more powerfully. Here Cody, the hero of the plains and vanquisher of the wilderness, rounds up a remnant herd for the entertainment of royalty. For a brief moment he brings to life the drama of the past to show it off

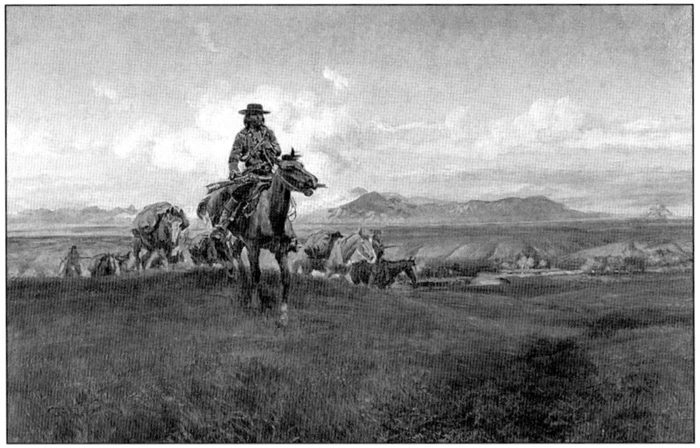

Romance Makers, 1918,
oil on canvas, 21.5 x 35.5 inches.
The Snite Museum of Art
Gift of C.R. Smith

for a visitor from afar who is willing to pay the tab for the experience. And here, at the behest of an eastern patron, Russell freezes on canvas that superficial reenactment—the condensation of reality that was mythic, even as it unfolded on the Nebraska prairie.

The implication of this was not lost on Russell. He painted *The Romance Makers* in 1918 and suggested, in the heroic proportions of the rider in front, that perhaps the plainsmen and their ilk were consciously riding into a storybook future. He suggested that they knew they were making history, and as a result sat taller in their saddles, rode harder, and dared more boldly so that they might figure more prominently in the history they were creating. At least Russell painted them as if they foresaw the epic that would envelop a whole nation's conscience—an epic they had told with their lives and to which Charlie Russell would devote his own. It was the West that has passed.

Russell was not interested in the story of the local smelter workers in Great Falls or in the woes of the Montana farmers or miners, but there were some obvious characters with whom he identified—the present-day cowboy and Indian whose ancestors had peopled his beloved era in a form reckoned as pure. By 1919 the scenery and its players had changed. Russell preferred to look past them into bygone times. "Cow folks are scare now," he wrote to George Farr that year. "Most of my old friends either rode for ore owned irons many of them have crossed the big range but they left tracks in history that the farmer cant plow under...goode or bad they were regular men and Americas last frontiersmen." But he could not ignore their modern manifestations, which, for the cowboy, took the form of movie actors and rodeo performers. At that time Russell declared himself, at least publicly, as scornful of such contrivances. The movies were too unrealistic and exaggerated, while the rodeos hosted events that no true cowboy would understand or tolerate. "There ain't such a thing as 'bulldogging' a steer on the range," he told a Minneapolis reporter in 1919. "All that started with a fake show. I know line riding and broncho busting. But bulldogging! And all the rest of that stuff. Bunk!"

However, there was more sympathy in Russell's heart than greeted the newspaperman's ear. He had supported the Calgary Stampede since its beginnings in 1912, and in the same year that he confessed his dissatisfaction with the fabric of rodeo, he and Nancy sent an exhibition of sale works to Calgary valued at more than $100,000 and widely publicized as such. He contributed a sketch for the letterhead of the stampede and produced a number of explosive paintings, such as *A Rodeo Rider Loses*, representing his enthusiasm for the sport. In an expression of affectionate jest, he even put himself in the saddle as a contestant.

Along with Frank Linderman, Russell was a vocal and persuasive advocate of Indian rights. Together the two men helped get the Cree and Chippewa established on the Rocky Boy Reservation in Montana. Although he worked hard to win victory for such social causes, these themes rarely entered his work directly. The reason, he explained, was that his audience was primarily eastern. "If I depended on my home state for commissions and sales, " he commented in 1919, "I would starve. In the east they like my pictures." And the easterners were willing to pay the prices Nancy placed on them.

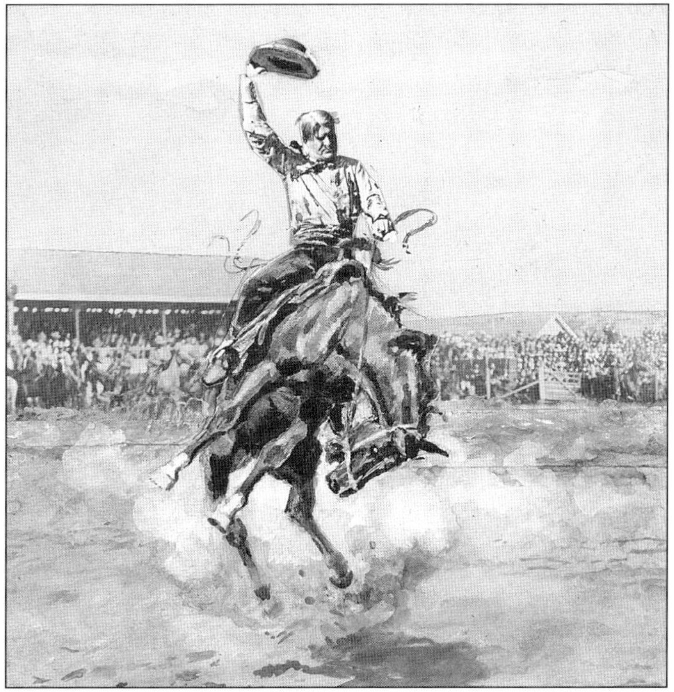

Russell on Bucking Horse, 1919,
photo and ink wash collage, 5.5 x 5.25 inches
Buffalo Bill Historical Center
Gift of William E. Weiss

Russell's success in the East, combined with his stated inability to support himself in the West, proved once again symptomatic of the prevailing paradox of the artist's career. When the Russells had guests over for dinner, Charlie would more often than not cook for them out in the log-cabin studio. The fireplace and an old Dutch oven were his tools, and he prided himself on the authentic western fare he had learned to make from Jake Hoover or some range camp cook. But the beans in the pot and the apples for the baked dessert were paid for by the sale of bronzes at Tiffany's or paintings sold at Folsom Galleries to some captain of industry from Pennsylvania or New York. His patrons, for the most part, were people he did not know or really care to get to know. He confessed to being rather uneasy in the company of easterners. He had escaped into the West as a youth and was now, by virtue of the innocence afforded him in those reclusive haunts, shielded from the implications of his market. Nancy served to insulate him further from those realities, so he could forget, or at least pretend to forget, not only that he was being supported by the bosses of the very civilization he despised, but that he had, in fact, been born into a family that prospered by exploiting the land and promoting expansion.

And what of the images that he purveyed to this enthusiastic clientele? Why were they so popular back beyond the big Missouri? And why did Russell's success with those images in the East undoubtedly depress him so much that eventually, in his later years, associates and family saw a certain hardness and cynicism develop. The images were popular because they were not of the transfor-

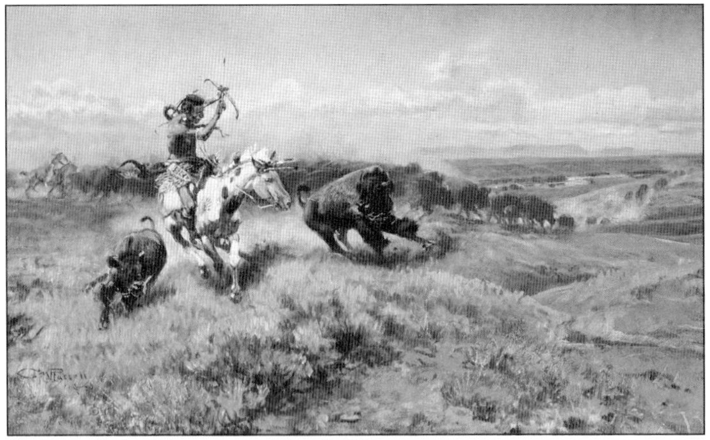

Horse of the Hunter or *Fresh Meat,* 1919
oil on canvas, 15 x 24 inches.
Private Collection.

mation that so agonized the artist but rather of the myth. As historian Robert V. Hine has observed, "Strip the West of its racial ugliness, forget its insistent irresponsibility, and drape the whole in self-reliant individualism, moralizing nature, and fervent nationalism, and America had found its image." What Russell provided for his audience was not the West as it was but rather the West refashioned in his historical mind's eye. His genius therefore centered on an ability to relay the message of nostalgic glorification.

And why did Russell's success produce an eventual bitterness within him? Frustration no doubt came in knowing the truth, of having lived through the years of transformation and having been a part of them. The irony had not been lost on him. It only drove him further into the recesses of the past for a justification of the present. His efforts ultimately resulted in the purging of social guilt and, as such, struck a responsive chord in the collective twentieth-century American imagination. The cathartic note of his pictorial requiem was apparent even as he exercised his most provocative brushstrokes or shaped his most evocative figure.

What he said of his eastern clientele (particularly in Pittsburgh, where he maintained an enthusiastic group of collectors) was that "they may not be so strong on art but they are real men and they like real life." What they liked, of course, was not real life at all but the illusions of past glories as Russell was wont to give them. *Fresh Meat*, painted in 1919, had nothing to do with current Indian issues, aside from Russell's employment of local Indians as models. It called up the triumph of noble horsemen over nature and repeated compositions and themes he had successfully exploited years earlier in Surround.

The Minneapolis Institute of Art held a special exhibition of Russell's work in the winter of 1919. The local press suggested that his buffalo-hunt paintings had "historical value" and that *The Romance Makers* profited from the bright theatrical back lighting he favored in the work of Maxfield Parrish, his favorite fellow painter. Yet they concluded that Russell's style must be regarded as strictly individual, separated from all other art movements of the day by "the big simplicity of his nature." He was, as Etelline Bennett had written in the spring of 1919, "painting the old West as it was, for a generation to whom it will be only a tradition." The task was worthy of the lifework of any artist, and Russell proved up to the task.

Charles M. Russell: The Artist in His Prime

BY BRIAN DIPPIE

He painted sitting down, shoulders slouched slightly forward, left hand holding his palette, arm resting on his knee, chin jutted out, mouth set, staring straight ahead, as though he could find the answers on the other side of the canvas. He made rough preliminary sketches and basic compositional studies--though nothing like the detailed preliminary drawings a schooled artist relied upon. He would refer to the works of others, and to photographs and the objects in his studio collection for specific information. He used live models infrequently, though he would sometimes assume a pose himself in front of a mirror, and routinely made wax models that might then be lit to produce highlights and shadows. He also employed an articulated cardboard cutout of a horse and rider ("a jointed hoss") that, he explained to his protege Joe De Yong, cast a shadow that "looks mighty natural."[1] When he was actually painting, Russell laid in the background then made changes as he went along. "I think its better to work all over your Picture not finish one figer and then another," he told De Yong. "It rests you."[2] He sometimes painted around figures, sizing heads, correcting faults in drawing, altering poses and positions, dealing with problems as they arose. He even moved figures about, as is evident in some of his early oils and watercolors. The watercolors are a particular revelation: one sees the underdrawing clearly visible through the paint overlay, which often substantially modifies the original sketch.

Even in his mature work Russell proceeded intuitively. He was never scientific about the arrangement of pigments on his palette, as Bill Gollings, a Sheridan cowboy artist of his acquaintance, was, nor did he know "a warm color from a cool one."[3] But he knew instinctively when things were right. A Great Falls neighbor who was also an artist remembered watching him at work:

"All at once Russell leaned back in his chair and let his hand--the one holding the brush--rest listlessly on his knee. He sat there some time studying the picture. Then he leaned forward and dipped his brush in scarlet paint and gave one dab to a figure; it sprang into view like magic. Charlie turned and smiled at me. Not a word was spoken. We both felt the satisfaction of the moment".[4]

And he knew when things were wrong as well. His cousin's son, Fergus Mead, spent part of the summer of 1911 at Bull Head Lodge on Lake McDonald, and recalled that Russell "painted every day--and mostly all day. And I swear to God he never stopped talking--spinning yarns":

"Charley used to sit on a little camp stool wither out on the porch of the big cabin, overlooking the lake, or inside if the weather was cool. Paint and talk. Every few minutes he'd swing around with his back to the canvas and study his work in a little hand mirror. It was easier, he said, than getting up and walking across the room to get distance. Also, of course, it reversed the picture and betrayed any bad drawing.

I remember that during my visit he was working on a picture of a couple of riders coming round the brow of a mountain trail. He fussed and fumed more over that picture--a small one--than he did over anything else he was doing at the time. Finally, after studying it for a long time, he shook his head sadly, mixed up a bunch of gray paint and started obliterating the entire picture. When we asked him how come, he showed us that if one of those men had stood up, he'd been about nine feet tall."[5]

Russell painted until he approximated what he saw in his mind's eye; the correspondence was never perfect. The year before he died, he claimed to have painted many wonderful pictures in his mind but, disappointingly, not yet one on canvas.[6]

Russell's legion of admirers would disagree. Indeed, Russell had hit his stride as an artist shortly after the turn of the century. He always had an observant eye, a feeling for human and animal anatomy, and a peerless ability to convey motion. Visits East, and regular association with the trained professional illustrators he called friends, enhanced his natural gifts. In 1916, at the peak of his powers, he offered a bit of advice to Joe De Yong:

"I think you can learn from watching other men work
but not onley one man
then study nature
when you paint hosses watch them
reflecded lights
I modled before I came west
eas[i]er"[7]

Some of Russell's greatest action pictures showing studies of men and animals locked in violent combat were painted at a time when his drafting skills exceeded his concern with "reflecded lights" and color. *The Cinch Ring* (plate #15) and *At Rope's End*, the latter a favorite exhibition piece, both date from 1909. Their "stout" tones, as Russell called them, are faithful to the sagebrush-strewn expanses of the northern plains, and their settings as harsh and basic as the action shown.[8] In sharp contrast are two rainbow-hued paintings done in 1921, *Wagons* (plate #29) and *Wolf and the Beaver*, whose magical landscapes are rendered in shimmering yellows and fiery oranges, turquoise and magenta, pinks and cobalt blue.

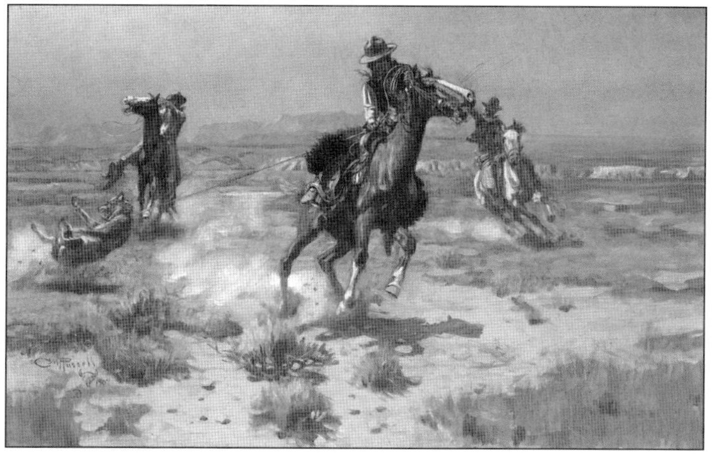

At Rope's End, 1909, oil on canvas, 22 x 32 inches.
Private Collection, Colorado.

Things also grew quiet in much of Russell's mature work; action yielded to mood as a hush settled over the land. Lambent light suffused some pictures; in others, a penetrating late-day glare illuminated the background and cast the foreground in deep shadow. Figures sprang into rounded life, rising above the horizon line in heroic relief against Montana's Big Sky. (The outlaw in *Wolf and the Beaver*, as a fugitive on the run, must skulk like a wolf below the horizon line, avoiding exposure.) Contemporaries recognized the remarkable change in Russell's art. Philip G. Cole, a major collector, was uninterested in paintings done "as far back as 1899." "Many of his best things were done many many years ago," he acknowledged to Nancy, but "as a general rule his early things were not up to the things he did after 1900."[9] The transformation Cole detected had not come about by accident.

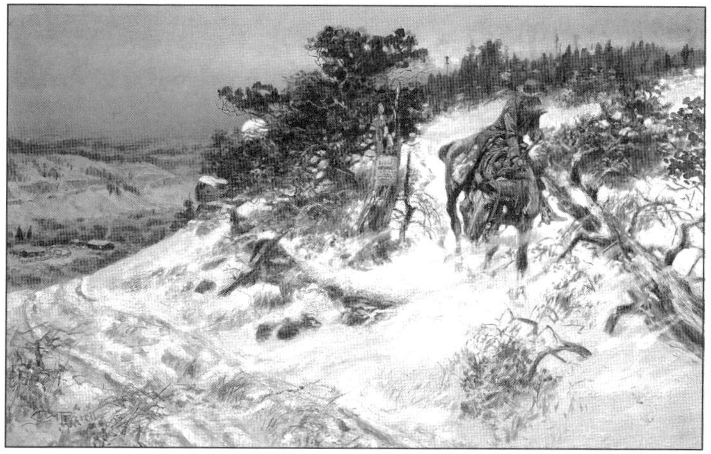

Wolf and the Beaver, 1909, oil on canvas, 23.5 x 35.5 inches.
Private Collection, California.

In the early 1900s, the Russells were still unworldly. Both admitted that the Cowboy Artist's reputation did not travel far across the Mississippi. In an interview published in the Anaconda Standard on December 15, 1901, Russell remarked, "There's nothing in the east for me. What do eastern people care about my pictures? Why, they wouldn't give 50 cents a dozen for them. It is the western people who understand them and the western people are the only ones who will want my pictures. . . . It would be useless for me to go East. I am going to stay right here and paint things as I see them in nature."[10] But getting exposure in the East was Nancy's priority after she took full charge of the business end of her husband's career. In 1902, she placed eight watercolors with William Macbeth, whose New York gallery specialized in "the work of American artists," as its letterhead stated. "One reason we have tried to send you what you wanted as soon as possable was becaus we wanted to get Mr. Russell[s] pictures started in New York," Nancy informed Macbeth. "There are more peopel who would buy and show his work so he would become beter knowen in the East." For Nancy, such exposure was the means to an unchanging end: higher prices for Russell art. When Macbeth balked at her demands and returned a batch of paintings as too expensive, she agreed that for the present Charles M. Russell would "hafto stay this side of Chacago where he and his work are knowen."[11] But Nancy did not retreat on her prices, nor on her desire to conquer the East.

Events moved rapidly in 1903. The Russells left Great Falls in October to visit his family in Saint Louis and see about having his work displayed at the Saint Louis World's Fair in 1904. At the invitation of an established illustrator of their acquaintance, John N. Marchand, they continued on to New York City. The experience opened their eyes. Opportunities beckoned in New York, notably in the field of illustration, and they were back again before the year was out for a protracted stay. Russell made friends easily and enjoyed the company of fellow artists. For the first time in his life, he had the opportunity to observe trained professionals at work and to absorb the technical information that so profoundly transformed his work. New York became a regular stop on the Russells' travels, and by 1910 Nancy was angling for a one-man show at a New York gallery. Because Russell had been under exclusive contract with the Brown & Bigelow calendar company since 1908 "where they use the copyright and we retain the originals," she explained to William Macbeth, they had a collection of paintings on hand suitable for exhibition.[12] Moreover, the Brown & Bigelow prints had given Russell's art the sought-for exposure in the East which, presumably, would translate into sales. Nancy's initiative paid off when "The West That Has Passed," a one-man exhibition featuring thirteen oils, twelve watercolors, and six bronzes, opened at New York's Folsom Galleries on April 12, 1911. It marked Russell's artistic coming of age. Previously Nancy had focused on greater productivity and rather arbitrary price increases to advance their income; New York taught her that exhibition quality pieces showing Russell at his best provided a surer path to prosperity, since a rising reputation elevated prices naturally. This was one of many calculations that figured into her management of his career--and that directly impacted on his art after 1911.

In 1912 Russell held his first international exhibition at (fittingly) the first Calgary Stampede. It was an unqualified success. Nancy sold thirteen of the twenty pictures catalogued, five to a single patron. This pretty much settled them on another Canadian exhibition the next year, in Winnipeg, where a local critic summed up Russell's recent artistic development: "That he is susceptible to experience as well as environment is plainly shown in his pictures. One has but to study his earlier work and compare them with those painted in the past two or three years. His later work is superior in every way."[13] The Canadian exhibitions in 1912 and 1913 served as stepping stones to Russell's only exhibition abroad, at the Dore Galleries in London in 1914. The English critics were mixed about his art, but the most perceptive praised his horses, his "great power of suggesting movement," his Western candor and light, and his seamless fusion of romance and realism.[14] Russell returned from England a considerable celebrity, and between February 1915 and April 1916 held major exhibitions in Chicago, New York, San Francisco, Pittsburgh, and Chicago and New York again. This hectic schedule abruptly ended when the Russells adopted a son, Jack Cooper Russell, in December 1916, beginning a three year hiatus in travel and exhibitions that was welcomed by Charlie, if not by Nancy. Commissions kept him busy enough, and staying at home was obviously to his taste; she fretted over finances, however, and grew increasingly restless with the inactivity. In late August 1919 they hit the road again, attending the second Calgary Stampede and continuing on to Saskatoon in September and Minneapolis in December. After 1919 there would be no further respites for Charlie until poor health intervened in the summer of 1923, and death in 1926.

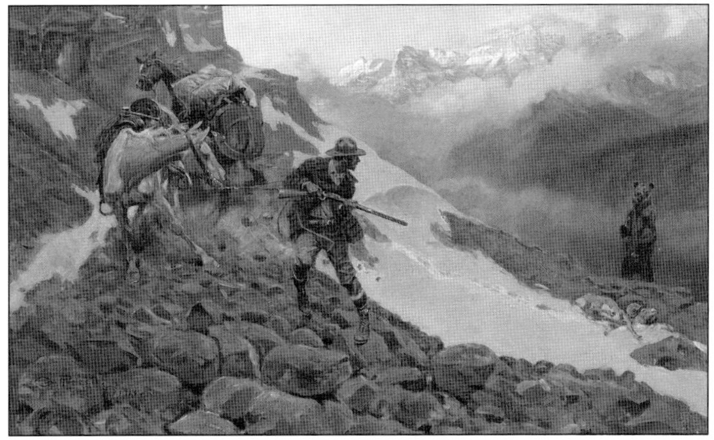

Whose Meat?, 1914, oil on canvas, 30,25 x 48.75 inches. Private Collection, California.

Exhibition catalogs from the years 1909 to 1923 provide a revealing record of Russell in his prime. These were his greatest years as an artist as he produced a string of masterpieces and gave definitive form to that vision we still think of as Charlie Russell's West. The catalogs also trace an important shift in his artistic focus. Of the twenty paintings he exhibited at Calgary in 1912, eight featured Indians and eight cowboys. Thirteen sold. Seven were Indian subjects, one showing a dance, the rest showing parties of warriors posed on a promontory or moving across the plains. Five were cowboy subjects, only one not an action piece. The thirteenth picture sold was of a man-bear confrontation--a Russell staple (*Whose Meat?*, for example) at future exhibitions. By the time Russell returned to Calgary in 1919 the balance of subjects he exhibited reflected sales patterns as well as personal preference. The catalog listed twenty-four oil paintings.

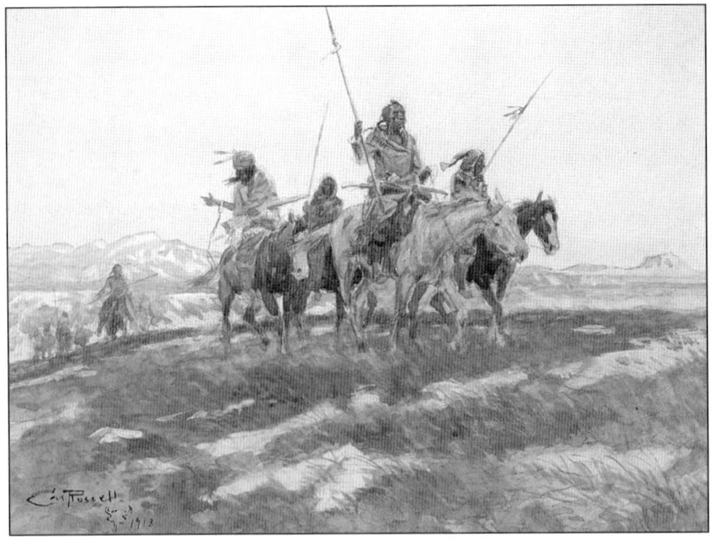

Piegan Hunting Party, 1913,
watercolor, 10.625 x 13..625 inches
Private Collection.

Four were hunting scenes, three involving bears, and one was a wildlife study of blacktail deer. Three of the paintings (with an obvious Canadian appeal) showed the North-West Mounted Police, two featured mountain men, and another depicted a sheriff making an arrest. Cowboys figured in three paintings, Indians in ten, indicating just how much the Cowboy Artist had shifted to Indian subjects. The cowboy paintings were all action pieces--a rider on a bucking bronco and two roping scenes. In contrast, eight of the ten Indian pictures involved no overt action, showing mounted warriors perched on a bluff or moving magisterially across an illimitable space, masters of their own domain. *Piegan Hunting Party*, *Indian Party* (plate #18) and *Mandan Warrior* are squarely in this tradition. After the Russells began wintering each year in California in 1920, Russell sometimes substituted Navajos for plains Indians to appeal to local taste. The Indian, he said, was "the onley real American," and as such the perfect symbol of that open land and freedom that he celebrated in his exhibitions of "The West That Has Passed."[15]

Practical considerations besides subject matter affected Russell's mature art since art, as Nancy liked to say, was a business. She had to be resourceful, organizing advance publicity, getting stories planted in the local papers where Charlie was exhibiting, and holding up her end in business negotiations over commissions, copyrights and prices for direct sales. When a prospective Wall Street client tried to argue her down from a quoted price, Nancy replied that it was impossible "for us to consider the offer which you have very kindly repeated because, strange as it may seem, we, in our line of endeavor, are trying to operate our business affairs upon a business basis." [16] Nothing, in short, happened by chance. Even the size and medium of exhibition pieces reflected Nancy's sales experience and her evalutation of the market.

In a fascinating 1922 letter to the manager of a lithography firm interested in commissioning a series of historical paintings for purposes of reproduction, Nancy specified a few of the calculations that entered into the business of Russell art. First, a commission had to fall within his range and style and liking, and she was pleased to report that he was "most enthusiastic" about the proposal. "Painting the life of the western frontiers has been his work for thirty years," she stated, "and his long study and observation of western history has particularly fitted him for such a commission." Having consulted Charlie, Nancy suggested possible subjects, noting that Buffalo Bill Cody, Kit Carson and Lewis and Clark had been overdone (certainly Russell had contributed his mite!). She then turned to "a very important matter." The client had suggested vertical compositions, about thirty by forty inches in size, to facilitate reproduction. But "Mr. Russell has always felt that upright compositions greatly limit the scope of action," Nancy explained:

"For instance it is, in his opinion, impossible to do justice to, say, an Indian fight where the breadth of convas is narrower than the length. Of course where only a single figure or a very small group is involved, the same difficulty is not encountered.'

'Mr. Russell, as you probably know, has done considerable work for calendar houses. Brown & Bigelow and the Osborne Company have always used 24 x 36 canvases with excellent reults for their purposes. My own suggestion would be to use canvases 40 x 50, with the composition so arranged as to permit elimination of space on each side, sufficient to bring the picture to the proportions you require, and my reasons for suggesting this are as follows:

First--Mr. Russell does infinitely better work on a wide canvas, where he has sufficient scope for his landscape, and the width of these canvases can be cut to include the action of the picture in reproduction without loss from the illustration or story standpoint. This has frequently been done by the calendar houses above mentioned.'

'Second--The value of the canvases to the owner is, I should say, one hundred per cent greater on the wider canvas, where the proper amount of landscape is provided as a setting for the action. Much of the charm of Mr. Russell's work is lost if he has to crowd his composition into too narrow limits. Western landscape is big and must be treated in a big way."[17]

Nancy was right about the nature of Russell reproductions. Some of his most famous prints (*When Blackfeet and Sioux Meet*, *Red Man's Wireless*, *Wagon Boss*, *Sun Worshippers*, *Sagebrush Sport* and *Jerked Down*, for example) center the action at the expense of background and, in a few instances, peripheral figures. Sometimes Russell's "Big Sky" became a low ceiling, and the substantial settings that he favored shrank as the borders closed in. Charlie accepted these changes, and even anticipated them by signing his name well inside a picture's margins to accommodate reduction. But the resulting prints, with their tight focus, have created

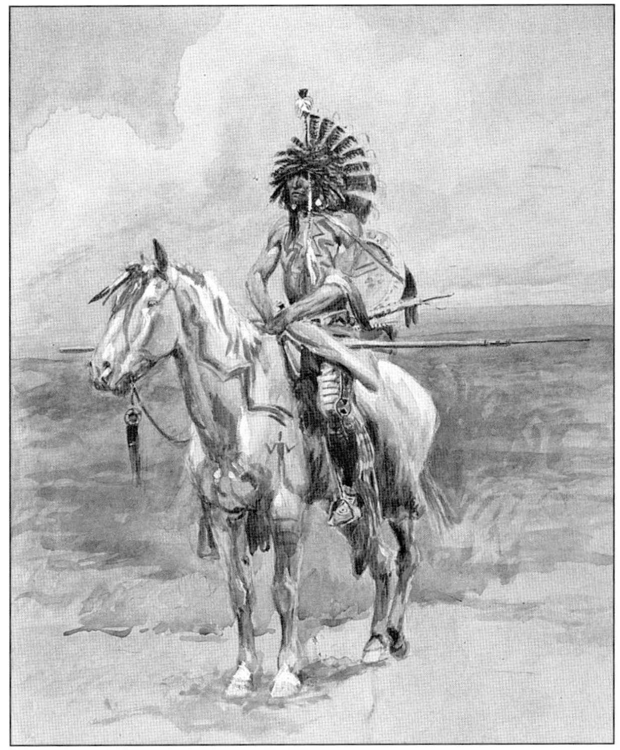

Mandan Warrior, 1906
watercolor on cardboard,
17 x 11 inches
Private Collection.

misunderstanding about his actual more spacious compositions, and have confused his meaning. To Russell, the Old West was an expansive, magic land, and his art faithfully mirrored his vision.

Nancy also explained to their prospective patron in 1922 that Russell was "very much opposed to sending out a preliminary sketch of a painting, as when he completes the painting it is quite likely to be very different from the first idea. In other words he requires entire freedom in working out a subject."[18] In fact, Russell had received many commissions over the years, and when pressed had produced working sketches and accepted the patrons' right of refusal. This was a sensitive point with Nancy. She did not like to send out work on speculation. Even while actively seeking illustrating assignments on their early visits to New York, Nancy was adamant that Charlie could not be paid as a novice, or treated as one.[19] Nor could he accept commissions for work that would be unsaleable were it rejected. "From your letters," she scolded a client in 1904, "you would think Mr Russell had nothing to do but try to pleas [sic] you and waist so much time and you look at the work then return same as if you had not ordered it at all."[20]

Nancy was more flexible where private commissions were concerned. In 1912 Malcolm Mackay ordered a painting of an old-time calf roundup. It had to be three by five feet in frame to fit the space available. Charlie obliged with a "very rough" sketch for Mackay's approval. In forwarding it, Nancy cautioned: "It may convey to you some notion of the composition but Chas. creates as he goes so would probably change things around to better advantage when actually working on the picture."[21] More pretentious commissions required more pretentious preliminary sketches. Russell had to submit a design to fulfill contractural obligations specified in his 1911 commission from the State of Montana for a mural to decorate the House of Representatives chamber in Helena. He did, though what officials approved bore only a family resemblance to the finished mural, *Lewis and Clark Meeting the Flathead Indians at Ross' Hole* (page 2).[22] Russell also prepared a preliminary oil sketch for his commission from the Montana Club, the superb *When the Land Belonged to God* (page 4).[23] But no commission was more pretentious--or, from a financial standpoint, more rewarding--than that from Edward L. Doheny to paint a two-part mural that would be thirty inches high and over twenty feet long. Nancy, having sold *The Wolf and the*

Beaver to the Dohenys in the spring of 1924, had the bit in her teeth by the fall; while she managed an exhibition in Duluth that December, Charlie stayed home in Great Falls to work on an oil painting and, he assured her, the designs the Dohenys required. He completed four preparatory sketches and Nancy took them with her to Los Angeles in April to await the Dohenys' decision. The commission was so lucrative--a purported $30,000--and Nancy so desperate to procure it, that Charlie had swallowed his pride (and muffled his disdain for "progress") by including the oil derricks Mr. Doheny as a prominent oil-man required in his mural. But Charlie honored his principles by relegating them to an obscure spot in the background.[24]

When it came time to paint the Doheny mural in the spring of 1926, Russell was too tired and too ill to enjoy his success. The Doheny commission established a record price for his work; it also established the critical intersection between art and commerce in his career. Art was a business, as Nancy insisted. But art also remained an outlet for Charlie Russell's deepest convictions. He felt the passing of the Old West as a personal loss, and, in his advancing years, made his art his own pathway back to yesterday. It provided an emotional release that transcended the pressures of success while permitting him to remain true to himself. The West, Russell told an old cowboy friend in 1922, "was a sweetheart of yours and mine, a wild maid with maney lovers. She . . . is an old woman now but we still love her."[25] That heartfelt message, coupled with a hard-won technical mastery, was the essence of Charles M. Russell's mature art.

NOTES

1. C. M. Russell note to Joe De Yong [January 1916], De Yong Papers, National Cowboy Hall of Fame, Oklahoma City, Oklahoma; illustrated in Joe De Yong (Scottsdale: Main Trail Galleries, 1980), p. 50.
2. C. M. Russell note to Joe De Yong [1916], De Yong Papers, C. M. Russell Museum, Great Falls, Montana.
3. E. W. (Bill) Gollings to Joe De Yong, January 13, 1924, December 5, 1925, De Yong Papers, C. M. Russell Museum; and Joe De Yong, "Charlie and Me . . . We Run Together Fine," Persimmon Hill 11, #3-4 (1982): 72.
4. Jessie Lincoln Mitchell, "C. M. Russell--The White Indian," Montana, the Magazine of Western History 10 (Winter 1960): 8.
5. Fergus Mead to James B. Rankin, May 10, 1938, James Brownlee Rankin Papers, Montana Historical Society, Helena.
6. Frank M. Chapman, Jr., "The Man Behind the Brush," Country Life 50 (August 1926): 37.
7. C. M. Russell note to Joe De Yong [January 1916], De Yong Papers, C. M. Russell Museum.
8. "Cowboy Artist Paints as He Talks, Lives," Minneapolis Journal, December 14, 1919.
9. Philip G. Cole to Nancy C. Russell, March 18, 1930, Mary 19, 1930, Helen and Homer E. Britzman Collection, Taylor Museum for Southwestern Studies, Colorado Springs Fine Arts Center, Colorado Springs, Colorado.
10. Typescript copy, Rankin Papers.
11. Nancy C. Russell to William Macbeth, December 12, December 24, 1902, Macbeth Gallery Correspondence, Archives of American Art: NMc
12. Nancy C. Russell to William Macbeth, December 6, 1909, and Cora W. Taylor (for Caspar Whitney) to Macbeth, May 21, 1910, Macbeth Gallery Correspondence.
13. C. St. J.-B., "Cowboy Artist at the Stampede," Winnipeg Free Press, August 12, 1913.
14. "The Cowboy Artist," Evening Standard (London), April 7, 1914; also T.L., "Cowboy-Painter: The Wild West in Bond-Street," Daily Mail (London), April 10, 1914.
15. C. M. Russell to Charles N. Pray, January 5, 1914, in Brian W. Dippie, ed., Charles M. Russell, Word Painter: Letters 1887-1926 (Fort Worth: Amon Carter Museum, in association with Harry N. Abrams, New York, 1993), p. 188.
16. Nancy C. Russell to George F. Baker, November 28, 1919, Britzman Collection.
17. Nancy C. Russell to H. S. Morgan, November 15, 1922, carbon copy, Britzman Collection.
18. Ibid.
19. Joseph Keppler to James B. Rankin, April 17, 1939, Rankin Papers.
20. Nancy C. Russell to Mr. H. Behrens, October 14, 1904, handwritten draft, Britzman Collection.
21. Malcolm S. Mackay to Nancy C. Russell, July 16 [1912], and Nancy C. Russell to Mackay, September 24, 1912, Britzman Collection.
22. See Dippie, ed., Charles M. Russell, Word Painter, pp. 162-63. Russell may have had to alter his original design because of a contractural confusion over the size of his mural. Russell's contract specified a painting 12' x 14', an error since what was desired was a painting 24' 9" x 11' 7-1/2". See Agreement, between the State of Montana and Charles M. Russell, July 24, 1911, Britzman Collection; Edwin L. Norris to Nancy C. Russell, January 12, 1912, copy, and C. M. Russell to A. J. Galen, Attorney General, Helena, January 23, 1912, Charles M. Russell research materials, Montana Historical Society, microfilm reel 3.
23. See Peter H. Hassrick, Charles M. Russell (New York: Harry N. Abrams, in association with the National Museum of American Art, Smithsonian Institution, Washington, D.C., 1989), pp. 111-12.
24. See Joe De Yong to his mother, April 11, 1924, De Yong Papers, National Cowboy Hall of Fame; Dippie, ed., Charles M. Russell, Word Painter, pp. 360-61, 368-70; Robert O. Schad, "The Estelle Doheny Collection," The New Colophon: A Book-Collectors' Miscellany (New York: Privately printed, 1950), pp. 232, 238; M. Hal Sussmann, "Russell Murals Unveiled," Southwest Art 18 (May 1989): 60-63. I am grateful to Professor Patricia M. Burnham, The University of Texas at Austin, for information on the Doheny murals.
25. C. M. Russell inscription (ca. 1922) in Richard R. Kilroy's copy of Rawhide Rawlins Stories (1921); in Frederic G. Renner, Paper Talk: Illustrated Letters of Charles M. Russell (Fort Worth: Amon Carter Museum of Western Art, 1962), p. 64.

THE PAINTINGS

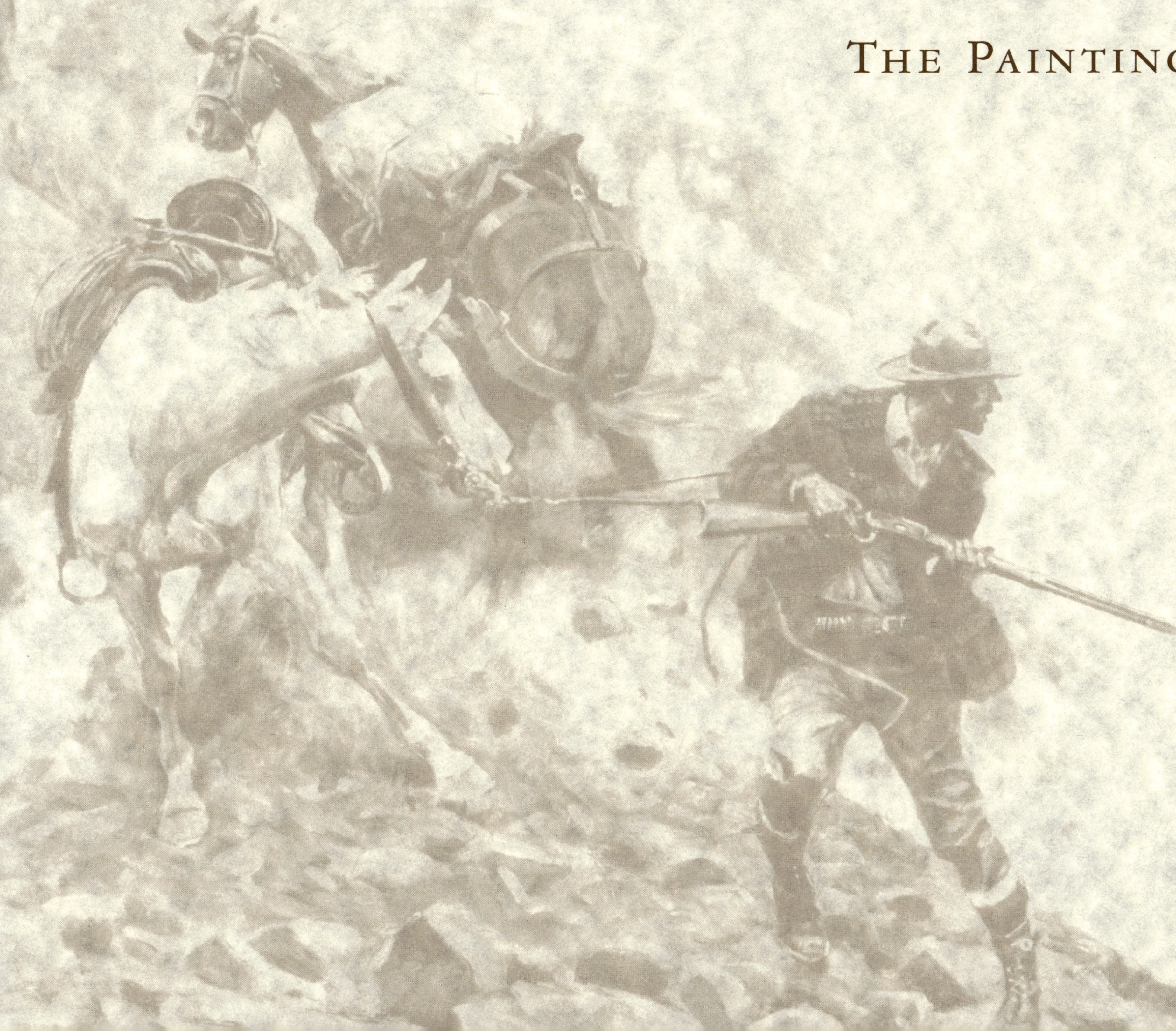

PAINTING PLATES

Title / Year

1. Indians on Plains, 1903
watercolor on paper
7 1/4 x 19 1/2 inches
signed and dated lower left: CM Russell/skull cipher/1903

PROVENANCE: Private Collection, California; {Mongerson Wunderlich Gallery, Chicago, Illinois}; Private Collection, Washington, D.C.

As a self-taught artist, Russell's only art instructors had been nature and his keen powers of observation. In 1903, he received his first opportunity to observe trained illustrators at work and to absorb the technical information that was to profoundly transform his art. As a result of advice and exposure from eastern artists and publishers, his craftsmanship and handling of color greatly improved. Russell had already begun to lighten his palette as early as 1897 and 1898. He became interested in obtaining desired effects with color alone. This transformation is particularly evident in his watercolors of the period such as *Indians on Plain* and *The Signal* (plate #2), in which he utilized a broader range of color in place of the earth tones that dominated his paintings throughout the 1800's.

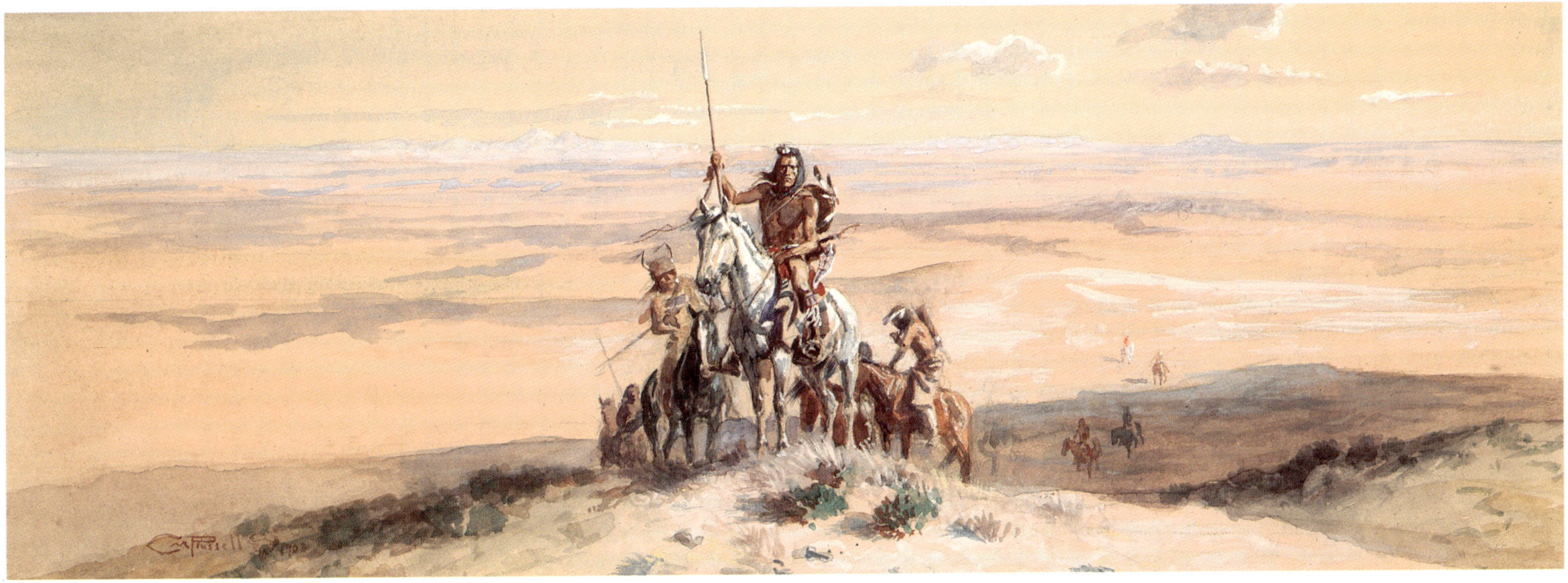

2. The Signal, 1903
watercolor and gouache on paper
14 x 19 3/4 inches
signed and dated lower left: CMR/skull cipher/1903

PROVENANCE: William A. Crowfoot, Miramir, Puerto Rico (1969); David DeFrancisca, South Laguna, California, (1977); William Morkill, Bellevue, Washington, (1977-1994).

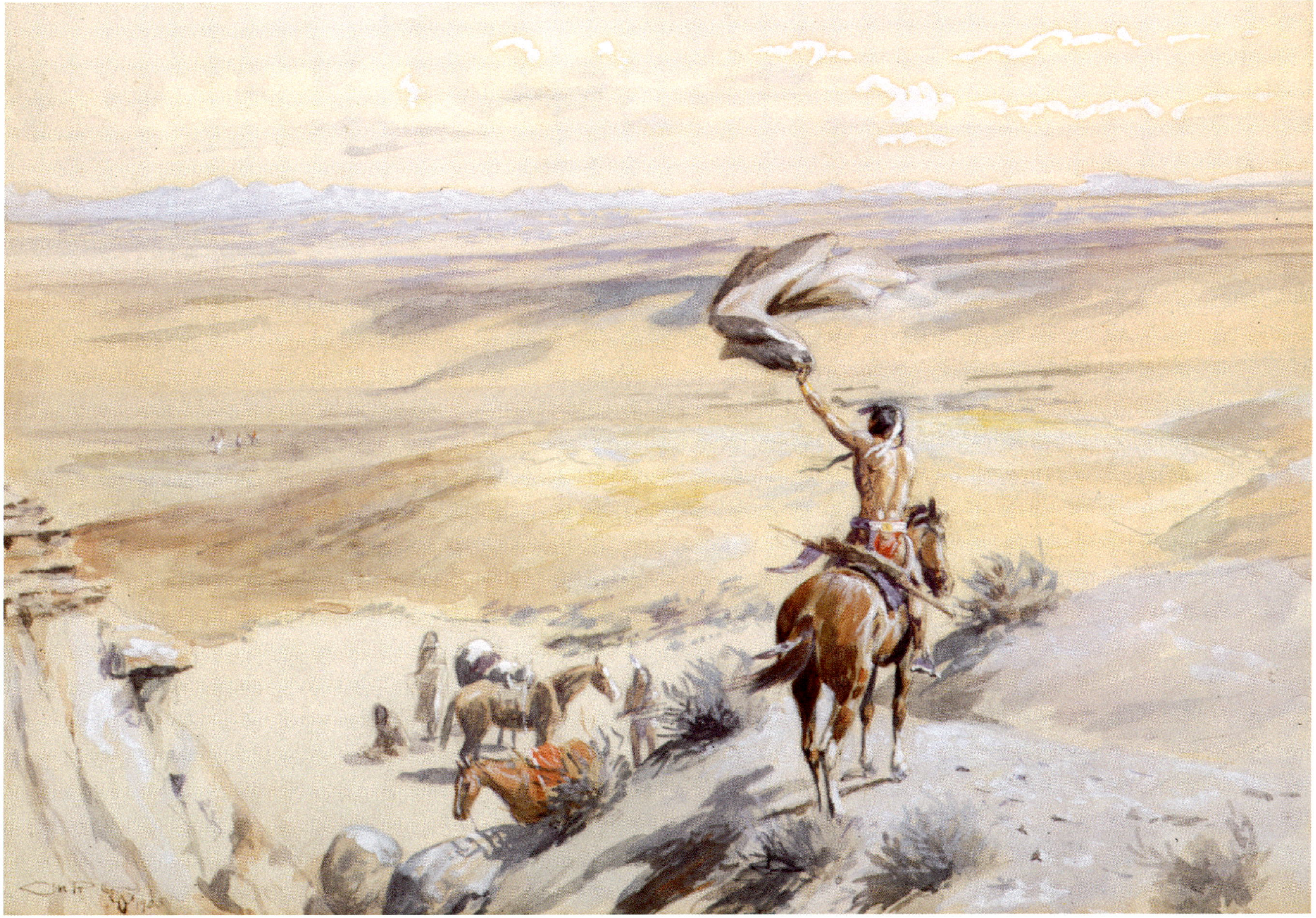

3. Big Horn Sheep, 1904
watercolor and gouache on paper
10 1/4 x 7 1/2 inches
signed and dated lower left: CM Russell/1904/skull cipher

PROVENANCE: Private Collection, Oklahoma.

By the time Russell had executed this watercolor, the Rocky Mountain sheep had been so widely hunted that their range had diminished to a few remote strips of mountainous terrain. Russell's masterful evocation of two rams fighting off the edge of a rocky precipice presaged one of his most accomplished studies of wild animals in bronze, *The Combat.*

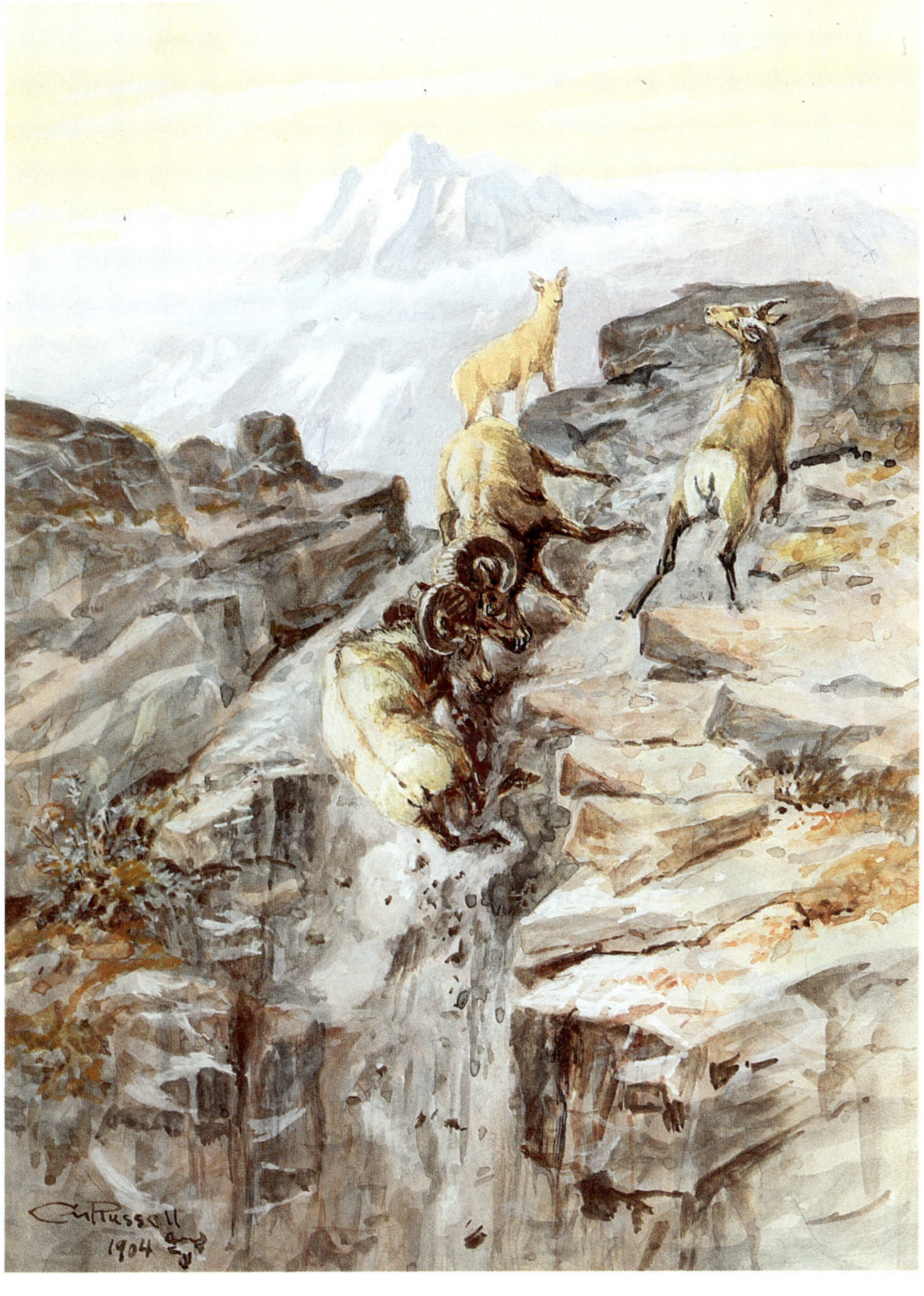
CMRussell
1904

4. *A Slick Rider,* 1905
watercolor on paper
16 x 13 1/2 inches
signed and dated lower left: CM Russell/1905/copyrighted

PROVENANCE: Frederic Hussey, circa 1905; Bill Magee, 1945; Stremmel Galleries, Ltd., Reno, Nevada; Ralph Tingle; {Gerald Peters Gallery, Santa Fe, New Mexico}; Private Collection, Montana, 1988.

From his initial canvases executed during the 1880s until late in his career, a favorite subject of Russell's was the bucking horse. His intimate knowledge and appreciation of ranch life led Russell to explore this theme on canvas and in bronze. *A Slick Rider* demonstrates his thorough understanding of human and animal anatomy in motion; rendered with the high degree of naturalism and authenticity his contemporaries were unable to match even with the advent of stop-action photography. The vertical composition centered around the image of horse and rider against a minimal background augments the visual impact of the scene.

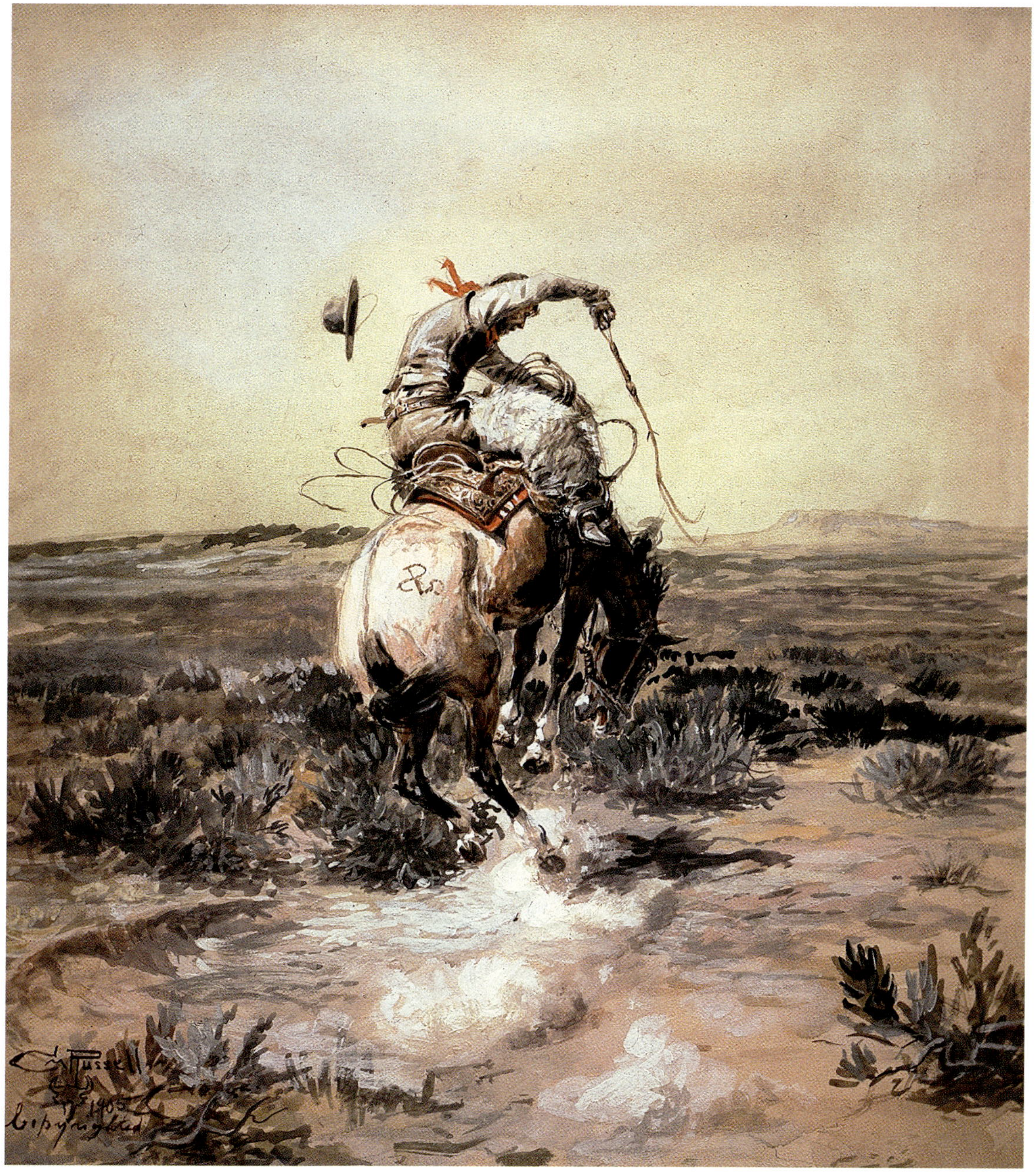

5. *Indian with Spear,* 1905
watercolor and gouache on paper
14 x 10 inches
signed and dated lower left: CM Russell/skull cipher/1905

PROVENANCE: Private Collection, Oklahoma.

A comparison of Russell's single figure studies, before and after the turn of the century, provides a revealing summary of his increasing technical expertise. By 1905, his handling of human and equine form had reached its peak, mainly due to his exposure to the New York art world over the winter of 1903-1904. The simple horse and rider composition in *Indian with Spear* reveals Russell's burgeoning sophistication as a draftsman and colorist. These new skills and innovations would later translate into the carefully finished, multi-figured paintings of the following decade.

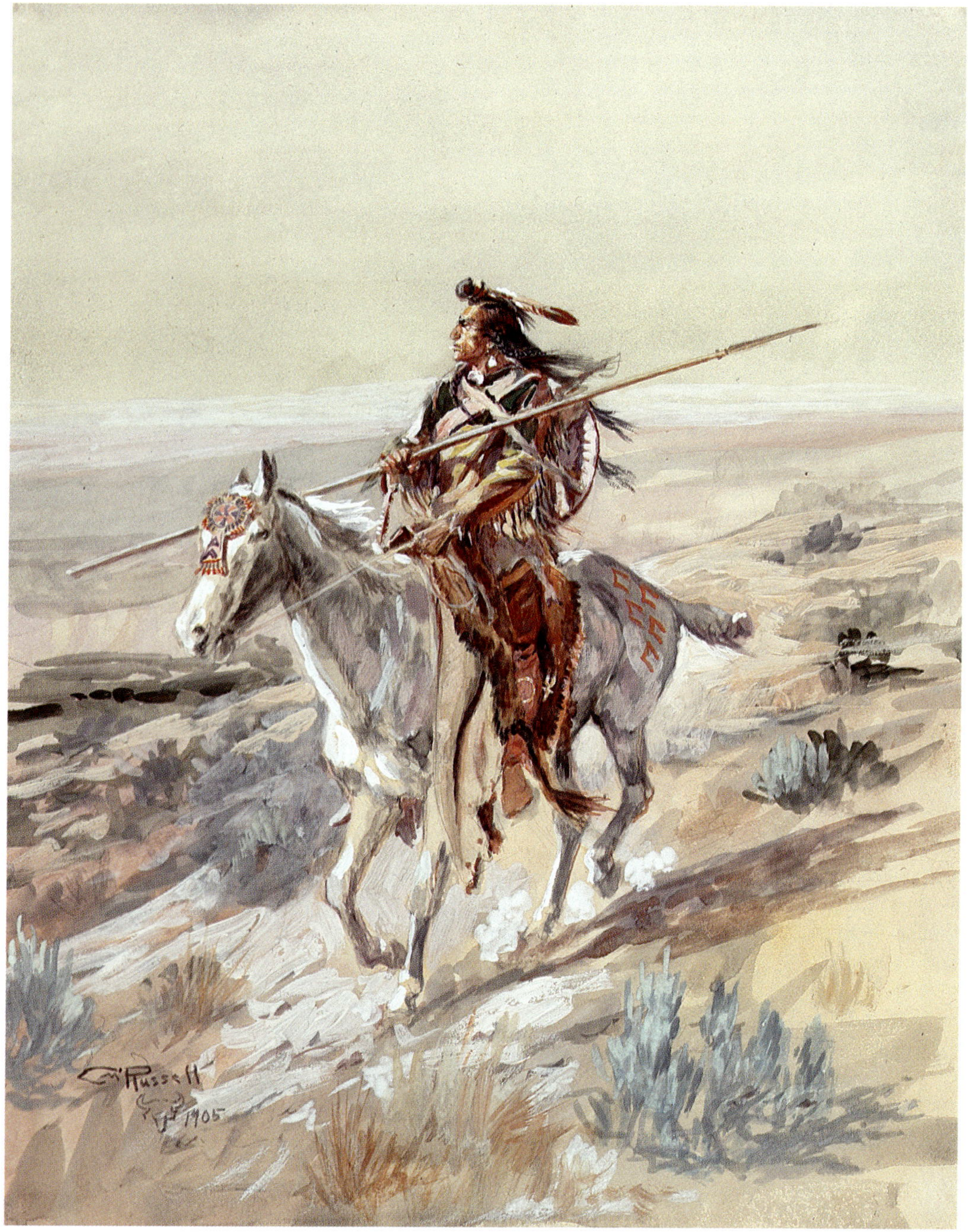
CMRussell
1905

6. *Blackfeet Burning Crow Buffalo Range,* 1905
watercolor on paper
13 3/8 x 19 1/2 inches
signed and dated lower left: CM Russell/skull cipher/1905

PROVENANCE: Mrs. Andrew Davis Collection, Butte, Montana; Estate of W.E. Weiss, Montana.

REFERENCES: Buffalo Bill Historical Center Exhibition catalogue, Buffalo Bill Memorial Association, Cody, Wyoming c. 1959; Preserving The Heritage Of The Old West exhibition catalogue, May 1961, Buffalo Bill Historical Center, Cody Wyoming, pg.2; Exhibition of Paintings, Drawings and Sculpture by Notable Documentary Artists of the Old West exhibition catalogue, May 1 to September 15, 1962, The Gallery of Western Art, Buffalo Bill Historical Center, Cody Wyoming, pg. 10; Cattleman, 30:5, "Charles Russell Famous Cowboy Artist of Montana," by A.M. Hurting, October, 1943, pg. 34; Montana, The Magazine of Western History, 8:3, (Summer, 1958), "My Partner, Charlie," by Con Price, pg. 63; True West, 4:3, (January-February, 1957)[3]; Illustrated in "The Cowboy Artist," Ridgely Calendar Co., Great Falls, MT., c.1922; A Bibliography of the Published Works of Charles M. Russell , by Karl Yost & Frederic G. Renner, University of Nebraska Press, Lincoln, 1971, pp. 50, 52, 54, 79, 89, 90, 104, 132, 147, 161, 195, 247; Brian W. Dippie, "'I Feel that I am Improving Right Along': Continuity and Change in Charles M. Russell's Art," Montana: The Magazine of Western History 38 (Summer 1988); Peter Hassrick, Charles M. Russell, Harry Abrahms Publishers, Inc. in association with The National Museum of American Art, 1989, p. 81.

In his determination to remain uninfluenced by art schools because he felt it was better to remain an "unspoiled genius", Russell found himself technically limited. He was receiving criticism on his works being weak and washy, lacking many technical fineries. Fortunately, these problems were surmountable, as Charles Russell was an exceptionally fast study and an adaptable student. In the years following his valuable first trip to New York, his technical abilities soared. Colors and light played a magical hand in creating his later watercolors. The beguiling freshness and natural charm of these works led Mariam White of the Fine Arts Journal to comment that Russell was "no longer a painter of stern realism, but rather a delineator of the poetical." (Hassrick 81)

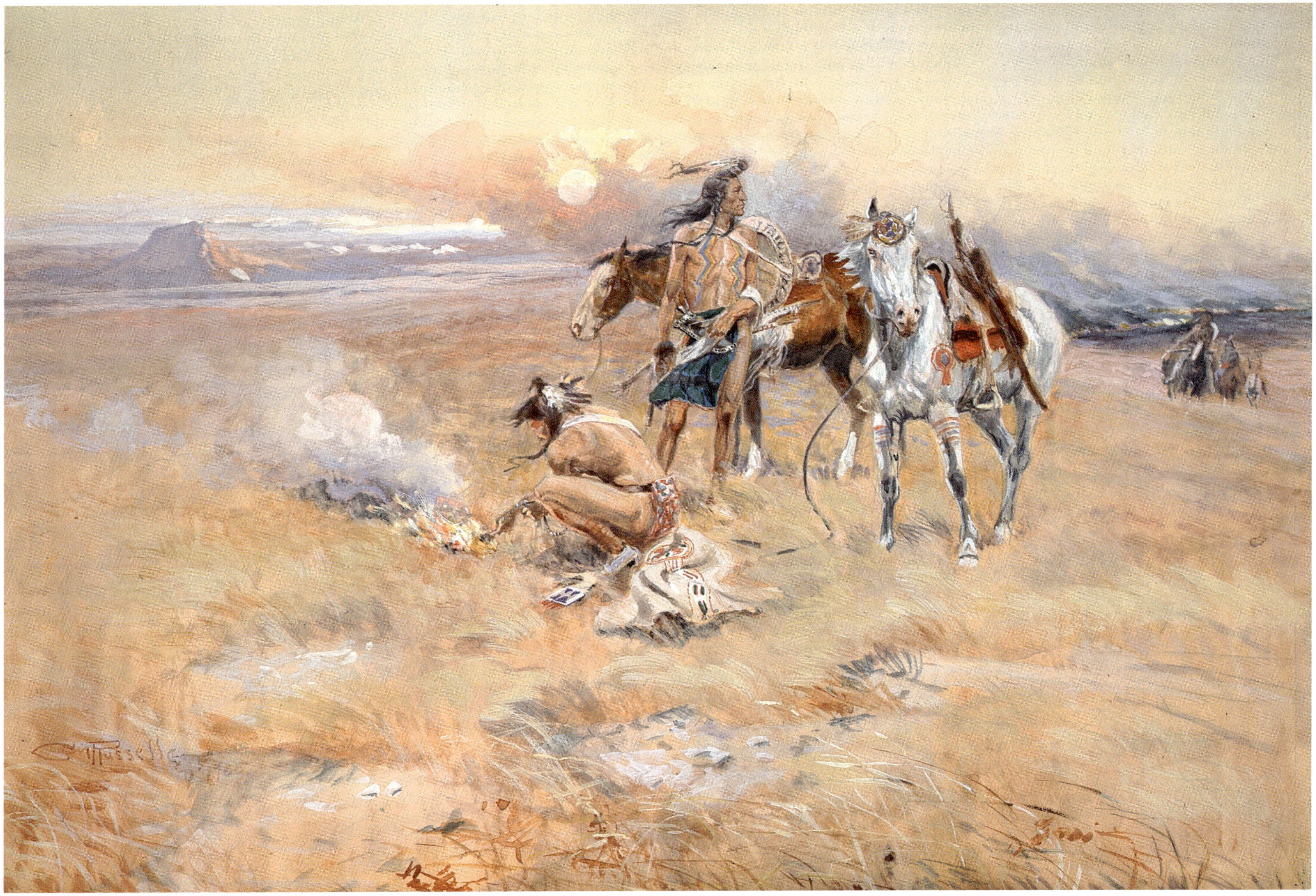

7. *A Cree Indian, c.*1905
oil on canvas
22 x 17 inches
signed lower left: CMR

PROVENANCE: The Artist; William Green Dows; Sutherland and Francis Dows; Henrietta Dows Arnold; {Wunderlich and Peters Galleries}, Private Collection, Milwaukee, Wisconsin.

REFERENCES: Bozeman Daily Chronicle, August 28, 1954, "Local Man's Charlie Russell Sketches Printed for The First Time"; C. M. Russell Gallery exhibition catalogue, c. 1955, Great Falls, MT., pg. 5; A Bibliography Of The Published Works Of Charles M. Russell, by Karl Yost & Frederic G. Renner, University of Nebraska Press, Lincoln, 1971, pp. 47, 111, 137, 138, 156, 157, 235, 238.

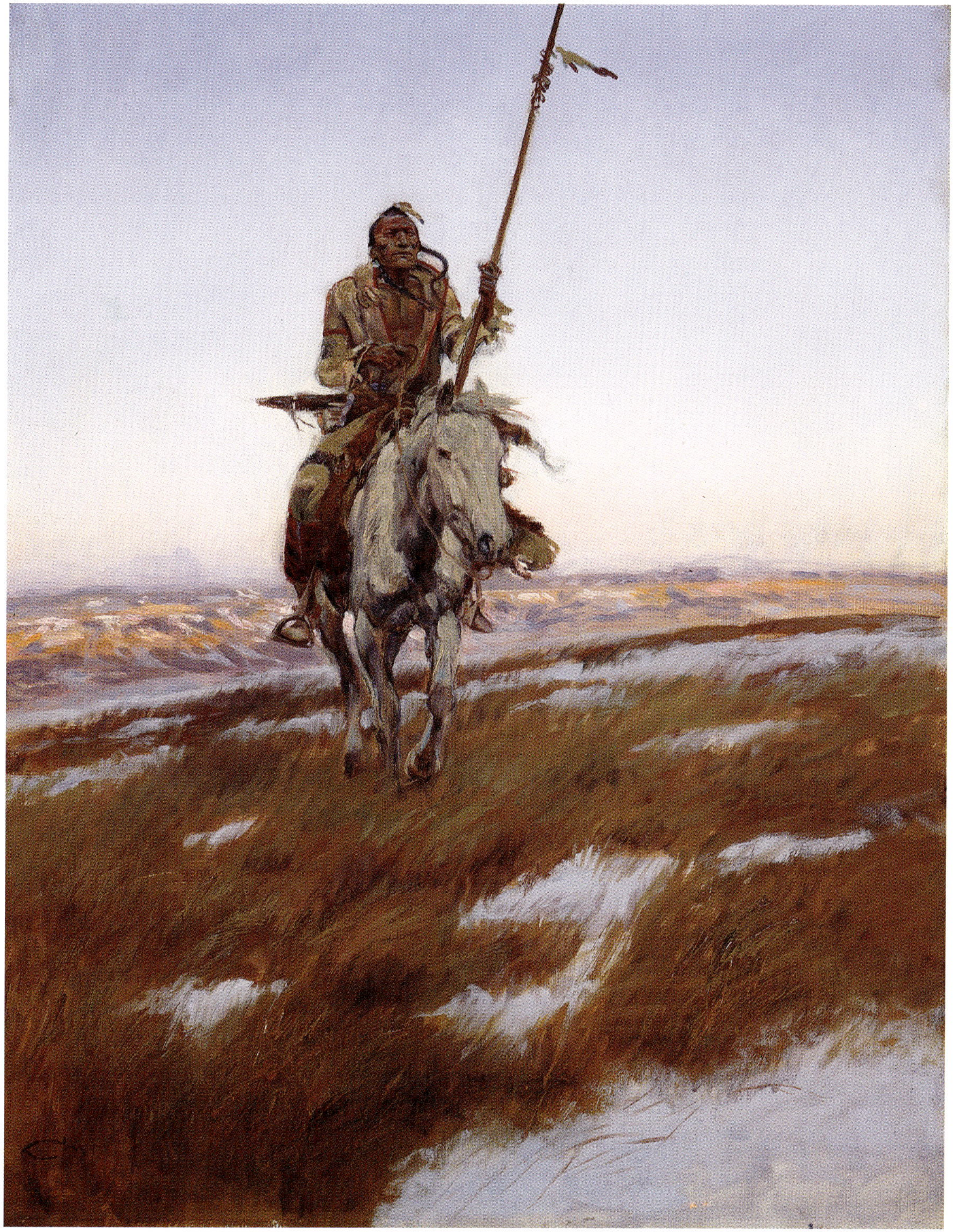

8. *Mandan Warrior,* 1906
watercolor on cardboard
17 x 11 inches
signed & dated lower left: C.M. Russell/1906 /skull cipher/copyright
inscription: *Mandan Warrior* below the image

PROVENANCE: The Artist; Edgar I. Holland, Los Angeles, California; Herbert Conrad (his son-in-law); Mrs. Herbert Conrad (his wife); Herbert & Jerry Conrad (her sons); Acquired by the present owner from the above, 1991.

EXHIBITIONS: Great Falls, Montana, C.M. Russell Museum, (on extended loan 1971-1991).

By the turn of the century, the Indian Wars had ended and the transition to reservation life was in progress throughout the Plains region. As the West of Russell's youth yielded to encroaching civilization, his artistic vision evolved away from stern realism and toward a more romantic style. The image of a single mounted warrior was a format Russell employed frequently and brilliantly manifested his nostalgic sentiments. Throughout his artistic career, he depicted one or more paintings of a lone warrior from every tribe with which he came in contact. Although many of Russell's contemporaries portrayed warrior-types, Russell's thorough knowledge of Native American culture led him to execute more than thirty individual paintings of Indians from some fifteen distinct tribes including *Mandan Warrior* and *A Cree Indian* (plate #7).

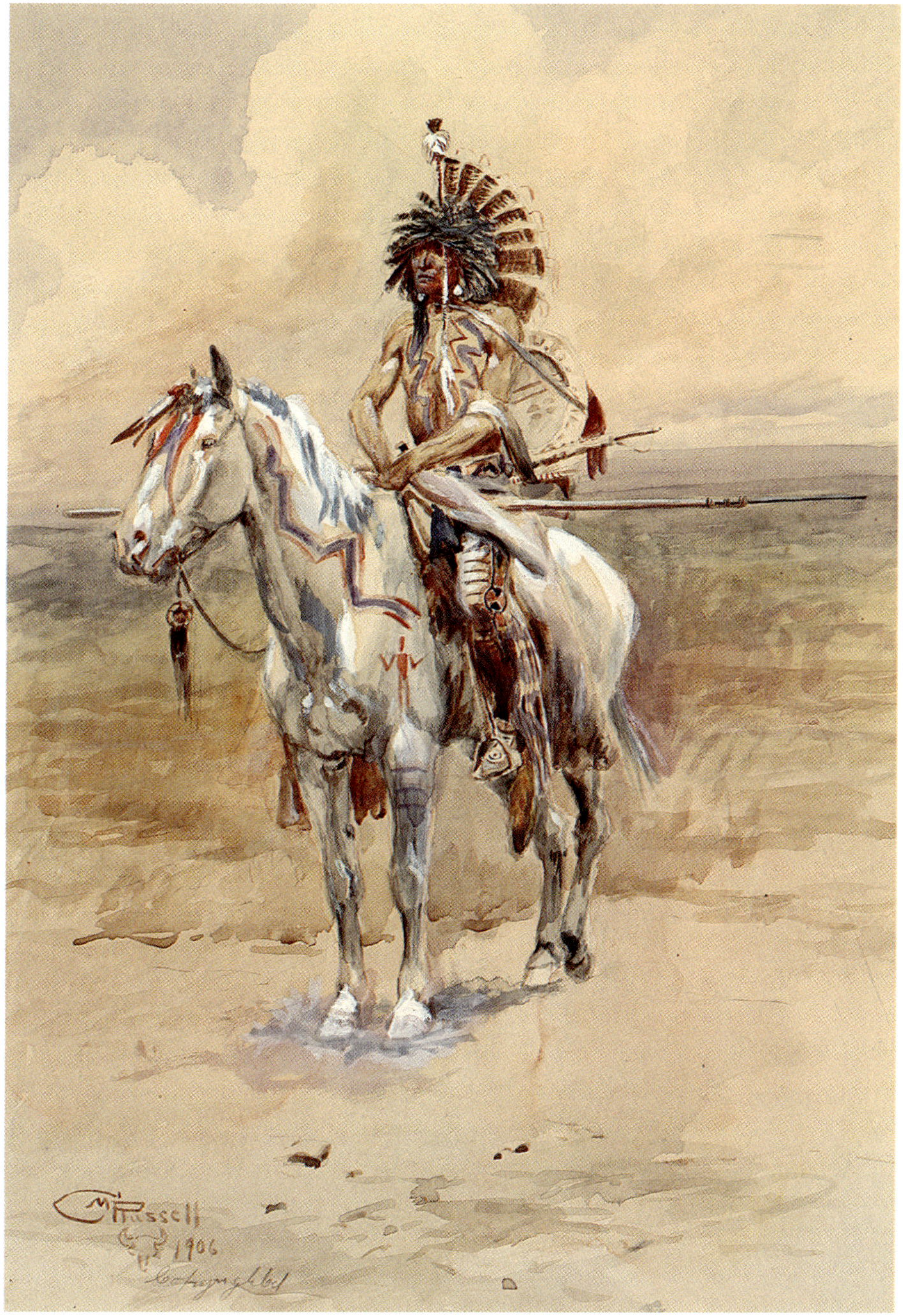
CM Russell
1906

9. *The Bison Trail,* 1908
watercolor on paper
6 1/2 x 10 1/2 inches
signed and dated lower left: CM Russell/1908/skull cipher

PROVENANCE: Private Collection, Oklahoma.

For Russell, the buffalo story assumed mythic proportions and came to represent the passing of the West and the advance of civilization. Since the beginning of his artistic career his depiction of the buffalo took many forms, from highly finished works to abbreviated sketches. He incorporated the outline drawing of a buffalo skull as part of his signature, identifying himself with the fate of the animal that once dominated the American landscape. Russell's sympathetic portrayal reveals his ability as animal painter as well as his reverence for the American Bison.

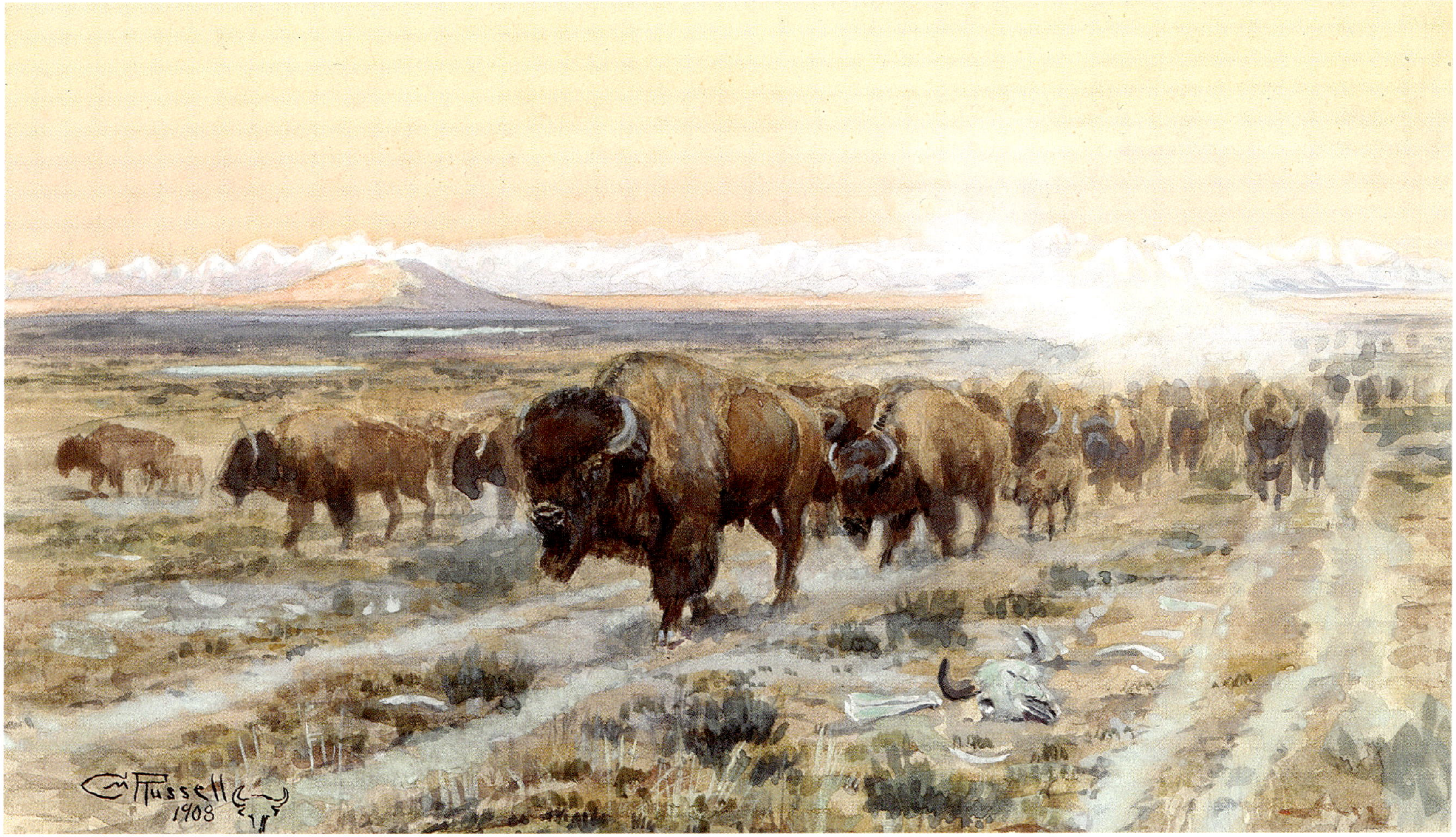

10. When the Plains Were His, 1906
oil on canvas
15 x 15 inches
signed and dated lower left: CM Russell/skull cipher/1906/copyright

PROVENANCE: Museum of Western Art, Denver, Colorado; Private Collection.

REFERENCES: Frontier Spirit, Museum of Western Art, Denver, Colorado, p.46; Peter Hassrick, Charles M. Russell, Henry Abrams Publishers, Inc., in association with The National Museum of American Art, New York, 1989, p.91.

In Charles M. Russell, Peter Hassrick explores the artist's depictions of Indian domestic themes. "He often and sympathetically portrayed the movement of the tribes' daily life within Indian camps, finding personal assurance as well as artistic challenges in these subjects. A favorite was the Indian women and children following in the wake of the hunters," as in *When the Plains Were His.* The Indian family, sensitively detailed and fancifully dressed, moves resolutely toward the viewer, as if reclaiming their land and native traditions. These romantically charged images recall a lost order of nature and an innocence that Russell deemed the best of all worlds.

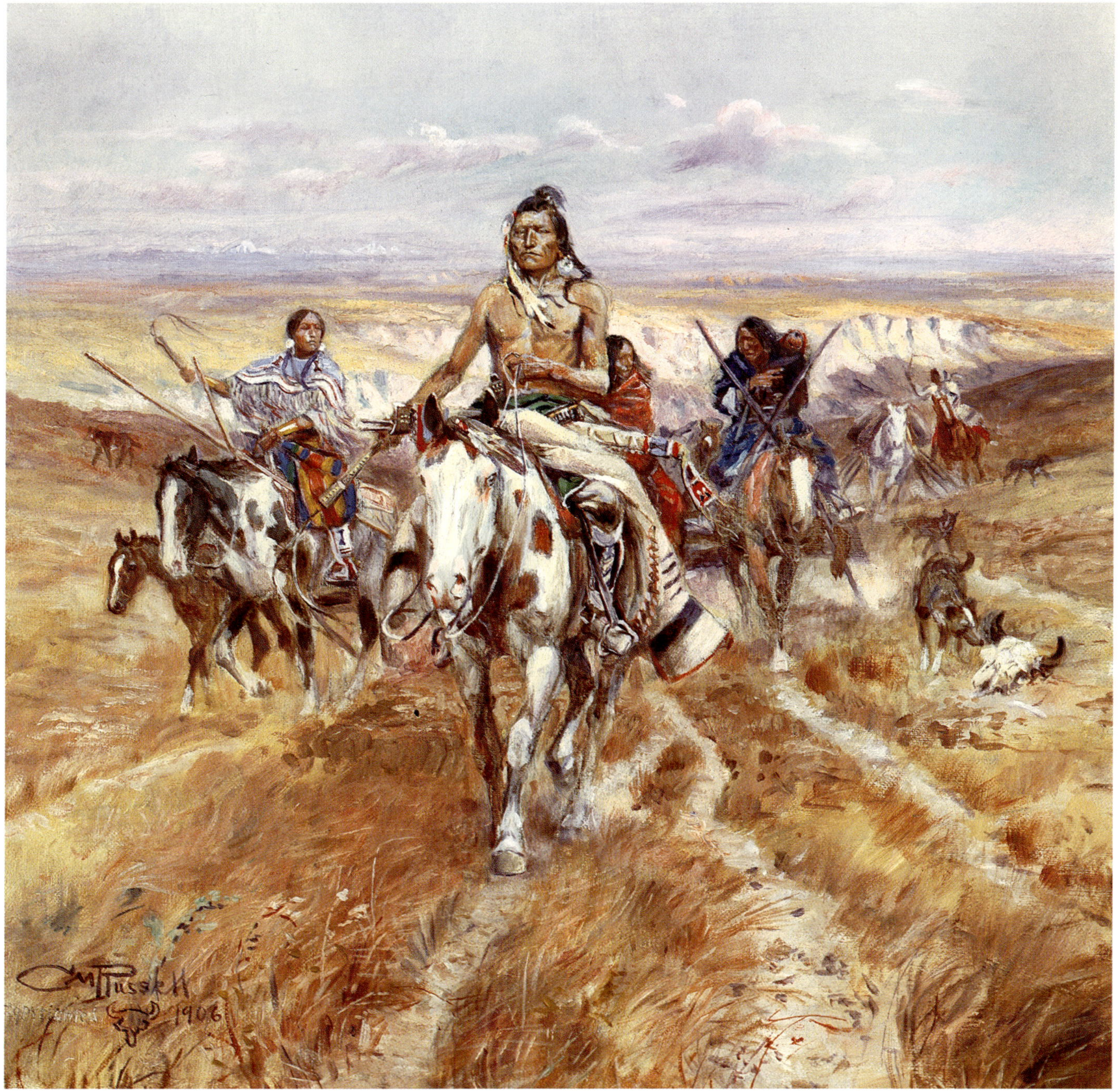
CM Russell
1906

11. Return of the Warriors, 1906
watercolor on canvas
11 5/8 x 16 inches
signed and dated lower left: CM Russell/skull cipher/1906/copyright

PROVENANCE: The artist to his father (perhaps as a wedding gift),1907; the elder Russell's widow in 1917; Homer Britzman; Mrs. Homer Britzman, Denver, Colorado; Hammer Brothers, New York, New York, 1957; Charles Ulrich and Josephine Bay Foundation; Buffalo Bill Historical Center, Cody, Wyoming; Museum of Western Art, Denver, Colorado; Collection of Wiley T. Buchanan, III.

REFERENCES: Charles M. Russell The Cowboy Artist, A biography by Ramon F. Adams and Homer E. Britzman. Trail's End Publishing Co., Pasadena, California, 1948, p. 160; Arizona Highways, "Genius in Chaps, The Life & Works of Charlie Russell," by H.E. Britzman, Nov. 1949, p.24, color; Chicago Tribune, Picture Section, cover (color), Jan. 1, 1950; Minneapolis Sunday Tribune, Section II, March 12, 1950, p.1; Gallery of Western Paintings, Raymond Carlson, ed. New York, London, Toronto: McGraw Hill Book Co., Inc., 1951, p. 14, color. Los Angeles Times, "Cowboy Painter Russell to Have Local Exhibit."

EXHIBITIONS: (*Private Collection of the Hammer Bros.*), the works of C.M. Russell from the collection of Homer E. Britzman in Trail's End Pasadena: Los Angeles Municipal Art Department, Tower Gallery, Los Angeles City Hall, Aug. 29-Sept. 13, 1957, California Palace of the Legion of Honor, Lincoln Park, San Francisco, Sept. 19-28, 1957, Historical Society of Montana. Charles M. Russell, Room of the State Museum, Oct. 1-12, 1957, The Trigg-C.M. Russell Foundation Inc. The C.M. Russell Gallery, Great Falls, Oct. 14-26, 1957, Calgary Allied Art Council, Coste House, Calgary, Canada, Nov. 1-17, 1957, The New York Historical Society, Central Park West, Dec. 17 - Feb. 2, 1958; Cornell Fine Arts Museum, Winter Park, FL., March 23-May 6, 1993.

The small party of Indians depicted in *Return of the Warriors* most likely portrays a buffalo scouting party. Their costumes, shields, and lances lend themselves toward ceremonial use rather than essential hunting accoutrements. These parties were carefully organized and led by an experienced warrior for the purpose of training teen-aged boys of the tribe. The composition is stylistically related to *When the Plains were His* and *Medicine Man,* with a central dominant figure moving forward into space balanced by a parade of figures following behind on either side.

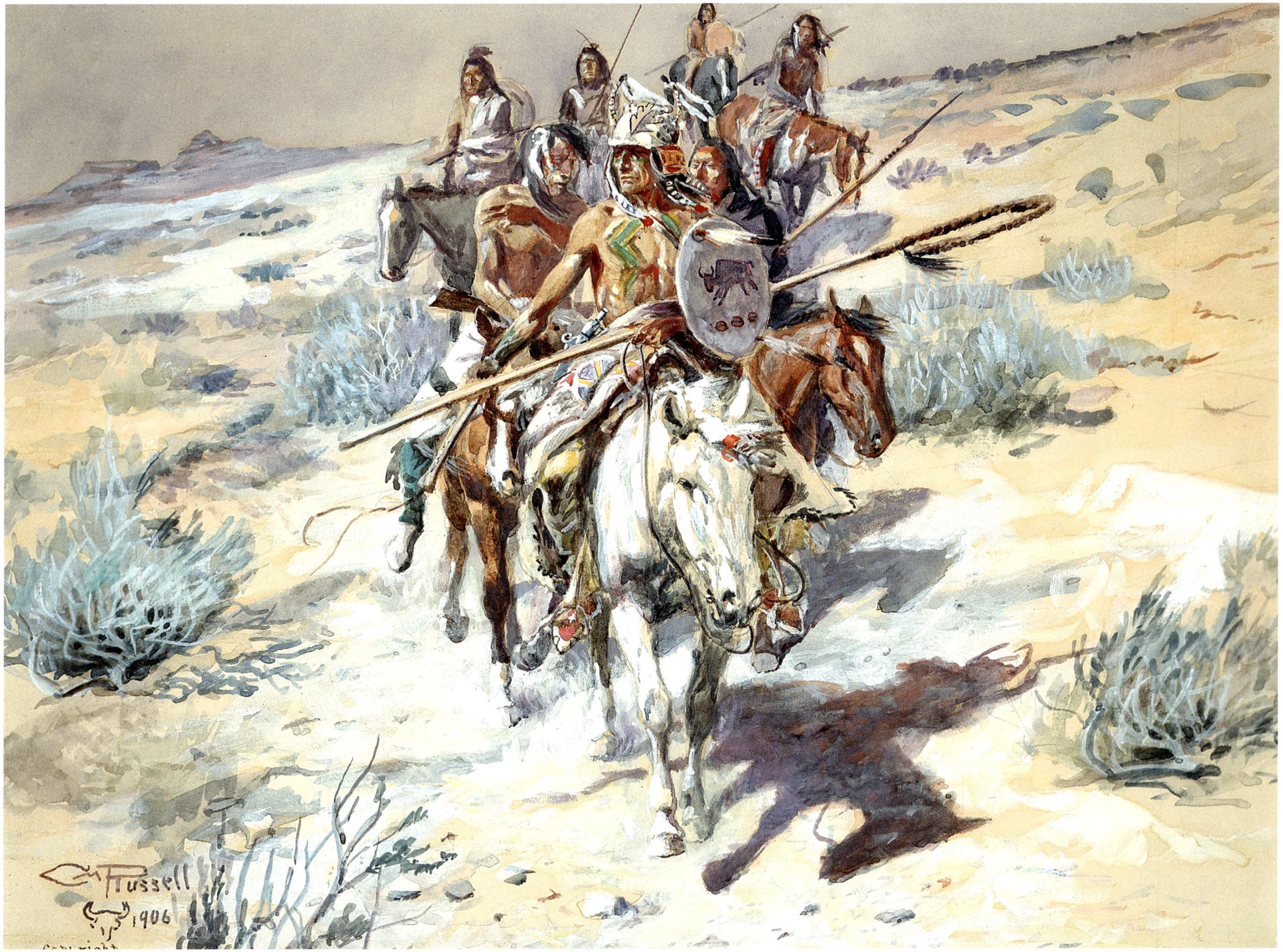
CM Russell
1906

12. The Truce, 1907
gouache and watercolor on paper
19 x 27 inches
signed and dated lower left: CM Russell/skull cipher/1907

PROVENANCE: The Artist to Dr. Hawkes, Great Falls, Montana; Nancy Jane Hawkes Moffitt (acquired through descent of the family); Rosenstock Galleries; Museum of Western Art, Denver, Colorado; {Gerald Peters Gallery, Santa Fe, New Mexico}; Private Collection, Montana.

REFERENCES: Frontier Spirit, Catalogue of the Collection of the Museum of Western Art, 1983, plate 61.

By the time Russell executed *The Truce*, he had already absorbed watercolor techniques introduced by fellow artists and art editors in New York during his visit in 1904. He began painting with a lighter palette and opaque white that enlivened his tinted washes. Russell's increasing mastery of the medium allowed him to experiment with light and atmospheric effects that foreshadowed many of his later, lyrical paintings.

Throughout his life, Russell identified with and revered Native American culture. He made frequent trips back to the reservations, inspired by the vivid color and proud native traditions he observed. *The Truce*, a highly finished work, recalls an earlier time when Indian and Anglo lived in a precarious but harmonious balance, partaking in the vast resources of the American West.

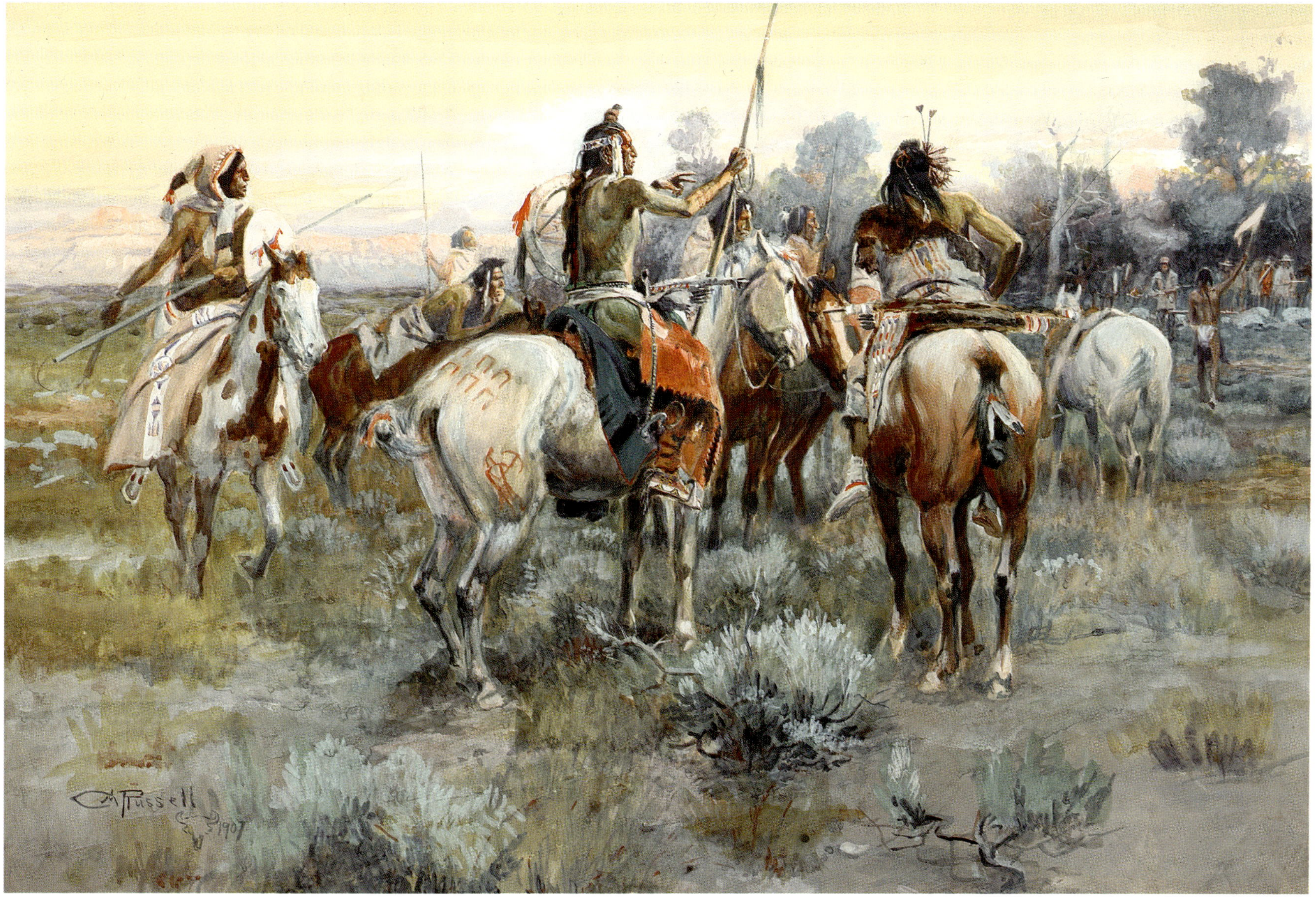
CM Russell
1907

13. Indian Camp-Lake McDonald, 1908
watercolor, gouache and pencil on prepared board
14 x 22 1/4 inches
signed and dated lower right: CM Russell/skull cipher/1908/copyright

PROVENANCE: Greer Garson Fogleson; {Gerald Peters Gallery, Santa Fe, New Mexico}; Larry and LeAnne Peterson, Big Sky Collection.

EXHIBITIONS: December, 1910, Charles Schatzlein (owner of a paint and art supply company and Russell's first dealer), Butte, Montana.

Though Russell remained committed to Western subjects throughout his career, after 1900 his paintings took on a more contemplative mood. Vigorous action yielded to scenes of man in harmony with nature as a result of the artist's exposure to the wave of Aestheticism sweeping across the canvases of the country's best artists. Russell, like his contemporaries George de Forest Brush and E.W. Deming, specialized in poetic evocations of Native Americans, a tradition originally established half a century earlier by Alfred Jacob Miller and John Mix Stanley.

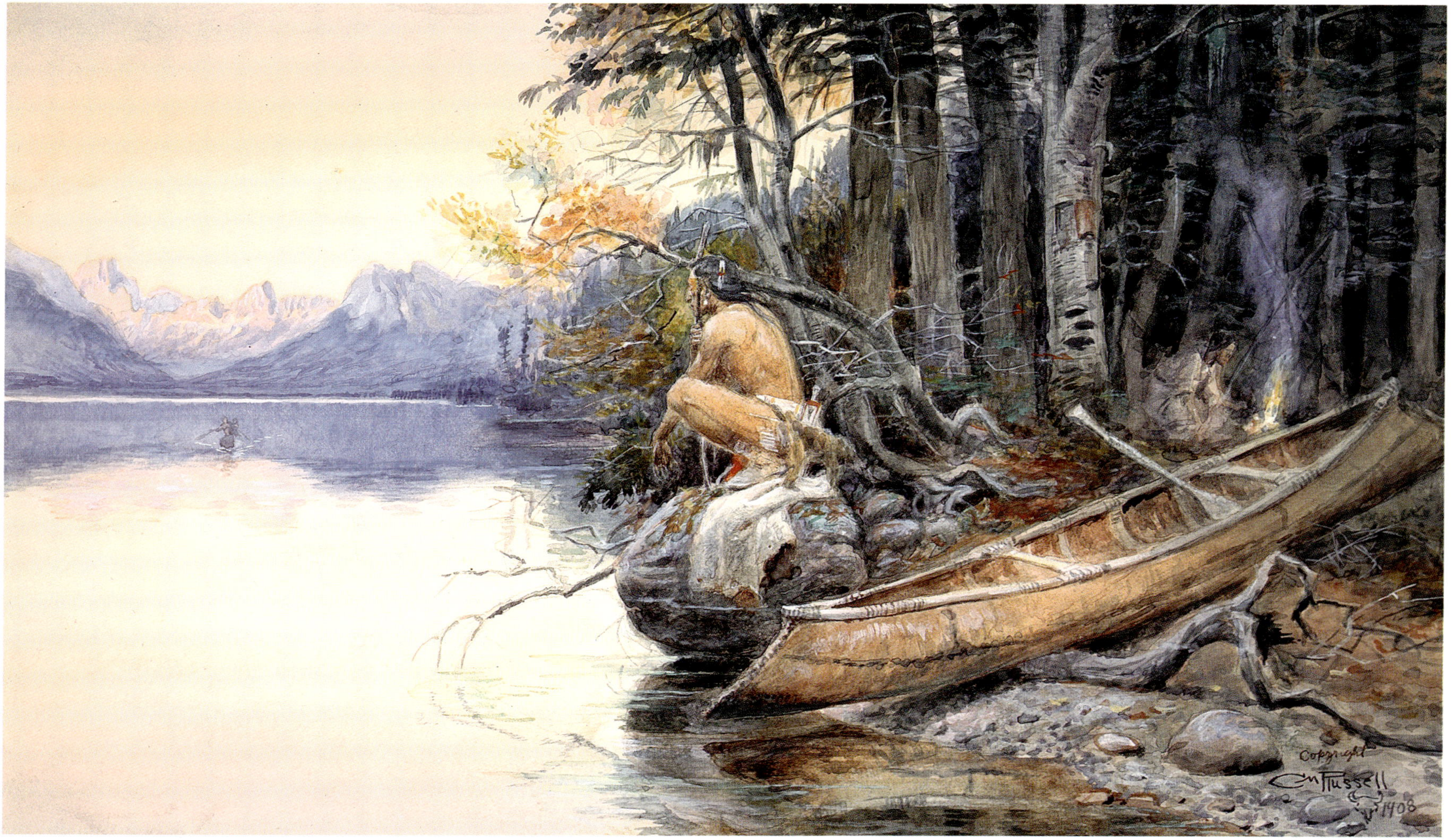
Copyright
CM Russell
1908

14. At Rope's End, 1909
oil on canvas
22 x 32 inches
signed and dated lower left: CM Russell/skull cipher/1909/copyright

PROVENANCE: The Artist to S.H. Keoughan, Denver, Colorado; The Estate of Walter McCune, Scottsdale, Arizona; Frederic Renner Paradise Valley, Arizona; {Gerald Peters Gallery, Santa Fe, New Mexico}; Private Collection, Texas; Private Collection, Colorado.

EXHIBITIONS: Eighth Montana State Fair, Helena, 1910; (*George W. Niedringhaus Exhibition*), St. Louis, 1910; Folsom Galleries, New York, New York 1912; Calgary Stampede, Calgary, Alberta, 1912; (*W.T. Ridgley Exhibition)*, Great Falls, Montana, 1912; (*Winnipeg Stampede*), Winnipeg, Manitoba, 1913; Thurber Galleries, Chicago, 1915; Thurber Galleries, Chicago, 1916; Folsom Galleries, Chicago, 1915; Thurber Galleries, Chicago, 1916; Folsom Galleries, New York, New York, 1916; Stendahl Art Gallery, Los Angeles, California, 1923; Library of Congress, Washington, D.C. 1983-84; (*American Cowboy Exhibit*), December 1983-October 1984, Institute of Texas Cultures, San Antonio, Texas, Denver Art Museum, Denver Colorado, Glenbow Museum, Calgary, Alberta, Canada, San Jose Museum of Art, San Jose, California; Denver Museum of Art, Denver, Colorado, February-April 1989.

REFERENCES: World's Work, July, 1911, "The Painter of the West that has passed. The work of Charles M. Russell, hunter, cowboy and artist, the painter of the cattle and Indian days," by Arthur Hoeber, p. 14628; World Newspaper, New York, April 9, 1911, N-8, "'Cowboy Artist,' Self Taught, Will Show in New York," illustrated; Karl Yost and Frederic Renner, A Bibliography of the Published Works of Charles M. Russell, 1971, p.108, 133.

Roping scenes constituted a major theme within the artist's oeuvre and their aesthetic drama and narrative appeal place them among his finest paintings. *At Rope's End* portrays a classic western scene through the use of strong compositional devices. The triangular figure arrangement, the line of the rope, and the broad landscape all work to unite the action across the picture plane. Russell painted these representations of men and animals locked in violent combat with a realism and fidelity to nature no other artist of his generation could equal.

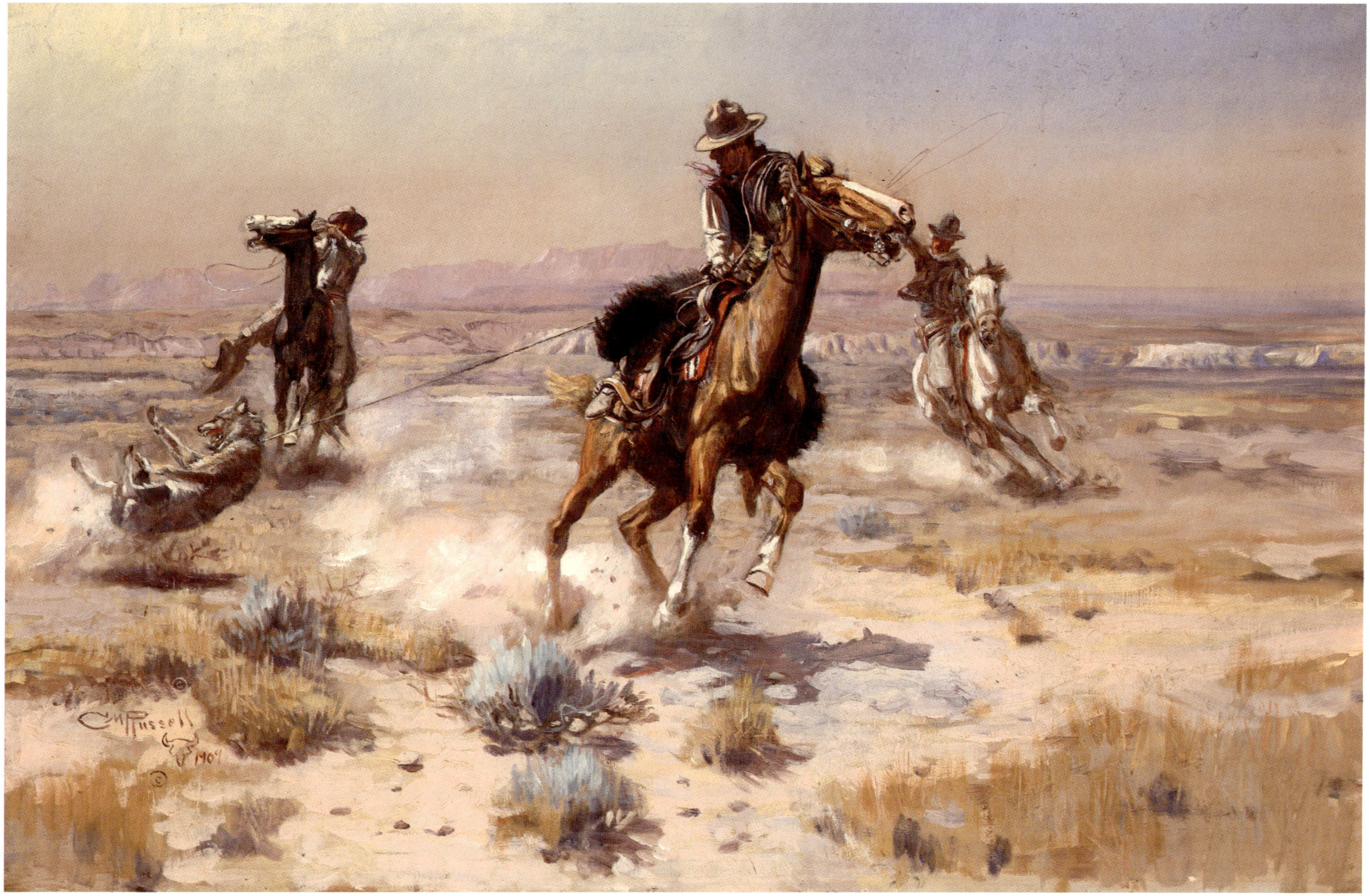

15. The Cinch Ring, 1909
oil on canvas
24 x 36 inches
signed and dated lower left: CM Russell/skull cipher/1909/copyright

PROVENANCE: Knoedler and Co., New York, New York; The National Cowboy Hall of Fame, Oklahoma City, Oklahoma; Private Collection, Denver, Colorado.

EXHIBITIONS: Brown & Bigelow, St. Paul, Minnesota, 1911, (probably exhibited as *A Loose Cinch*).

REFERENCES: Twelve Wonderful Pictures, C.M. Russell (nd, c.1920), print portfolio, illustrated; C.M. Russell Western Reproductions (c.1930), print portfolio, illustrated; Will Rogers (introduction) Just in Cowboy Boots (1940-1941) advertisement flyer, p. 20, illustrated; John Mariani, "Charles Russell," Western Horseman 16:1 (January, 1951), p.18-19; Western Horseman 16:12 (December, 1951), illustrated, verso cover; Harold McCracken, The Charles M. Russell Book, The Life an Work of the Cowboy Artist (1957), p.158-159, illustrated; Dean Krakel, Adventures in Western Art (1977), p. 85-86, 146-148, illustrated, p. 189.

Russell's ability to portray movement convincingly was one of his greatest talents, one he utilized to great effect in his roping scenes. *The Cinch Ring*, one of his most celebrated action canvases, illustrates how Russell translated action in the round onto a two-dimensional space. To a large extent, Russell's development as a sculptor aided his ability as a painter. He often used clay and wax models as studies for paintings to work out shadow effects, figure arrangement, and individual poses. Russell's Darwinian dramas involving man confronted by nature were a consistent theme throughout his important early works and served to define the myth of the American West.

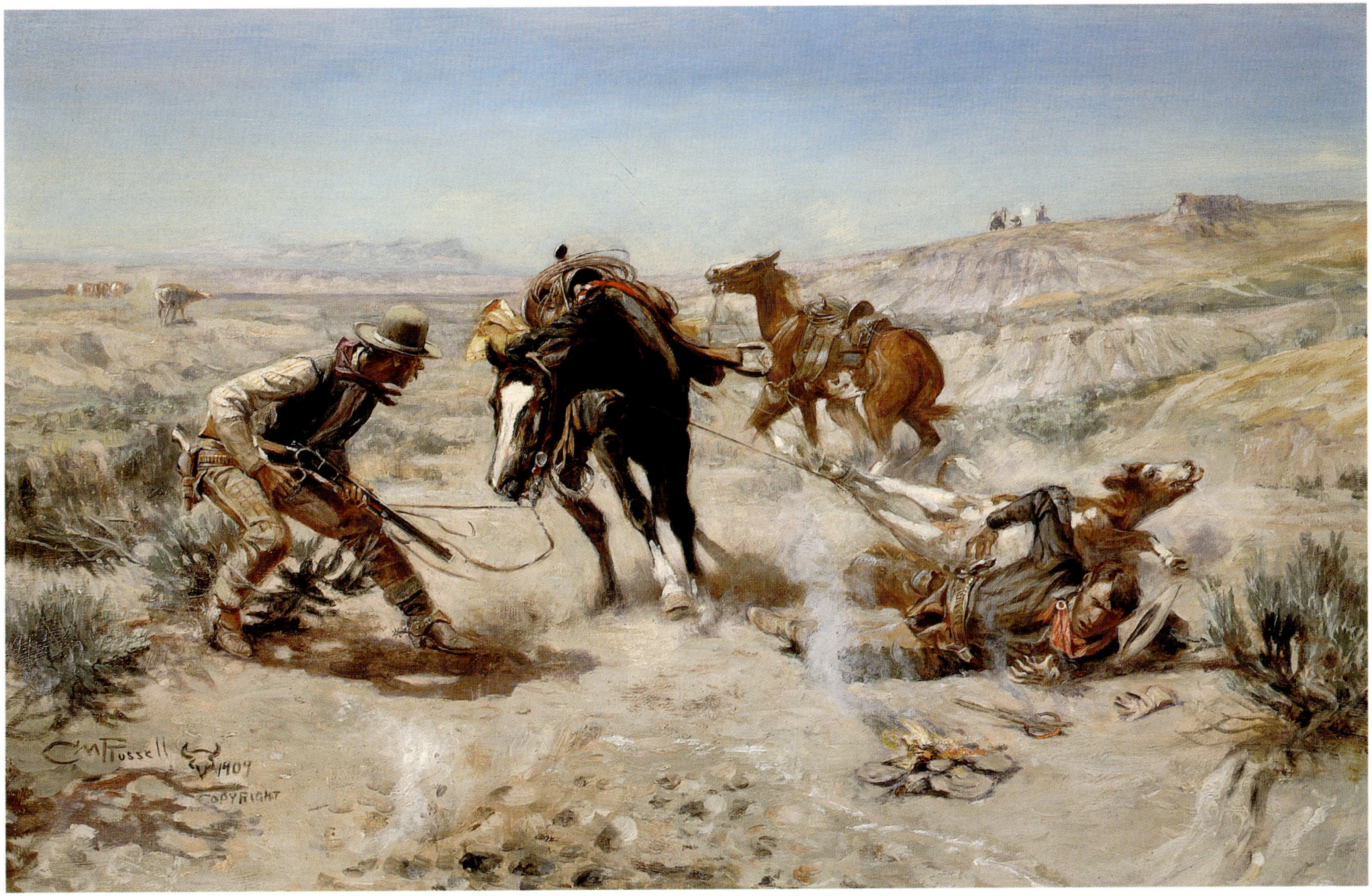
CM Russell 1909
COPYRIGHT

16. The Surround, 1911
oil on canvas
28 3/4 x 50 inches
signed and dated lower left: CM Russell/skull cipher/1911

PROVENANCE: The Artist to his wife; Britzman to C.R. Smith; Kennedy Galleries, New York; Private Collection.

EXHIBITIONS: (*Inaugural Exhibition*), June 25, 1965, The National Cowboy Hall of Fame and Western Heritage Center.

REFERENCES: Kennedy Galleries, Inc., Kennedy Quarterly, Vol. IV, No. I, "The Eye of the Traveler, an historical & artistic perspective of the American & Canadian frontiers in the work of outstanding 19th century artists." p. 60; Inaugural Exhibition, June 25, 1965 The National Cowboy Hall of Fame and Western Heritage Center, Oklahoma City, OK, p.18; Dunn's Review, (January, 1950), cover; Montana, The Magazine of Western History, Autumn 1958, "Modest Son of the Old West," by Joe De Yong, p. 16.; Spring 1964 (cover); The Book of the American West, Jay Monaghan Editor-In-Chief. New York: Julian Messner Inc., 1963; Karl Yost and Frederic Renner, A Bibliography of the Published Works of Charles M. Russell, University of Nebraska Press, Lincoln, NB, 1971, pp. 34, 57, 62, 81, 91, 95.

The Surround, Russell's title choice for this painting, depicts one type of buffalo hunt in which mounted hunters with bows and lances swooped down from all directions encircling a large herd of grazing buffalo. Though Russell never witnessed a surround, he observed the animals firsthand in a buffalo roundup around 1908. By the time *The Surround* was executed, Russell's development as a painter was apparent. He had mastered increasingly complex perspective and compositions, here involving several hunters, horses, and the violent collision of the herd. While Russell's buffalo imagery alone had symbolized the vanishing frontier for decades, the incorporation of the pre-reservation Indian heightened the sense of pathos associated with the transformed West.

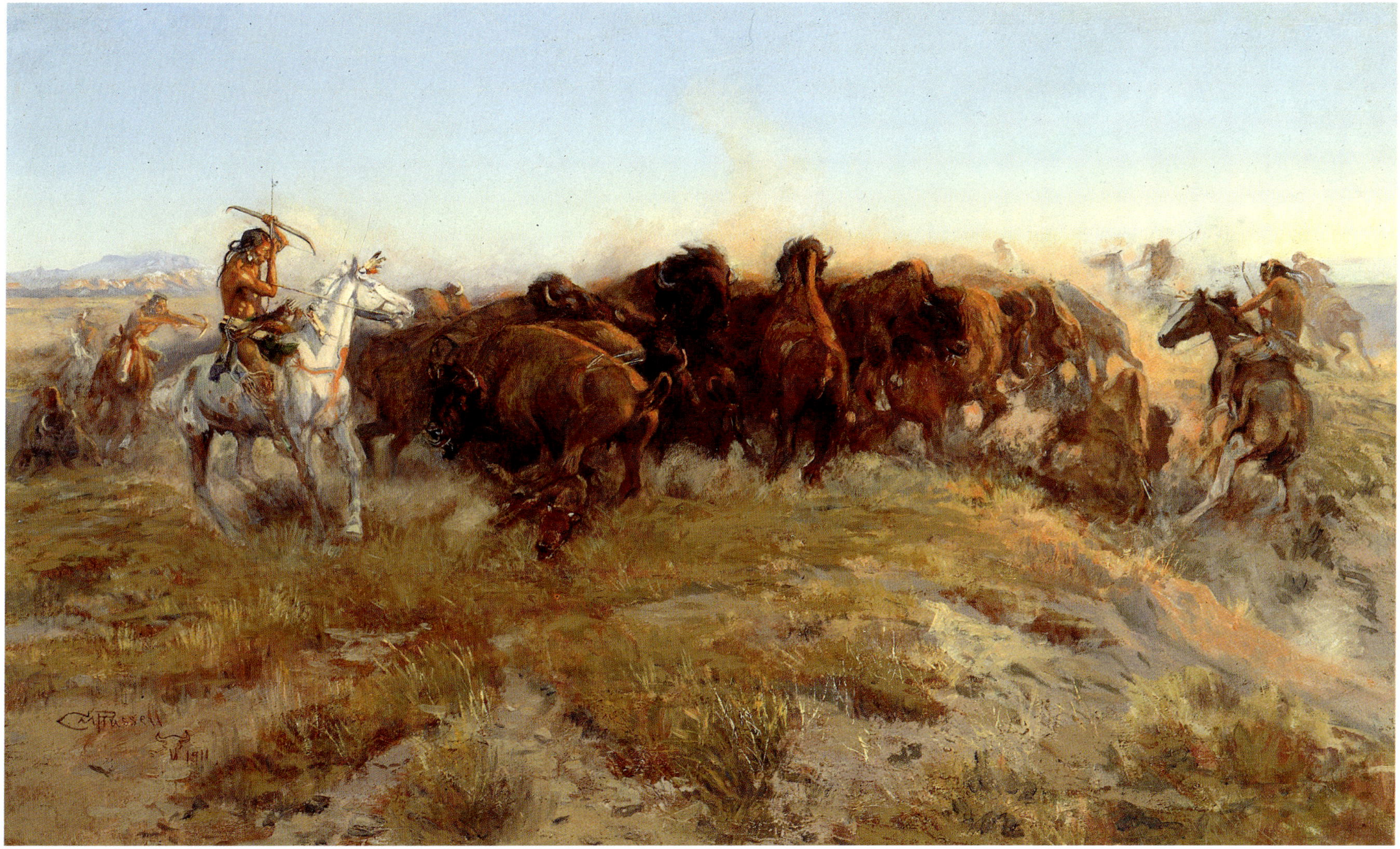

17. Piegan Hunting Party, 1913
watercolor on paper
10 5/8 x 13 5/8 inches
signed and dated lower left: CM Russell/skull cipher/1913

PROVENANCE: Private Collection, Oklahoma; {Gerald Peters Gallery, Santa Fe, New Mexico}; Private Collection.

The Piegan Indians, or "Poor Robes," originated as one of the Algonquin tribes of the American East. As the centuries passed, they migrated westward toward the Great Plains and became one of the three tribes in the large and powerful Blackfoot Confederacy. Dramatic and bold, they roamed from Wyoming up through Montana and north into the present Canadian provinces of Alberta and Saskatchewan.

In 1912, Russell held his first international exhibition at the Calgary Stampede. Paintings submitted for exhibition revealed a shift in his artistic focus. Many of the new subjects included parties of warriors posed heroically upon a promontory, or moving across the plains in harmony with the land they inhabited. *Piegan Hunting Party* and *Indian Party*, (plate #18) were executed during a period of stylistic experimentation when narrative and documentary concerns gave way to an interest in the subtleties of mood, color and light.

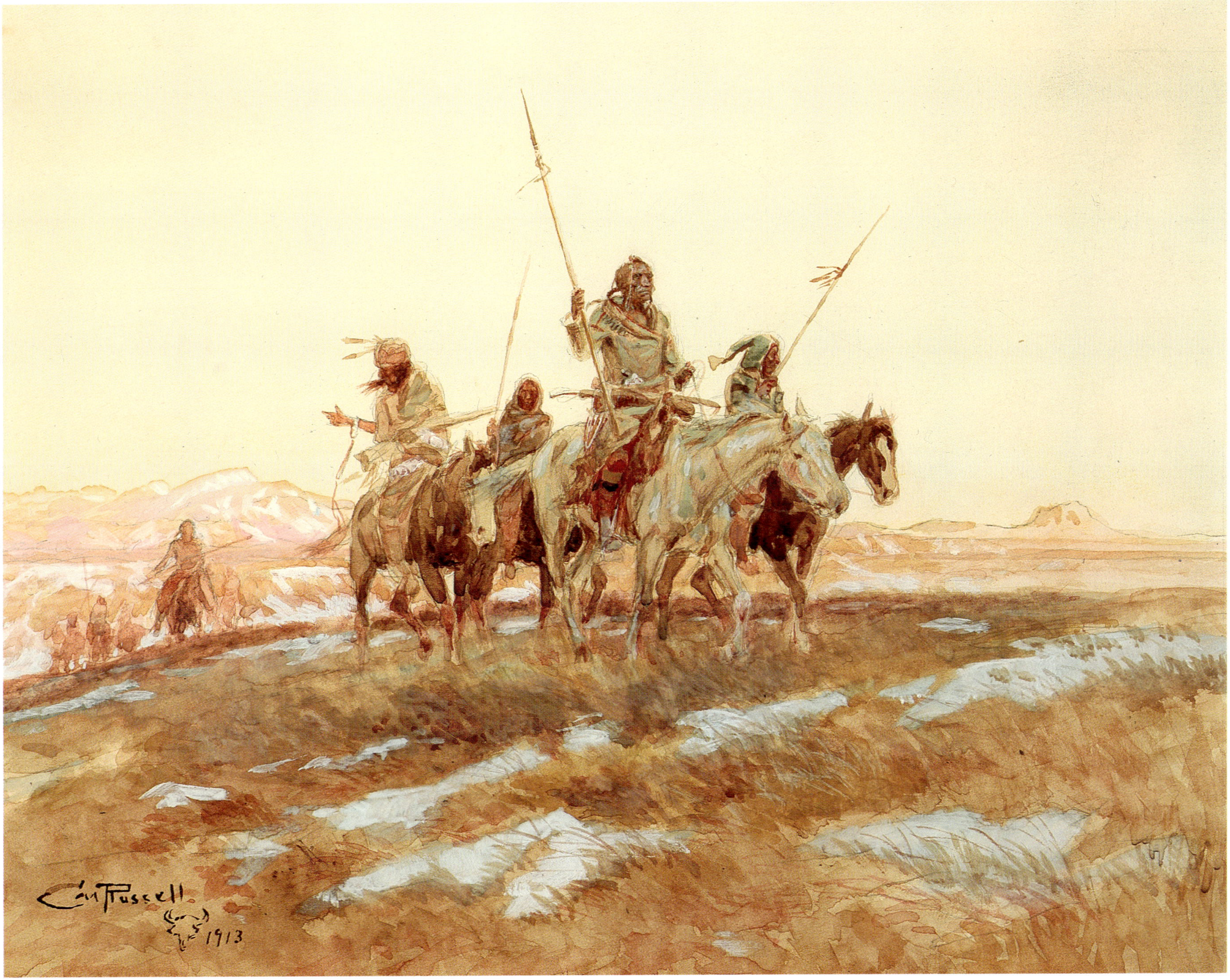
CM Russell
1913

18. Indian Party, 1915
watercolor on paper
12 x 19 inches
signed and dated lower left: CM Russell/skull cipher/1915/copyright

PROVENANCE: Private Collection; Peter Wray, Phoenix, Arizona; {Gerald Peters Gallery, Santa Fe, New Mexico}; Private Collection, Oklahoma.

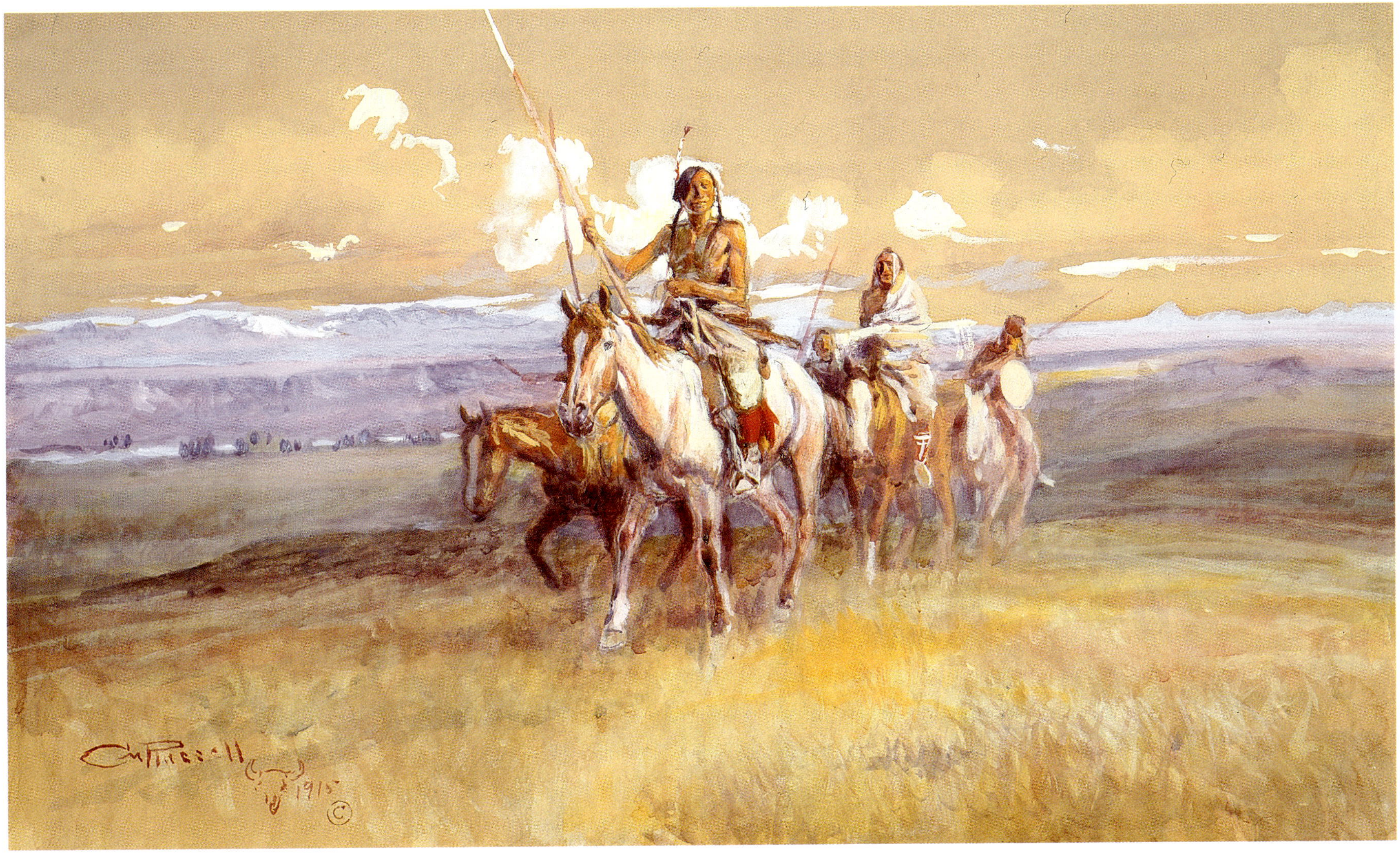

19. Signal Smoke, 1912/reworked in 1915
oil on canvas
36 x 30 inches
signed and dated lower left: CM Russell/skull cipher/1915

PROVENANCE: Estate of Nancy Russell; Earl C. Adams Collection; Estate of W.E. Weiss.

REFERENCES: Frederic Remington Centennial Exhibition and Paintings, Drawings and Sculpture by other Notable Documentary artists of The Old West and Plains Indian Art exhibition catalogue, May 1 to September 15, 1961; The Gallery of Western Art, Buffalo Bill Historical Center, Cody Wyoming, pg. 12; Karl Yost and Frederic G. Renner, A Bibliography of The Published Works of Charles M. Russell, University of Nebraska Press, Lincoln, NB,1971, pp. 52, 150.

Russell painted dozens of pictures of war parties, usually three to five men, on the move or on the lookout. The recurrent theme presents an opportunity to view Russell's continued evolution as a painter. *Signal Smoke*, one of his most ambitious works, was executed through a series of conscious design decisions. Throughout his career the artist delighted in representing the vast Montana geography and traditionally utilized a broad, horizontal format. *Signal Smoke*, one rare example of a vertical arrangement, achieves the same unity of composition characteristic of his wide-ranging landscapes. The brilliant light accentuates the figures in the strong asymmetrical composition, ingeniously framed by the raised lance and plume of smoke.

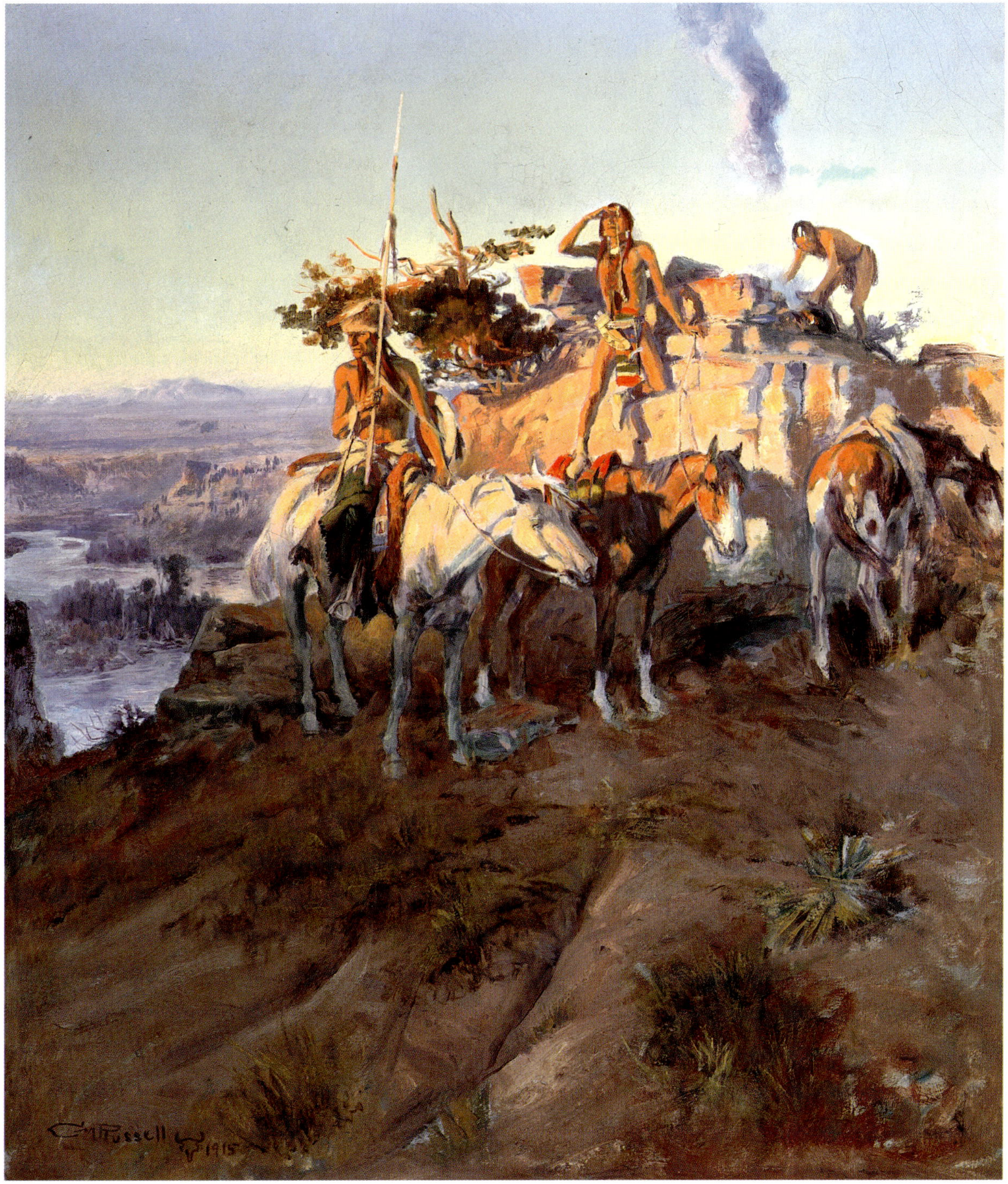
CMRussell
1915

20. Whose Meat?, 1914
oil on canvas
30 3/4 x 48 3/4 inches
signed and dated lower left: CM Russell/skull cipher/1914/copyright

PROVENANCE: Jack Bartfield, New York, 1980; Museum of Western Art, Denver, Colorado; {Gerald Peters Gallery, Santa Fe, New Mexico}; Private Collection, California.

EXHIBITIONS: Thurber Galleries, Chicago, Illinois, February, 1916; Folsom Galleries, New York, New York, 1916; Museum of Westward Expansion, St. Louis, Missouri, (*Charles M. Russell: American Artist*), April 2 - August 29, 1982; on loan to Buffalo Bill Historical Center, Cody, Wyoming.

REFERENCES: Helen R. Mackay, "Good Medicine," Montana, The Magazine of Western History (Spring 1957), p.32; Karl Yost and Frederick G. Renner, A Bibliography of the Published Works of Charles M. Russell, University of Nebraska Press, Lincoln, NB, (1971), pp. 89, 140, 151, 195, 234; Jefferson National Expansion Historical Association, Charles M. Russell: American Artist (1982), p.51; Persimmon Hill (Fall 1982), vol. 12, no. 1, p.75; Museum of Western Art, Frontier Spirit: Catalogue of the Collection of the Museum of Western Art,(1983), p. 101, illustrated, pl. 69; Brian W. Dippie, "'I Feel that I am Improving Right Along': Continuity and Change in Charles M. Russell's Art," Montana, The Magazine of Western History 38 (Summer 1988).

Russell upheld his distinction as a fine storyteller through a series of paintings devoted to the subject of "frontier-types," executed around 1915. These scenes, designed to have wide appeal to sportsmen, arrest the action at its apogee, leaving viewers to draw their own conclusions. This period represents the pinnacle of Russell's facility as a painter when his colors found harmony with eye and nature, and his draftsmanship allowed him to convey great drama in narrative and landscape with equal command. In *Whose Meat*, ultimate compositional control is achieved through the broad diagonal, unifying and heightening the dramatic tension animated by tottering horses and hunter.

Note: This painting was reproduced as a color print by The Osborne Company of Clifton, New Jersey, in 1925, and also issued as a color print by Brown and Bigelow, (date unknown). It was later issued by the Dick Jones Picture Company as part of a portfolio (size 20 x 13 inches), C.M. Russell: Western Reproductions, circa 1930, and as an art blotter by The Osborne Company in 1948.

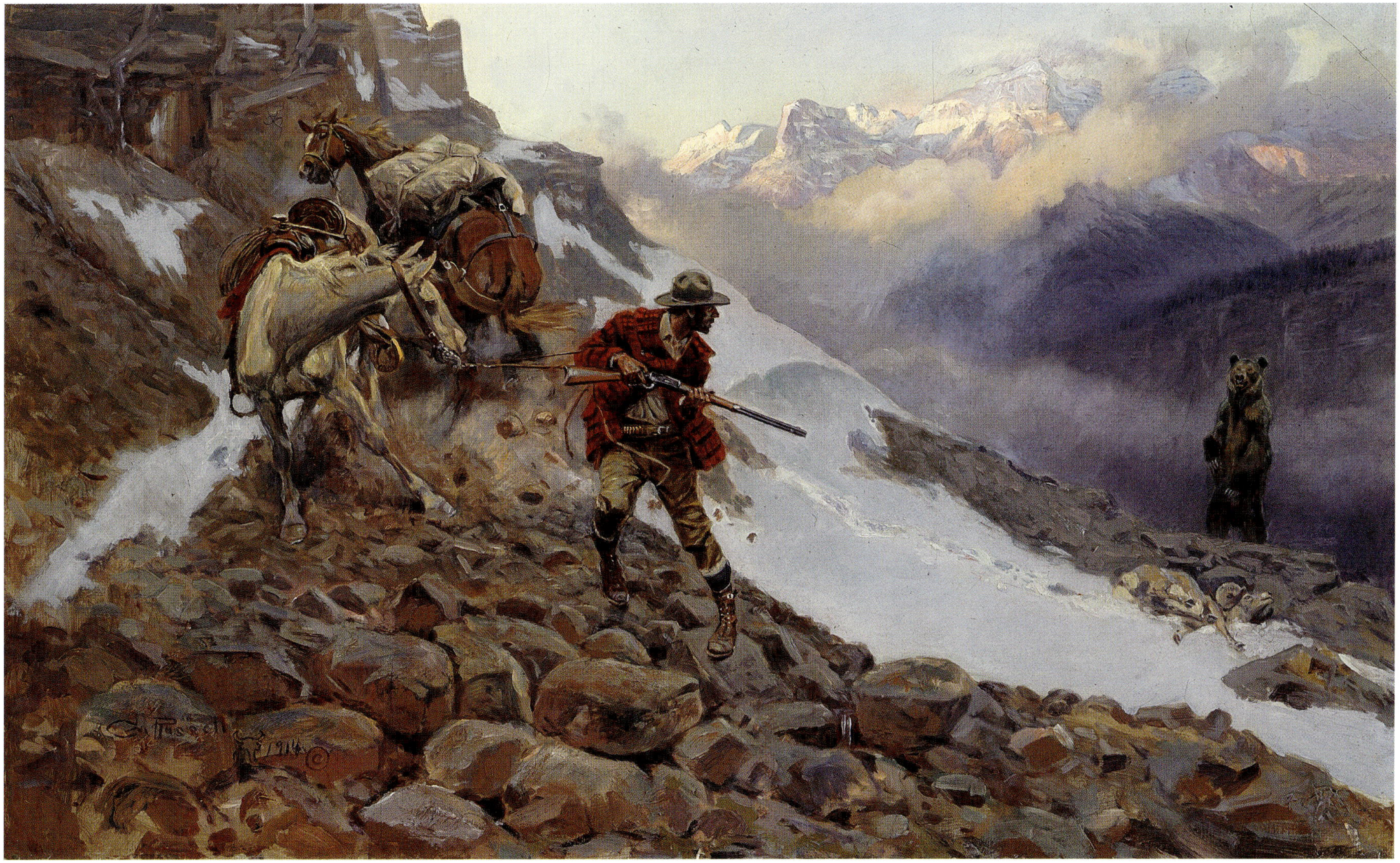

*21. Four Mounted Indians, c.*1914
watercolor on paper
13 1/2 x 20 inches
signed lower left: CM Russell/skull cipher

PROVENANCE: Private Collection; {Gerald Peters Gallery, Santa Fe, New Mexico}; Linda and Michael Keston, Los Angeles, California.

REFERENCES: Brian W. Dippie, Looking at Russell, Amon Carter Museum, Fort Worth, Texas, 1987.

In Looking at Russell, author Brian Dippie explores the parallels between European and American interest in Orientalism. Throughout the nineteenth century, the Far West had been to Americans what the Orient represented to Europeans. It was an age of exploration, discovery, and empire. Popular magazines carried tales of frontier escapades on the American plains as well as the Arabian desert, while Buffalo Bill's Wild West shows expanded to include Arab horsemen. Charles Russell was thoroughly responsive to such exotica, incorporating oriental subjects in his paintings and adopting a style steeped in romanticism. *Four Mounted Indians* reveals striking eastern similarities in the portrayal of dramatically clad Indians set in a romantic desert locale.

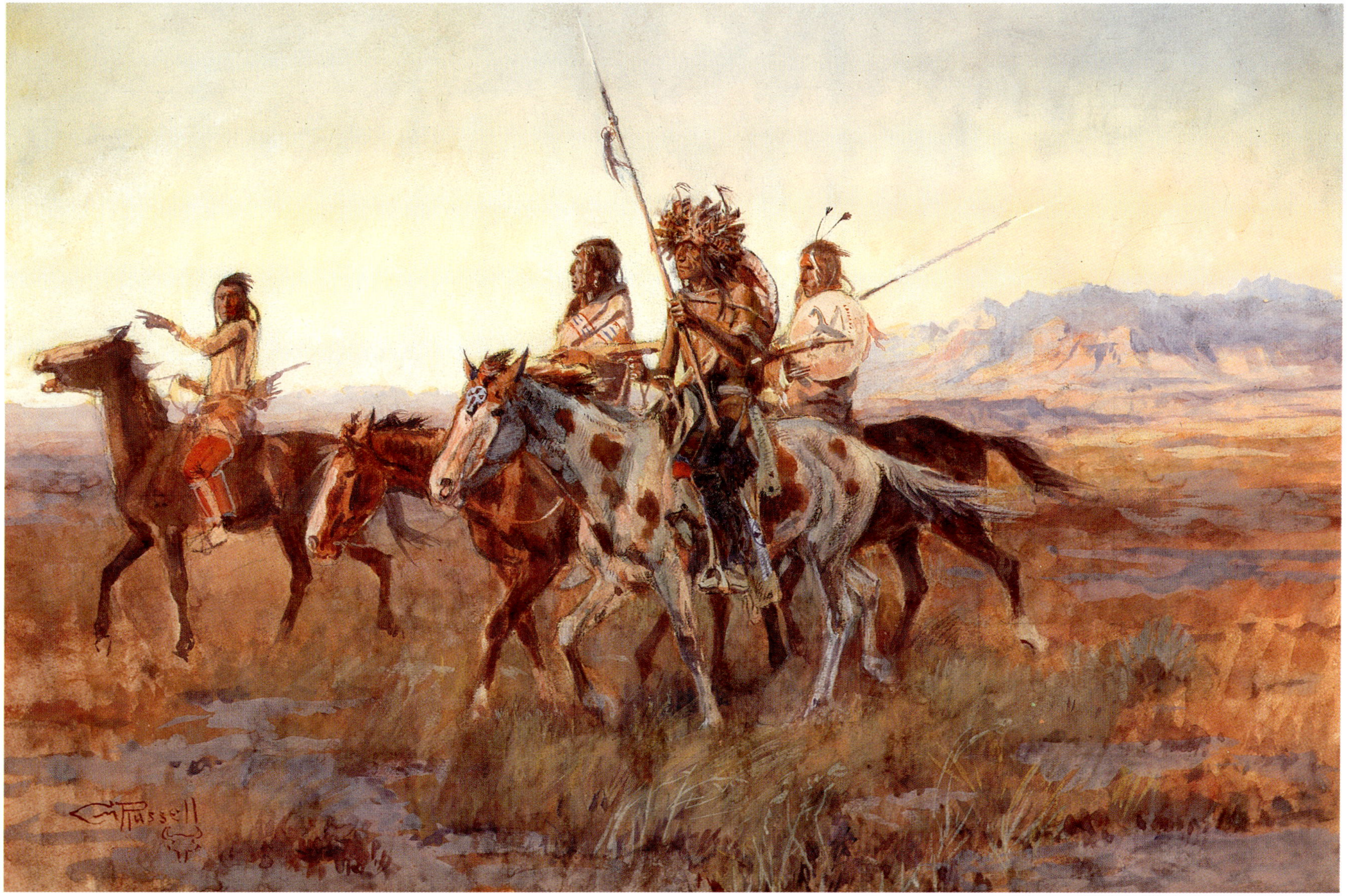

*22. The Lost Trail, c.*1915
gouache on paper
13 3/4 x 19 3/4 inches
signed lower left: CMR/skull cipher

PROVENANCE: Museum of Western Art, Denver, Colorado; {Gerald Peters Gallery, Santa Fe, New Mexico}; Private Collection, California.

REFERENCES: Brian W. Dippie, Looking at Russell, Amon Carter Museum, Fort Worth, Texas, 1987, p.101-102, ill. pl. 91; Brian W. Dippie, "'I Feel that I am Improving Right Along': Continuity and Change in Charles M. Russell's Art," Montana, The Magazine of Western History 38 (Summer 1988).

In Looking at Russell, author Brian Dippie comments on Russell's artistic influences. Although Carl Wimar was active in St. Louis decades earlier, his oil paintings were scattered throughout the city so that Russell would have had numerous opportunities to view them. As a young painter, Russell absorbed Wimar's subjects, compositions, poses, and handling of color. Wimar's influence is particularly apparent in comparing both artist's versions of *The Lost Trail*. Russell's painting, an obvious homage to Wimar, used the same pyramidal figure arrangement of mounted warriors with one marking tracks on the ground. Thus Russell reveals his roots in the romantic tradition originally established by Wimar and other pioneer western painters.

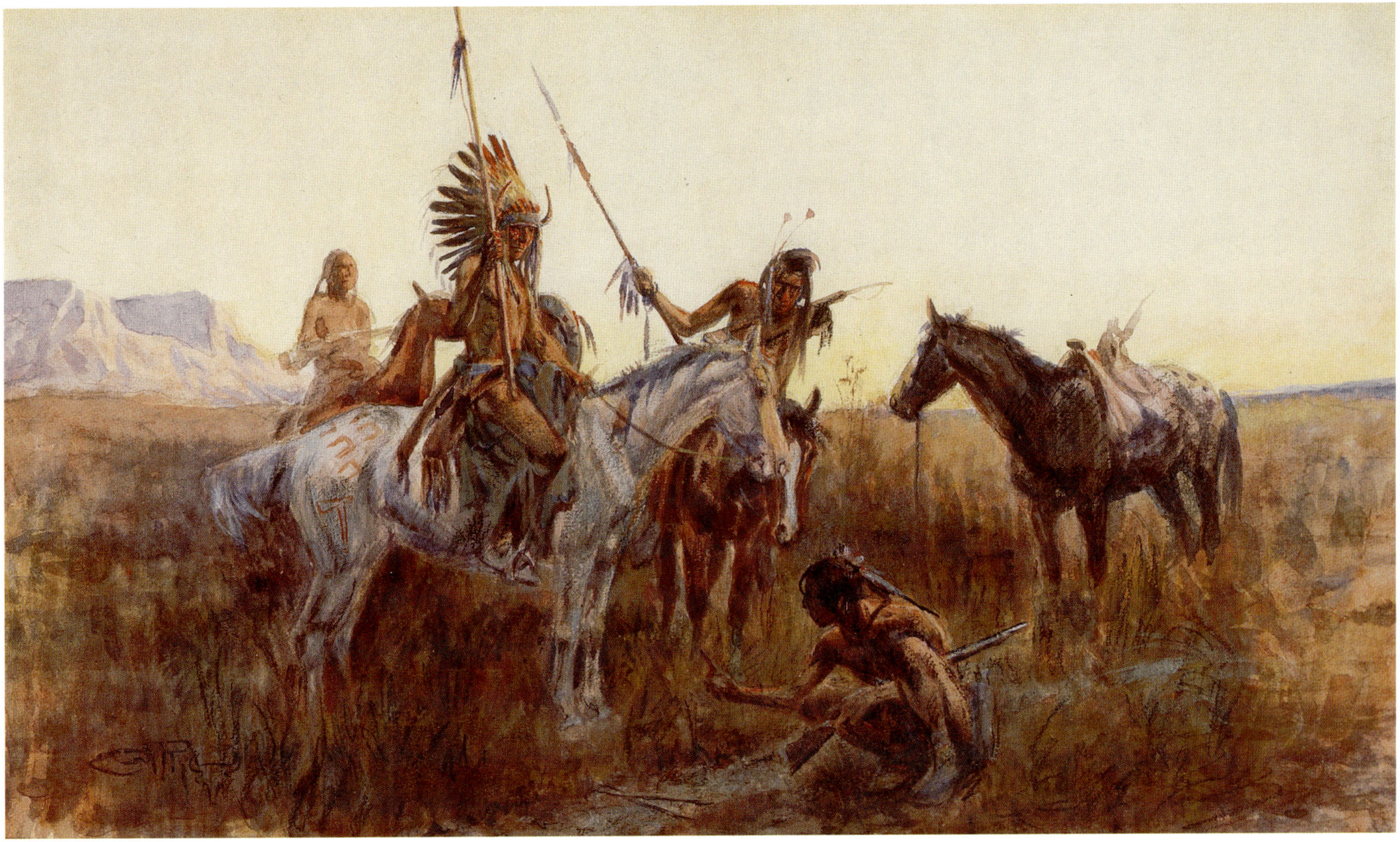

*23. Roping a Wolf, c.*1918
watercolor on paper
17 1/2 x 24 1/4 inches
signed lower left: CM Russell/skull cipher

PROVEANCE: Kennedey Galleries, New York; Private Collection, Jenkinstown, Pennsylvania, 1981; {Gerald Peters Gallery, Santa Fe, New Mexico}; Private Collection, Texas.

REFERENCES: Brian Dippie, Looking at Russell, Amon Carter Museum, Fort Worth, Texas, 1987.

Russell had a number of favorite subjects, variations of which he would paint or draw many times over. His roping subjects were executed both in oil and watercolor media, perhaps at different times, and always with different compositional results. For years, there were stories of white wolves of prodigious strength in the Judith Basin country that he knew well. With the destruction of their natural prey, the buffalo, wolves turned to the white man's cattle and soon became a serious problem to early Montana cowmen. Though present day sentiment finds the "sport" of roping wolves reprehensible, it was one of the diversions that offered excitement and challenge to cowboys around the turn of the century. Whether roping cattle, mustangs, wolves or grizzlies, these scenes occupied Russell's imagination throughout his artistic career and depicted moments of high drama and danger. He imbued his portrayals of old-time cowhands, both at work and play, with precision and insight.

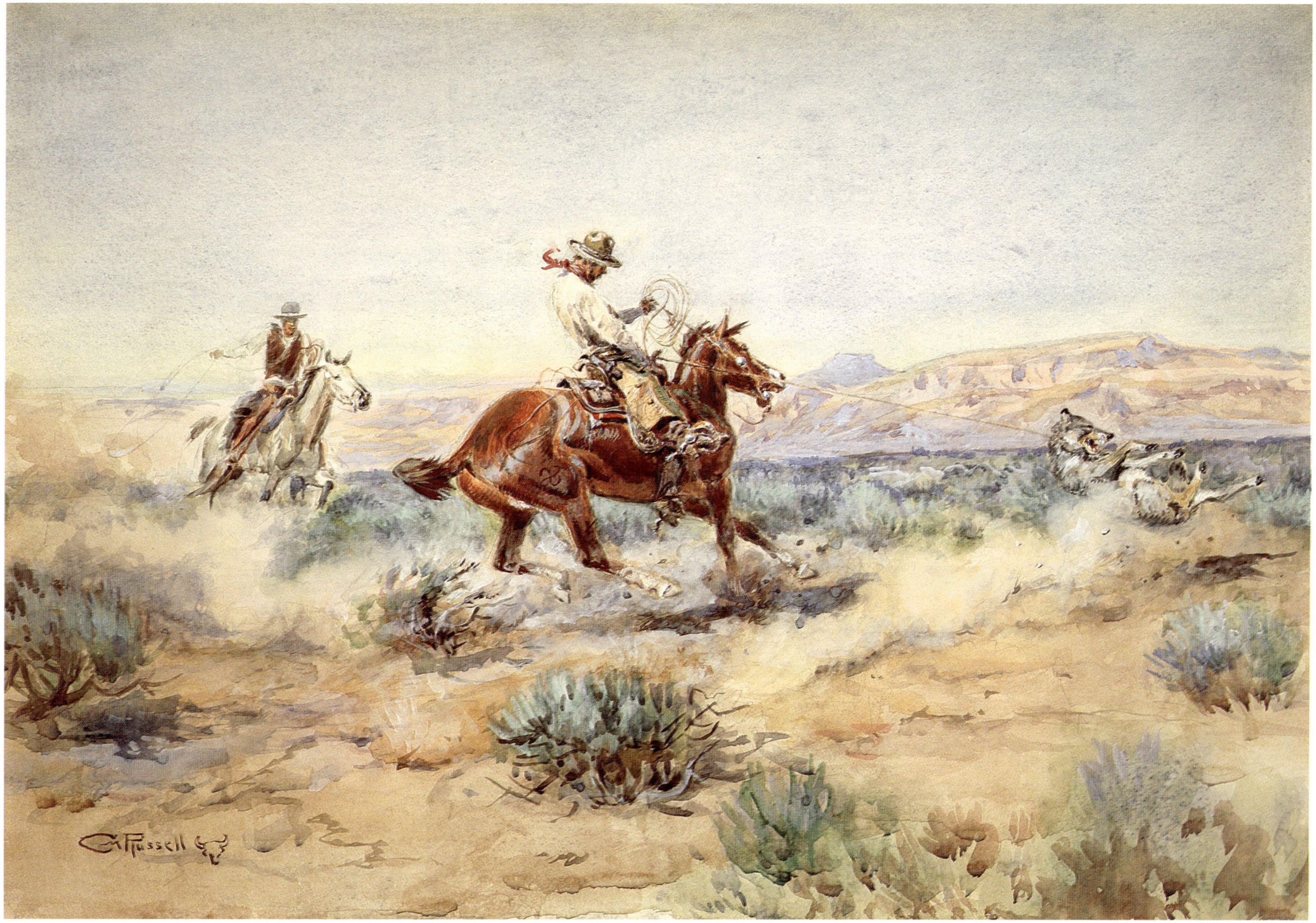
CMRussell

24. On the Prod, 1918
watercolor and gouache on paper
12 x 22 inches
signed and dated lower left: CM Russell/skull cipher/1918/copyright

PROVENANCE: Museum of Western Art, Denver, Colorado; Private Collection, Philadelphia, Pennsylvania.

EXHIBITIONS: Arthur H. Harlow, New York, New York, 1925.

REFERENCES: Frontier Spirit, Catalogue of the Collection of the Museum of Western Art, Denver, Colorado, 1983, plate 65.

On the Prod, rendered in 1918, represents a period in which Russell temporarily returned to the opaque watercolors he employed in *The Truce*. Much of Russell's superiority as a Western artist was due to the delicate balance of documentary realism and romantic myth he incorporated into his cowboy pictures. *On the Prod* combines the accuracy of every cowboy accouterment with the glorification of the frontier life he had known.

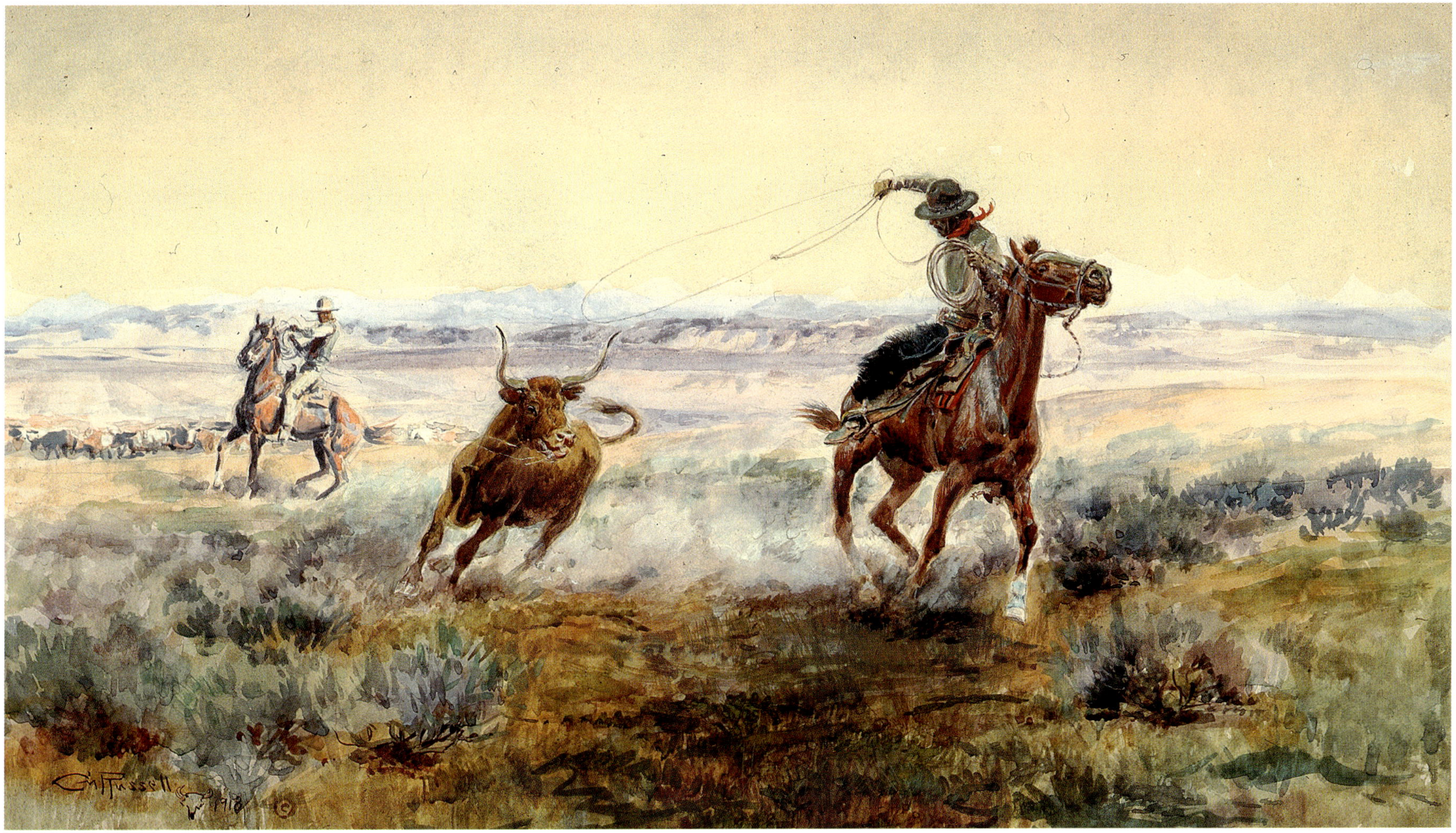

PHOTOGRAPH : James O. Milmoe

25. *Horse of the Hunters* or *Fresh Meat,* 1919
oil on canvas
15 x 24 inches
signed and dated lower left: CM Russell/skull cipher/copyright/1919

PROVENANCE: Collection of C. R. Smith; Private Collection.

REFERENCES: American Heritage, 15:2, (February 1964). [16]-[21], "How The Indian Got The Horse," by Francis Haines.

In 1908, Russell participated in roundup and transfer of a privately owned buffalo herd to the Canadian government. During the drive, he was charged by an angry bull and narrowly escaped injury. The experience inspired a number of paintings including this piece entitled *Fresh Meat*. Peter Hassrick noted in "The West that Has Passed" that when the painting was executed in 1919, it "had nothing to do with current Indian issues, aside from Russell's employment of local Indians as models." It called up the triumph of noble horsemen over nature and repeated compositions and themes he had successfully exploited years earlier in *The Surround*.

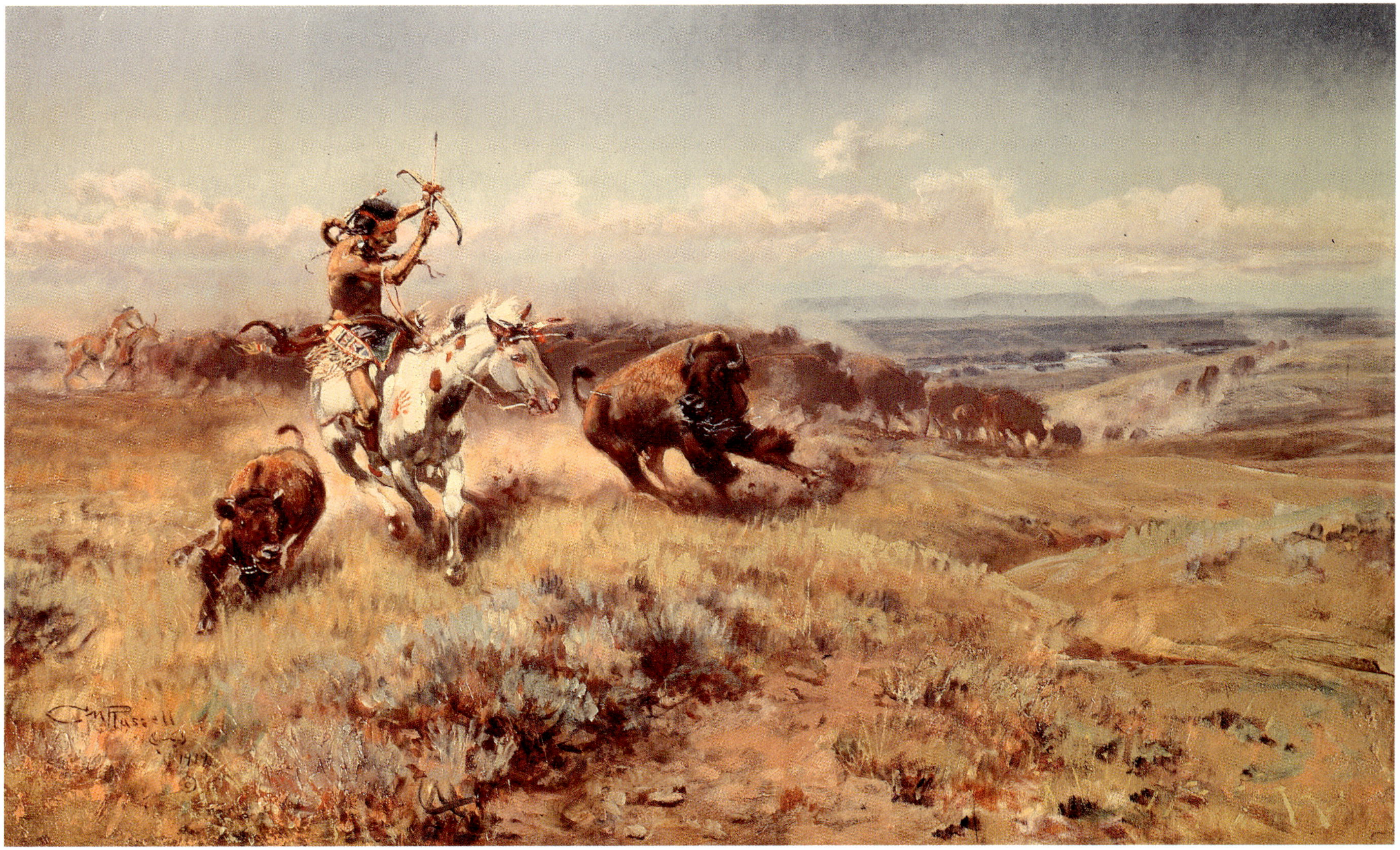

26. *Buffalo Hunt No. 40,* 1919
oil on canvas
30 x 48 1/2 inches
signed and dated lower left: CM Russell/skull cipher/copyright/1919

PROVENANCE: The Artist; H. Edward Manville, Pittsburgh, Pennsylvania; David B. Findlay Galleries, New York, New York; Amon Carter Museum, Ft. Worth, Texas; Private Collection.

EXHIBITIONS: Brown Palace Hotel, Denver, 1921; Stendahl Art Gallery, Los Angeles, California, 1923; Biltmore Salon, Los Angeles, 1924; Arthur H. Harlow, New York, New York, 1925.

REFERENCES: Los Angeles Times, April 8, 1923, rotogravure section, p. 9; Great Falls Leader, Montana Parade Section, March 19, 1961, Humble Way, 1:2 (April, 1962), "Monarach of the Old West," pp. 16-17; "Museum in Texas houses Russell, Remington art"; Karl Yost and Frederic Renner, A Bibliography of the Published Works of Charles M. Russell, University of Nebraska Press, Lincoln, NB, 1971, pp. Frederic G. Renner, Charles M. Russell: Paintings, Drawings, and Sculpture in the Amon Carter Museum, Harry N. Abrams, Inc. in association with the Amon Carter Museum of Western Art, 1974, illustrated pl. 199.; Brian Dippie, Looking at Russell, Amon Carter Museum, Fort Worth, Texas, 1987.

Of the recurrent themes in Russell's oeuvre, none was more fully explored than the buffalo hunt. The subject was one he returned to and developed by incorporating elements of agitation and physical agony that greatly improved the somewhat static compositions of his earlier buffalo hunt scenes. By 1919, Russell executed *Buffalo Hunt No. 40*, his most compelling painting on this theme.

This high drama integrates landscape and action, forcing the herd to respond to the terrain and the tumult of the chase. Within the flawless composition, bulls, calves and cows collide –representing the animal from every vantage point –while the strong pyramidal arrangement stabilizes the scene. *Buffalo Hunt #40* conveys Russell's remarkable skill in the utilization of light and space as well as the virtuosity with which the milling buffaloes are portrayed. This painting is most nearly related to *Buffalo Hunt #39*, currently housed at the Amon Carter Museum, and was executed to fulfill an exhibition requirement with the Minneapolis Institute in 1919.

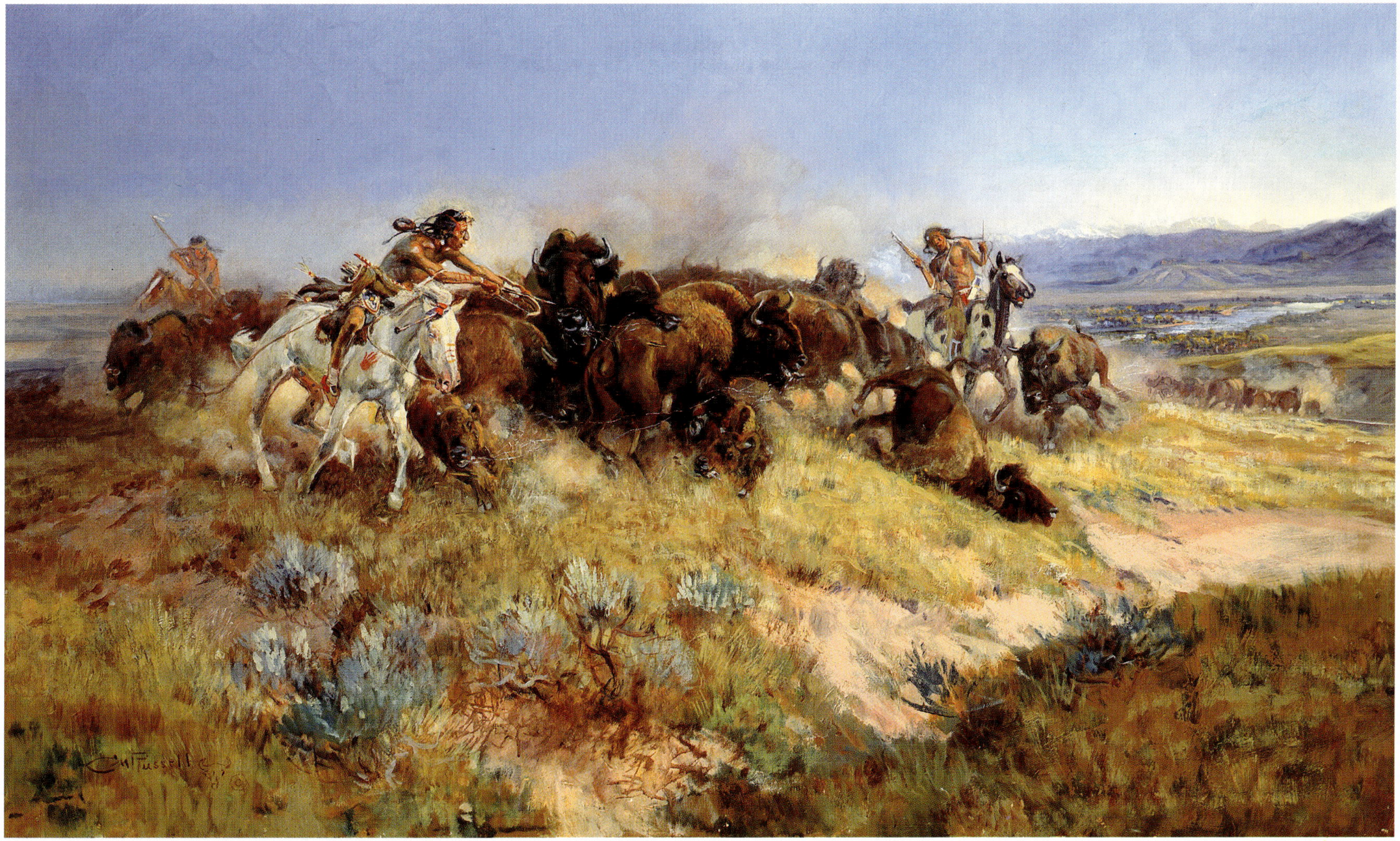

27. The Stranglers, 1920
oil on canvas
29 1/2 x 47 1/2 inches
signed lower left: CM Russell/skull cipher/copyright

PROVENANCE: Estate of Nancy Russell; Earl C. Adams Collection; Estate of W.E. Weiss, Wyoming.

EXHIBITIONS: Kanst Galleries, Los Angeles, 1921; Brown Palace Hotel, Denver, 1921; School of the Arts, Santa Barbara, 1923; Biltmore Salon, Los Angeles, 1924; Arthur H. Harlow, New York, New York, 1925; Corcoran Gallery of Art, Washington, D.C., 1925; Art League of Santa Barbara, Santa Barbara, 1927; Biltmore Salon, Los Angeles, 1927; Grand Central Art Galleries, New York, New York, 1927 & 1928; Robert C. Vose Galleries, Boston, 1928.

REFERENCES: Boston Globe, November 21, 1928, Paintings of Charles Russell on Exhibition; Exhibition of Paintings, Drawings, and Sculpture by Notable Artists of the Old West exhibition catalogue, May 1 to October 1, 1963, Whitney Gallery of Western Art, Buffalo Bill Historical Center, Cody Wyoming, pg. 12; Karl Yost and Frederic G. Renner, A Bibliography Of The Published Works Of Charles M. Russell, University of Nebraska Press, Lincoln, NB, 1971, pp. 56, 111.

As relayed by Brian Dippie, *The Stranglers* is not only a great action picture, but rarer yet, an action portrait of Will Rogers. In 1920, the Russells made their first extended vacation to California. Nancy's eyes were opened to an enticing new market for Charlie's art –Hollywood, where Westerns were all the rage. That November 26th, an unidentified newspaper reported that Russell was painting his old friend Will Rogers:

> The portrait shows the famous spinner of "illiterate jokes," on horseback, dexterously spinning the noose of his lariat over the back of a huge grizzly bear which has been thrown on its back on the ground by the rope of another mounted cowpuncher. The artist has taken as a background he sun-browned grass and sage of the Montana foothills, with the blue, broken outlines of the higher mountains showing in the distance. Action, color, and accuracy of detail are notable features of the picture. One almost expects to see the wide mouth of the cowboy humorist quirk up in the famous grin. "Bill told me he wanted a roping picture," says Mr. Russell, "so I'm painting this one for him."

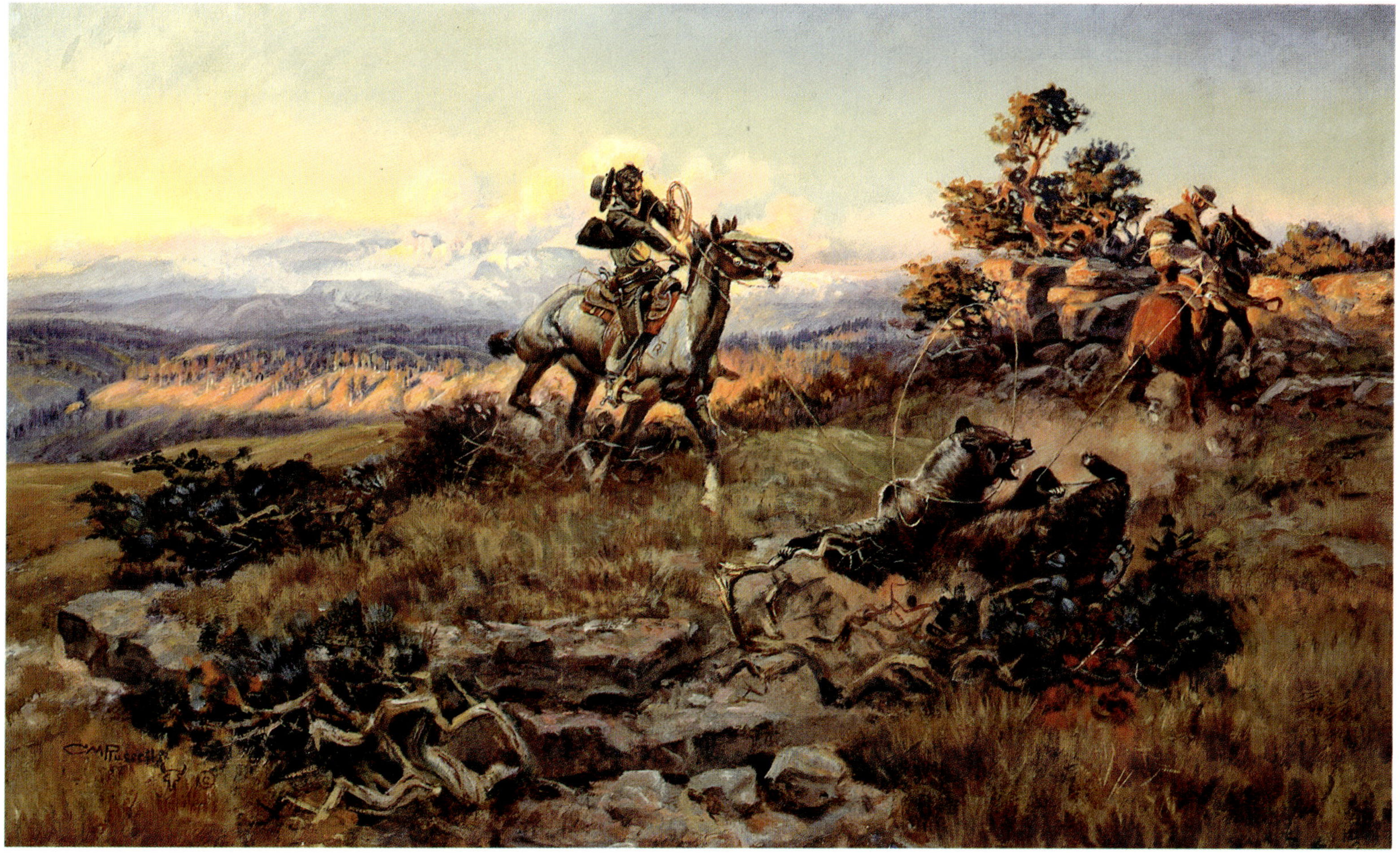

28. Planning the Attack, 1901
oil on canvas
24 x 36 inches
signed and dated: CM Russell/skull cipher/1901

PROVENANCE: The Artist; Private Collection, Montana; Private Collection.

As noted by art historian Alexander Nemerov, a number of paintings exist in which Russell has "juxtaposed adversaries, tokens of the old and new, the traditional and the technological, in a mannered relation of near and far." Representing two such works, *Planning the Attack* and *Wagons* picture the Native Americans in the foreground as they stop to observe the wagon train across the river in the distance. Always in these paintings the newer of the adversaries, the ones representing technological change and an end of the old days, appears in the background.

However similar in composition, a comparison of the two works reveals a striking transformation in style over the twenty year period. One of Russell's consummate early works, *Planning the Attack*, features relatively sophisticated compositional devices. The large pyramidal outcropping serves both as a backdrop for the primary Indian figures, as well as to integrate the distant landscape on the far left portion of the work. However by 1921, Russell had abandoned the stark realism that characterized his earlier work for a more lyrical style. *Wagons* (plate #29) represents the final evolution in Russell's career when he relied on color treatment and brushwork alone for unity of form.

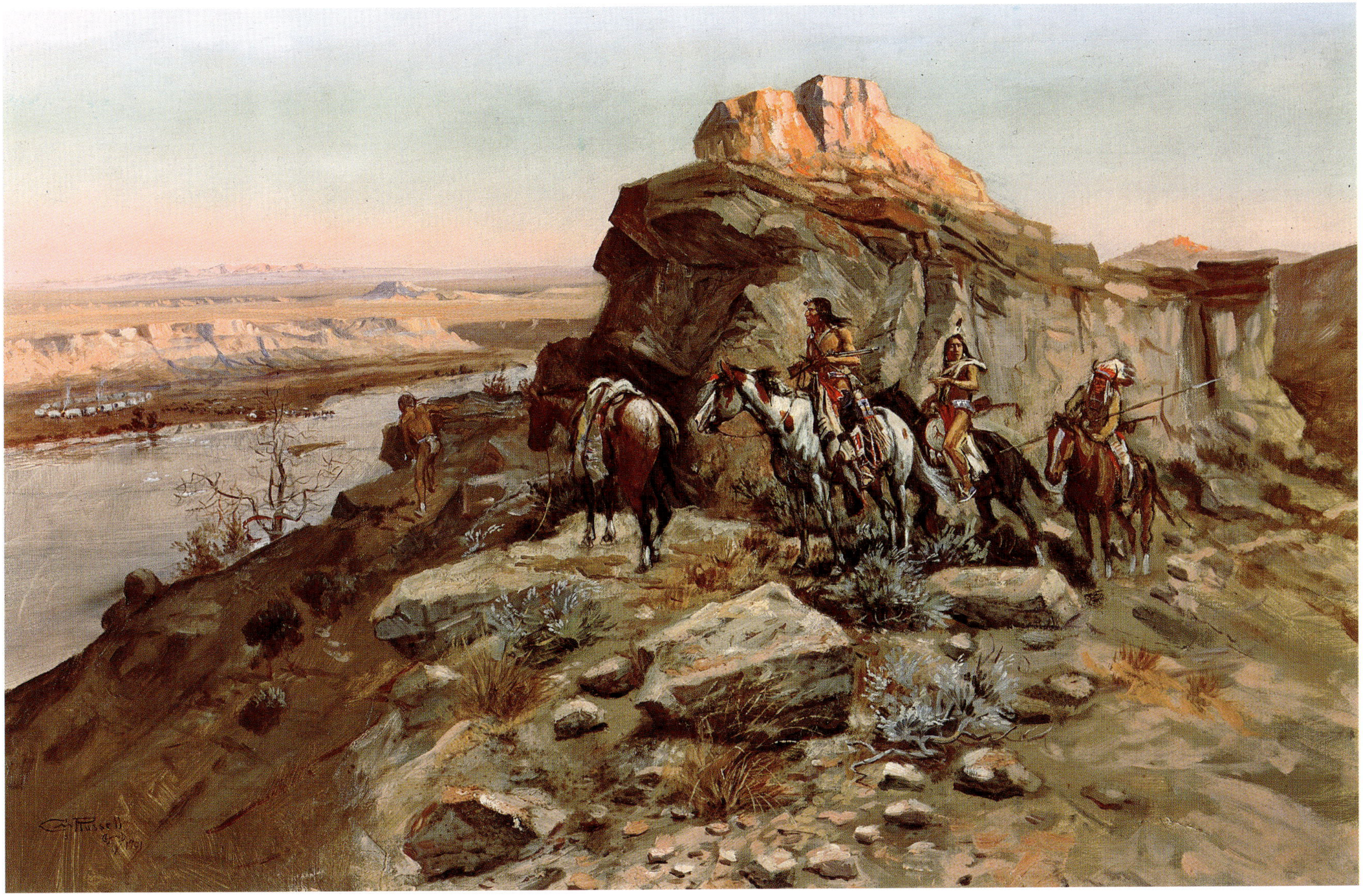

29. Wagons, 1921
oil on canvas
30 x 48 inches
signed lower left, dated lower right: CM Russell/skull cipher/1921

PROVENANCE: S.H. Keoughan, Denver; Kennedy Gallery, New York, New York; Private Collection, Dallas, Texas.

EXHIBITIONS: Brown Palace Hotel, Denver, Colorado, 1921; Stendahl Art Gallery, Los Angeles, California, 1922; School of the Arts Gallery, Santa Barbara, California, 1923; Stendahl Art Gallery, Los Angeles, California, 1923.

REFERENCES: Los Angeles Times, April 8, 1923, rotogravure section, p.9.; Karl Yost and Frederic Renner, A Bibliography of the Published Works of Charles M. Russell, University of Nebraska Press, Lincoln, NB, 1971, p.124.

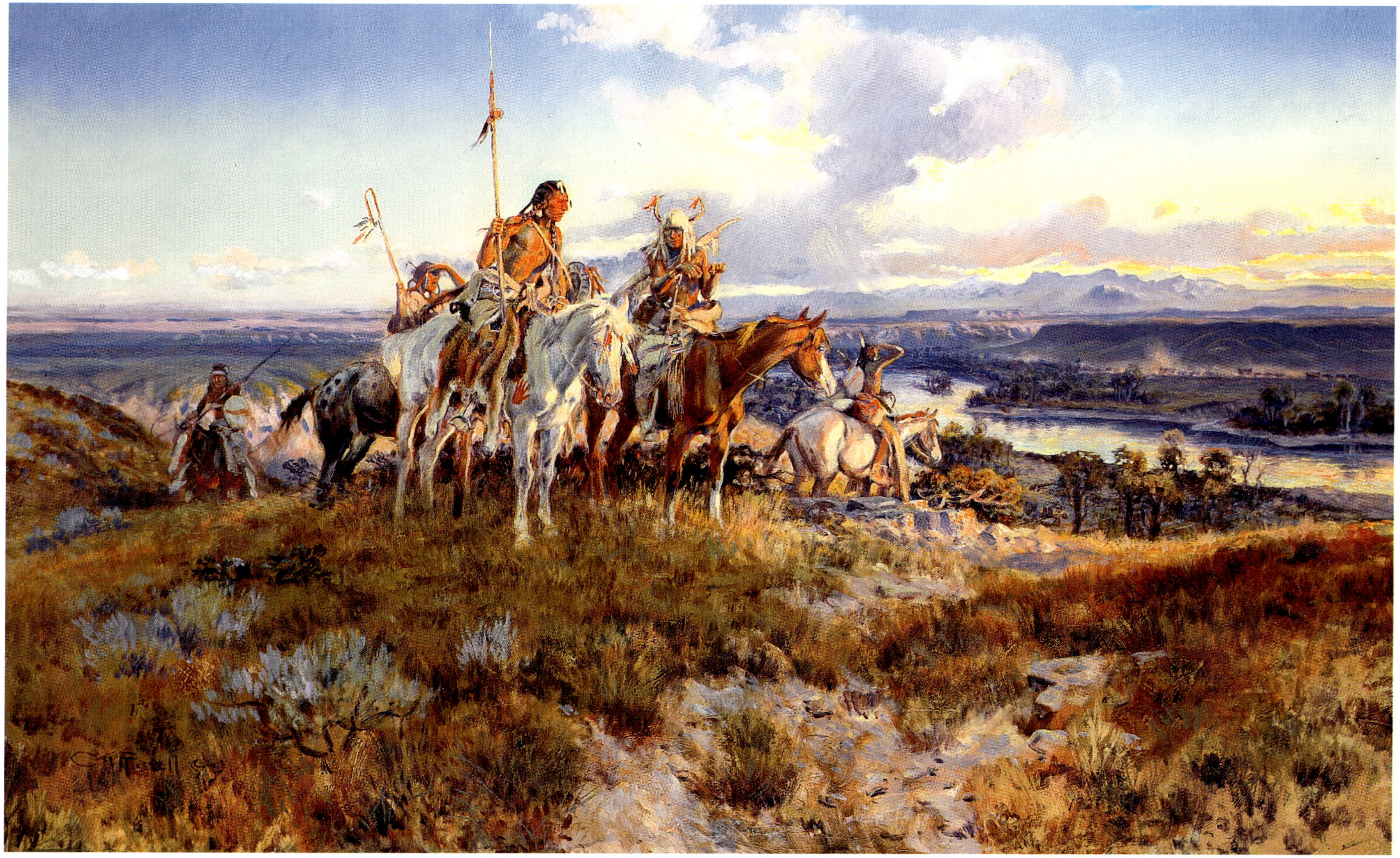

30. Wolf and the Beaver, 1921
oil on canvas
23 1/2 x 35 1/2 inches
signed lower left: CM Russell/skull cipher/copyright

PROVENANCE: Edward L. Doheney Estate, Los Angeles, California; St. John's Seminary, Camarillo, California; Robert Hefner, Oklahoma City, Oklahoma; Private Collection, California.

EXHIBITIONS: Brown Palace Hotel, Denver, November-December, 1921; Stendahl Art Gallery, Ambassador Hotel, Los Angeles, California, April, 1922; Special Exhibition of Paintings and Bronzes by Charles M. Russell, March 26-April 9, 1924, The Biltmore Salon, Los Angeles, California.

REFERENCES: Rocky Mountain News, December 4, 1921, "Roerich Paintings Arrive, Are Declared Revelation;" Karl Yost and Frederic Renner, A Bibliography of the Published Works of Charles M. Russell, University of Nebraska Press, Lincoln, NB, 1971, p. 31; M. Hal Sussmann, "Russell Murals Unveiled,: Southwest Art 18 (May 1989), p 62.

At the pinnacle of Russell's career, many of his most successful canvases involved the affectionate portrayal of paradox. The theme usually centered on a solitary man pitted against nature, forced to confront a moral dilemma. Here the lone fugitive, not unlike the lone wolf, skulks below the horizon line to avoid exposure both from harsh elements and would-be lawmen out to fetch a reward. In contrast, the beaver rests comfortably within the safe confines of its den below. The dilemma arises: should the outlaw continue on the trail away from the cozy house, or risk being apprehended by journeying to the cabin for shelter? The viewer is left to his or her own devices to decide. Obviously a metaphorical work, the drama is conveyed through brushwork, color and mood rather than the physical dynamics that characterized earlier narrative paintings.

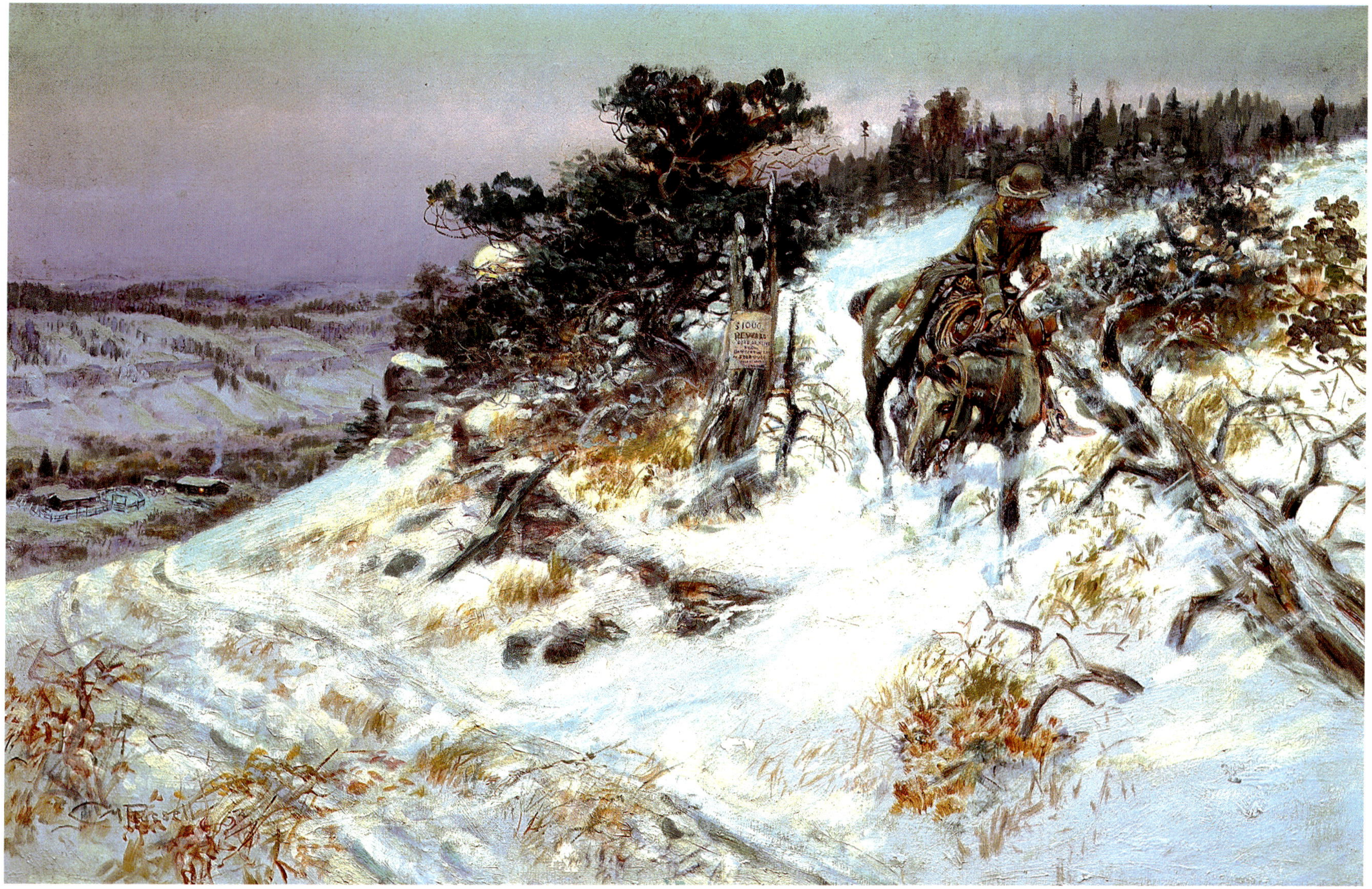
$1000
REWARD

31. Invocation to the Sun, 1922
watercolor on paper
11 x 17 inches
signed and dated lower left: To Jannette Kanst From CM Russell/skull cipher/1922

PROVENANCE: Private Collection; {Gerald Peters Gallery, Santa Fe, New Mexico}; Private Collection.

REFERENCES: Great Falls Daily Leader, December 31, 1954, "Two Russell Paintings on Loan Here for First Public Exhibition"; Karl Yost & Frederic G. Renner, A Bibliography of the Published Works of Charles M. Russell, University of Nebraska Press, Lincoln, NB, 1971, pp. 115, 149, 163, 194.

In February of 1920, the Russells journeyed to Southern California for the first time. They rented a house in Pasadena, where Nancy Russell arranged the first of many exhibitions in California. Kanst Gallery, a prestigious gallery in Hollywood Hills, would be host to an exhibition of six sculptures and twelve paintings of which *Invocation To The Sun* was one.

Though Russell was widely known for his action paintings, his later works were among the most compelling and personal statements within his oeuvre. He found freedom in simplification of form as details became secondary to mood. In many instances, the Indian leader was an older man approaching Russell's age. Here, the aged patriarch stands with arms outstretched toward the setting sun. Russell's awakening sense of color floods the scene with sunstruck effects, creating a mood of pure reverie.

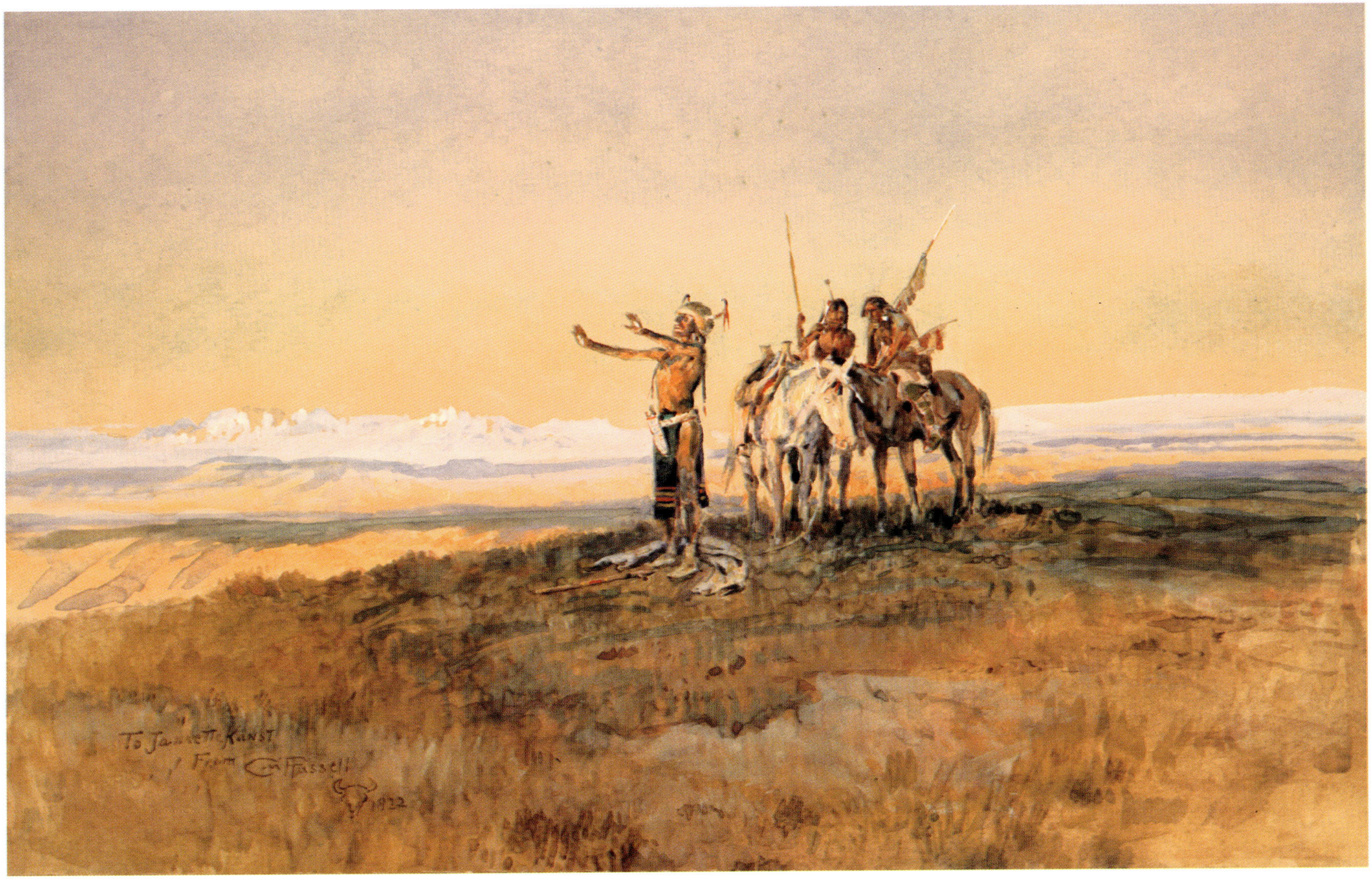

32. Worked Over, 1925
watercolor on paper
19 x 29 inches
signed and dated lower left: CM Russell /skull cipher/1925

PROVENANCE: Nancy Russell; National Cowboy Hall of Fame, Oklahoma City, Oklahoma; Private Collection, Denver, Colorado; {Gerald Peters Gallery, Santa Fe, New Mexico}; Private Collection, Texas.

EXHIBITIONS: Art League of Santa Barbara, Santa Barbara, California, 1927; Biltmore Salon, Los Angeles, California, 1927; Wildenstein & Co., New York, New York, (*How the West Was Won: Paintings Watercolors, and Bronzes by Frederic Remington and Charles M. Russell*) for the benefit of the Hospital for Special Surgery, May 22-June 22, 1968, no. 82; Gene Autry Western Heritage Museum, Los Angeles, California, The Butler Institute of American Art, Youngstown Ohio, Museum of Western Art, Denver, Colorado, The Eiteljorg Museum, Indianapolis, Indiana, and the Roanoke Museum, Roanoke, Virginia, (*The West Explored: The Gerald Peters Collection of Western American Art*), November, 1988-April, 1989.

REFERENCES: West 2 (May, 1926), frontispiece; Wildenstein & Co., How the West Was Won (1968), illustrated, no. 82; Karl Yost and Frederic Renner, A Bibliography of the Published Works of Charles M. Russell, University of Nebraska Press, Lincoln, NB, 1971, p. 106; Julie Schimmel, The West Explored: The Gerald Peters Collection of Western American Art (1988), p.59, illustrated, pl. 41.

Worked Over features two cowboys settled into their saddles, looking across a waterhole at a brindle cow with a roving calf. The cow is clearly branded *b*, while the calf's original brand had been changed to *B*. Hence the title of the painting refers to the unscrupulous rustler act of "working over" cattle.

This painting was executed by Charles Russell as a gift to his wife, Nancy. The title and subject are an allusion to their son adopted in 1916, and how they had to "work him over" to give him the Russell "brand." As Russell himself wrote to his good friend Con Price: "Maybe you dont know it Con but we got a boy at our house now he was a little two month slickear when we put our iron on him his name is Jack and he reminds me of Leslie (Con's son) when he was a baby." This painting hung over Nancy Russell's bed from 1926 until her death in May of 1940.

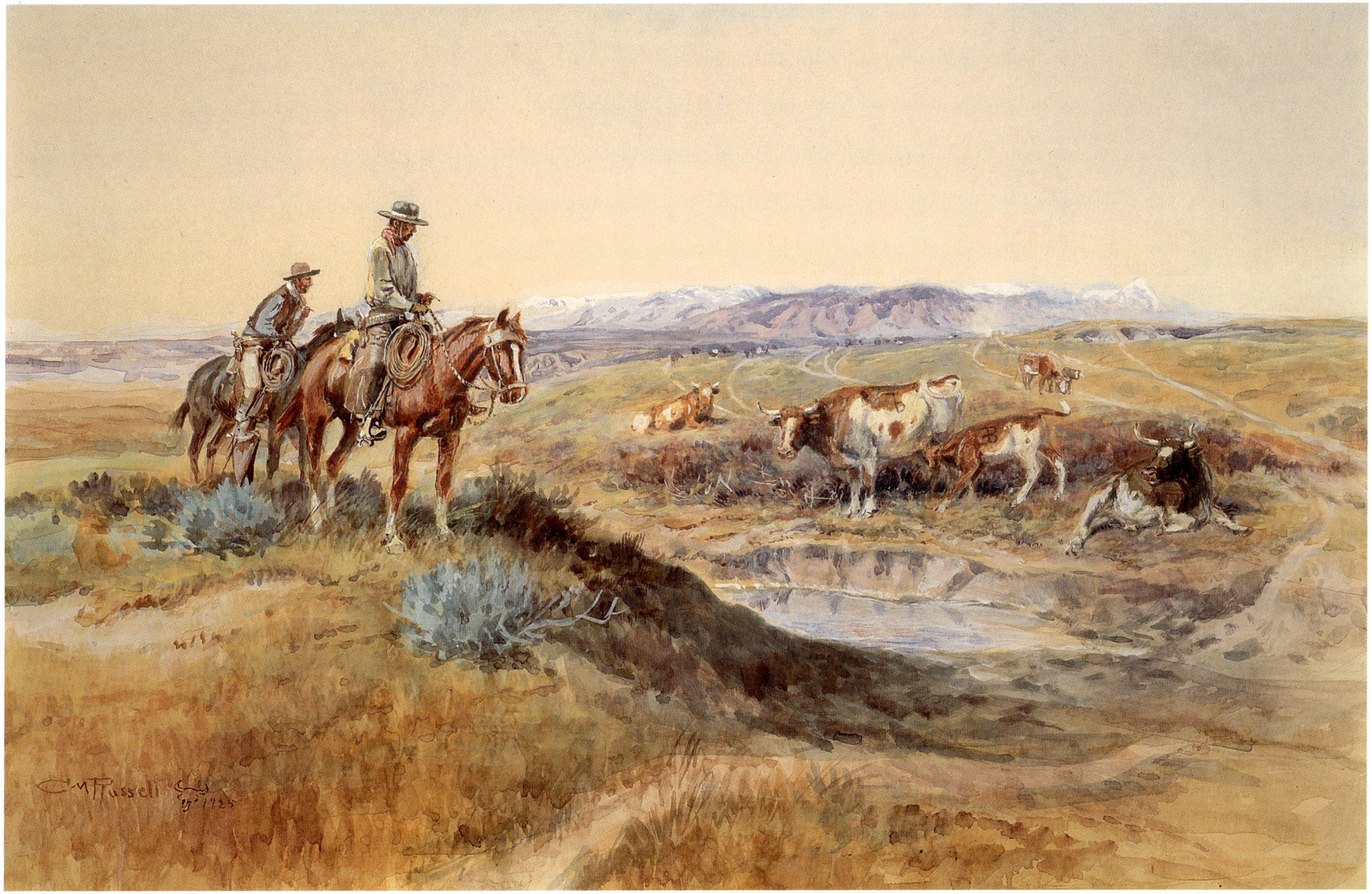

33. The Free Trader, 1925
oil on canvas
15 1/8 x 20 1/8 inches
signed lower left: CM Russell/skull cipher

PROVENANCE: Nancy Russell Estate, Pasadena, California (1940); C.R. Smith, New York, New York, (1941); H.R. Britzman, Pasadena, California, (1941); Private Collection, California.

EXHIBITIONS: Arthur H. Harlow, New York, New York, 1925; Corcoran Gallery of Art, Washington, DC; Apartment, 52 Gramercy Park, New York, New York, 1925; Art League of Santa Barbara, Santa Barbara, California, 1927; Biltmore Salon, Los Angeles, California, 1927.

REFERENCES: My Sixty Years on the Plains Trapping, Trading, and Indian Fighting, by W.T. Hamilton, New York, Forest and Stream Publishing Co., 1905, p. 178; Exhibition Catalogue from the Sale of the Collected Works of Frederic Remington and Charles M. Russell, J.W. Young, Chicago, c. February 1947, p.5; The Charles M. Russell Book, Harold McCracken, p. 42; Montana, The Magazine of Western History, Autumn issue, 1962; Karl Yost & Frederic G. Renner, A Bibliography of the Published Works of Charles M. Russell, University of Nebraska Press, Lincoln, NB, 1971, pgs. 10, 45, 46.

Although Russell seldom portrayed frontier-types in the nineteenth century, trappers, mountain men, and traders became frequent and apt symbols of his twentieth century sentiments. His identification with these men stemmed from his experience with a skilled hunter and trapper named Jake Hoover. At the age of sixteen, Russell became a keen observer of wildlife and grew to love the freedom the frontier afforded. His longing for this passing way of life is impressed upon canvases such as *Free Trader*, as enhanced by the buffalo skeleton prominently in the foreground. A horizontal format and bold backlighting set a dramatic stage for the heroic proportions of the lead rider, as if he envisioned the changes associated with civilization.

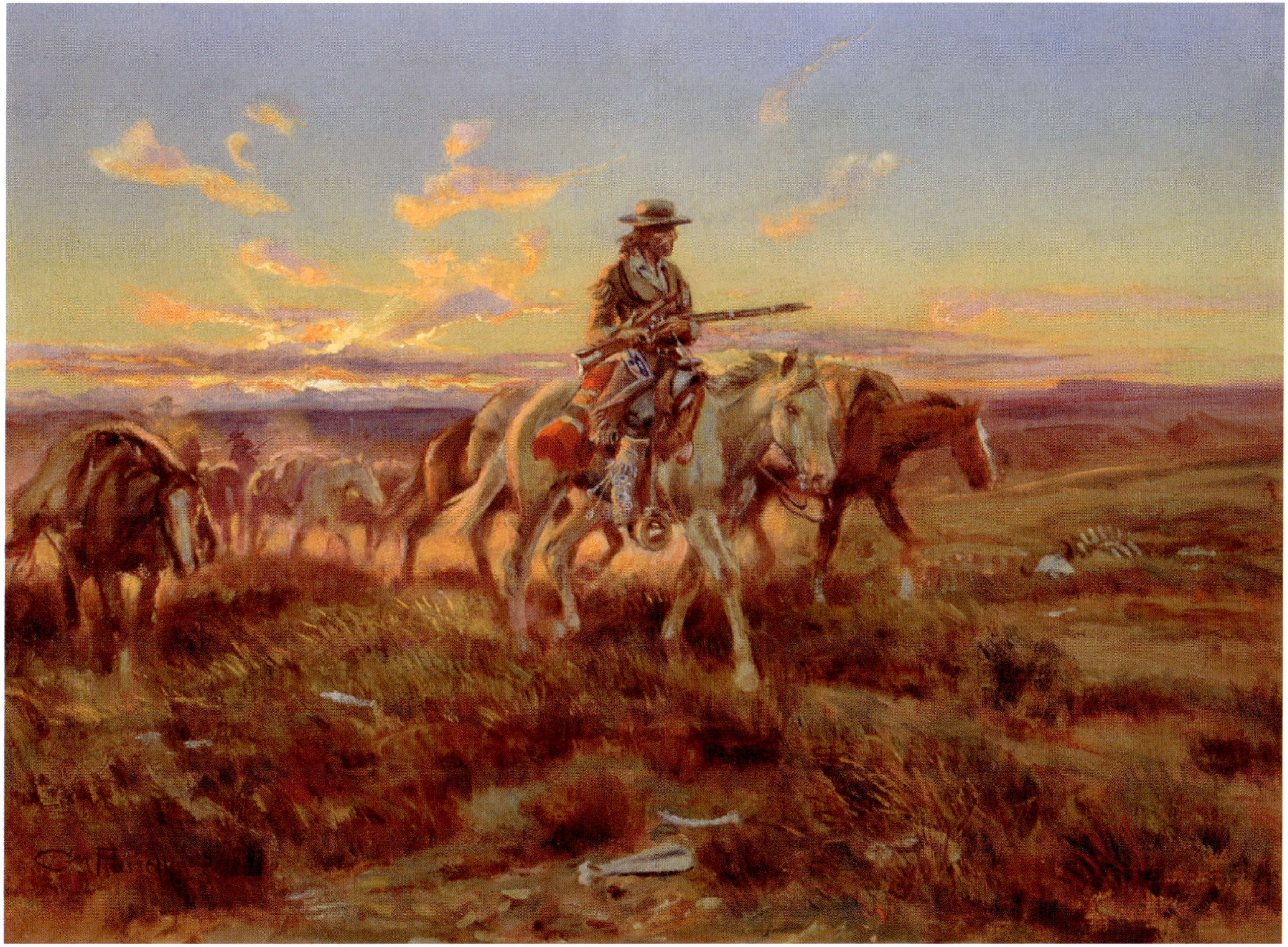

34. Mexico, 1925
watercolor on paper
18 1/2 x 28 1/2 inches
signed and dated lower left: CM Russell/skull cipher/1925

PROVENANCE: Nancy Russell, Pasadena, California; C.R. Smith, Washington, D.C.; George Miller; George Miller's son; Earl C. Adams, Los Angeles, California; The Adams Family Trust, San Marino, California; {Mongerson Wunderlich Gallery, Chicago, Illinois}; Private Collection, Chicago, Illinois.

EXHIBITIONS: Art League of Santa Barbara, Santa Barbara, 1927; Biltmore Salon, Los Angeles, 1927; (*The West Remembered: Artists and Images*), 1837-1973 [San Francisco: California Historical Society, 1973], p.64.

REFERENCES: Akron Topics, 5:55, (February 1927), 16, 30, "Scattered Precincts," by Fred Ayer.

Throughout his life and in his art, Russell represented and preserved the essence of the American West. The subject of Mexican *vaqueros*, the original cowboy, seemed a fitting one as the artist grew increasingly nostalgic for a past that survived only in his memories. He expressed his sentiments about the old days to his longtime friend Harry Stanford, "You have a good memory and knew the country when it was worth knowing, and men good ore bad that were regular men...Write about them and the land they lived in...when the nester turned this country grass side down the west we loved died..."

In Russell's superb watercolor titled *Mexico*, an errant steer is being looped and tied by the skilled vaqueros. The handling of the front horse and rider is the focus of the composition, full of detail and deft modeling. Though the theme was not new, it was a resonant one, providing a summary statement of Russell's dedication to preserving the myth of the West.

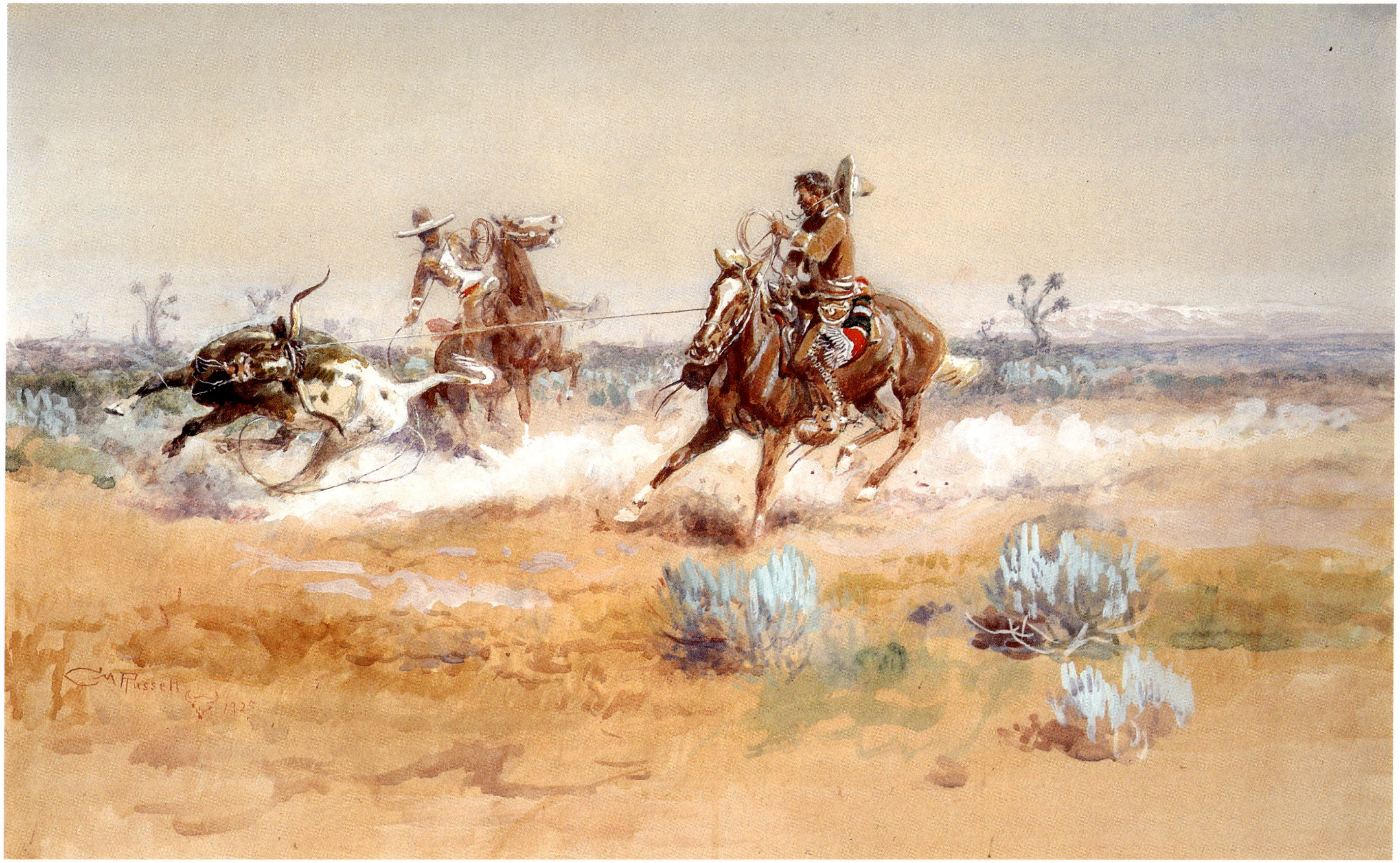

35. Navajo Trackers, 1926
watercolor on paper
18 x 29 1/4 inches
signed and dated lower left: CM Russell/skull cipher/1926

PROVENANCE: Museum of Western Art, Denver, Colorado; {Gerald Peters Gallery, Santa Fe, New Mexico}; Private Collection, Texas.

REFERENCES: Karl Yost and Frederic Renner, A Bibliography of the Published Works of Charles M. Russell, University of Mebraska Press, Lincoln, NB, 1971, p.80; Frontier Spirit, Catalogue of The Collection of the Museum of Western Art, Denver, Colorado, 1983, plate 28; Brian Dippie, Looking at Russell, Amon Carter Museum, Forth Worth, Texas, 1987, p.121.

During the final year of Charles Russell's life, he looked to the past for both inspiration and subject matter for his work. *Navajo Trackers* epitomizes the style and mood of Russell's last years of creativity. The horsemen seem a natural part of the landscape; their costumes reveal an interest in the exotic and brilliant application of color. Russell wrote of the Navajos to his friend Edward Borein, "at sundown a band of these American Arabs dropped down from the high country... most of these riders looked like the real thing in their high forked saddles and concho belts or turquoise necklaces and ear rings... they were not like the Indian I know but everything on them spelt wild people and horsemen in a mixture of dust and red sunlight it made a picture that will not let me forget Arizona." (Frontier Spirit 80)

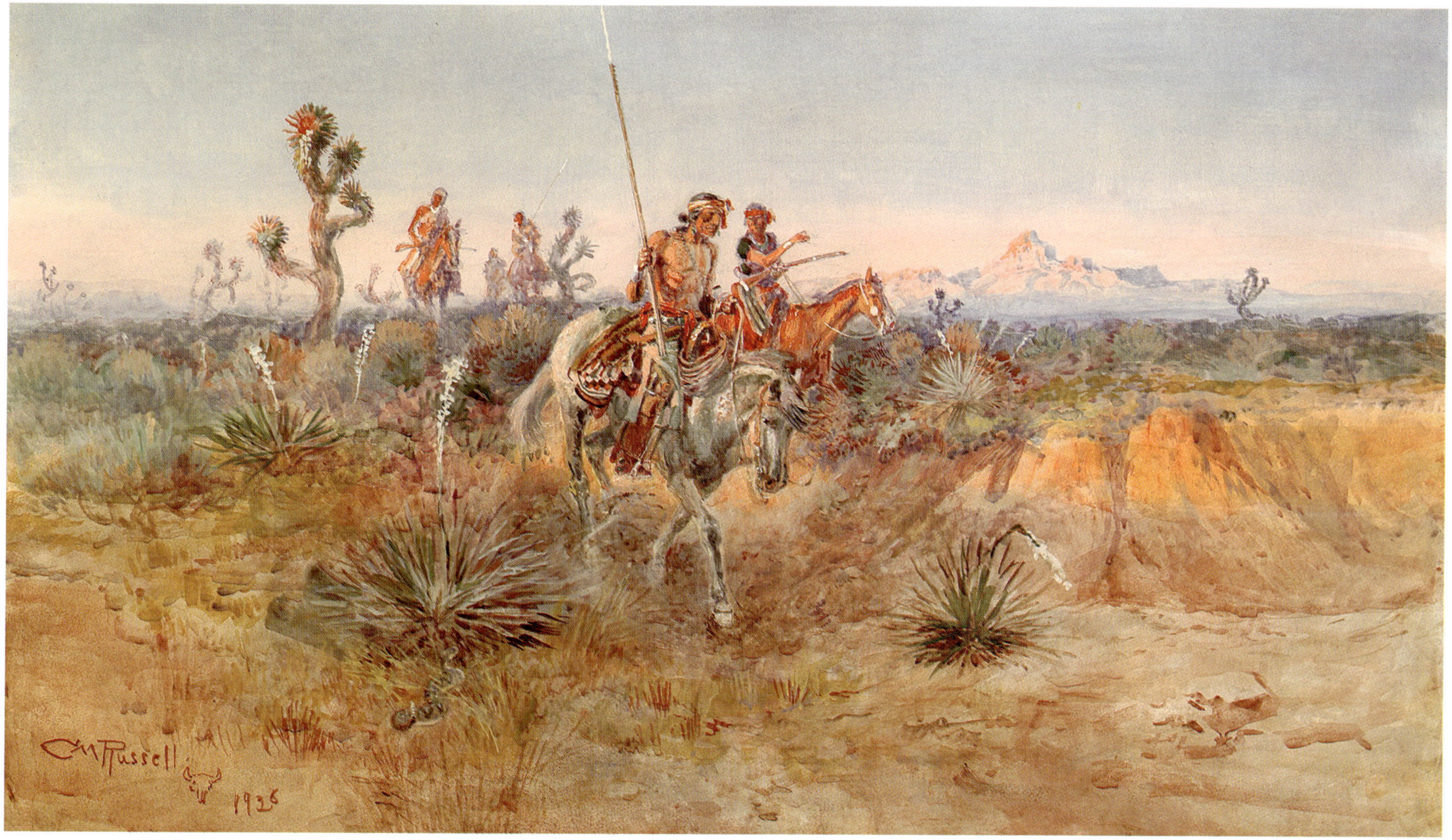
CMRussell
1926

36. *Four studies for "The History of the West" Series, c.*1926
watercolor
signed lower left: CMR/skull cipher
7 1/8 x 38 1/8 inches each

PROVENANCE: The Artist; Edward L. Doheny Estate, Los Angeles, California; Knoedler Galleries, New York, Nwe York; Private Collection: Private Collection, California.

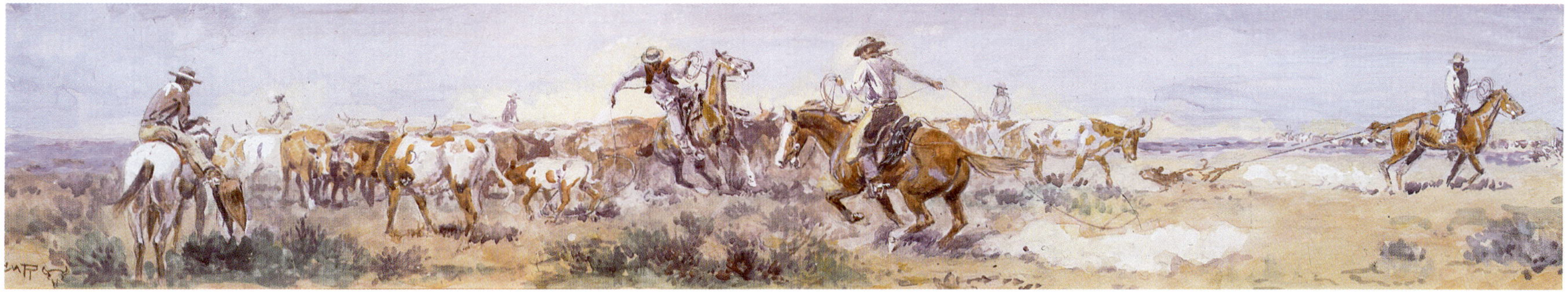

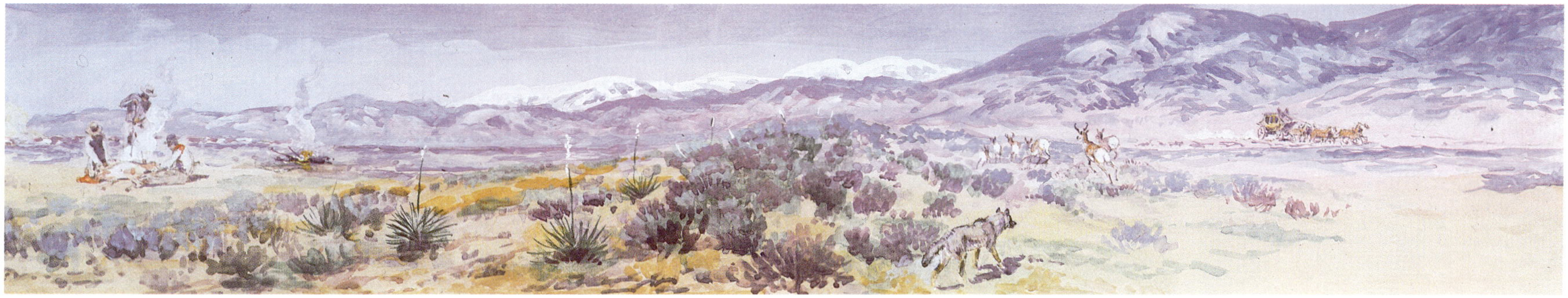

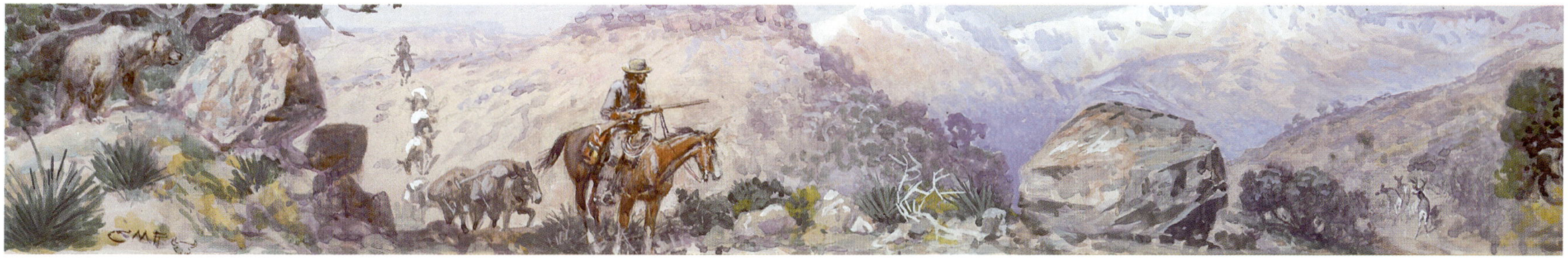

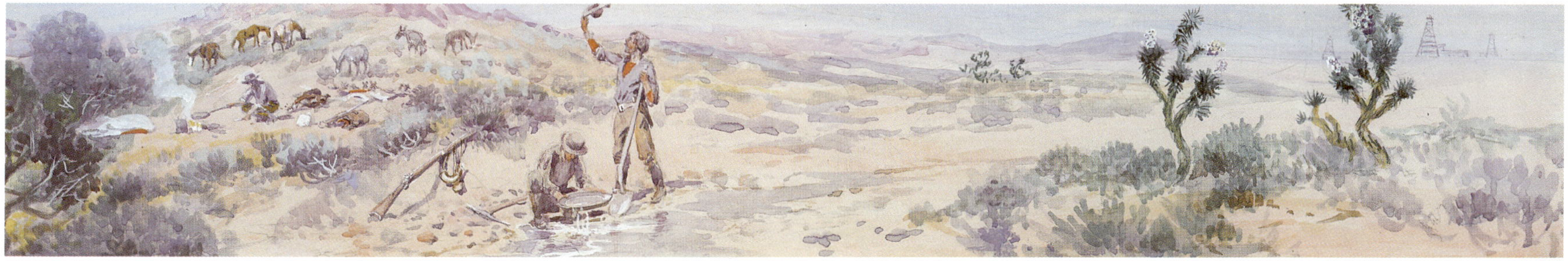

37. *The History of the West,* 1926
oil on canvas
30 inches x 20 feet (north panel)
30 inches x 23 feet (south panel)
signed and dated lower left: CM Russell/skull cipher/1926

PROVENANCE: Edward L. Doheny Estate, Los Angeles; St. John's Seminary, Camarillo, California; Robert Hefner, Oklahoma City, Oklahoma; Private Collection, New Mexico.

A frieze, commissioned by Mr. Doheny for his home in Los Angeles, is here divided between the north and south walls, with small extensions by an amateur artist added to fill the space at either end of each wall.

Starting with the panorama on the north wall, the story of the West unfolds with a round-up. While cowboys herd the calves, the branding irons are heating over a fire. A coyote stalks a buck with four does, and a six-horse stage coach moves along in the distance.

On the south wall, it is late afternoon and sunlight sheds a rosy glow on the mountains. Spring is indicated by snow on the peak, active waterfalls, and two flowering Joshua trees. A bear peers over rocky outcroppings at a pack train. The lead rider lifts his rifle to take aim at the buck and two does on the opposite slope. Three horses and three mules graze beyond the campfire where a cowboy is making coffee, with gear and tarpaulin laid out for the night. In the foreground, to the right, a miner sifts his gold-pan over the stream. His companion, leaning on a shovel, waves towards the approaching pack train.

The frieze was completed in April, 1926. Charles Russell died the following October. It was probably his last important work.

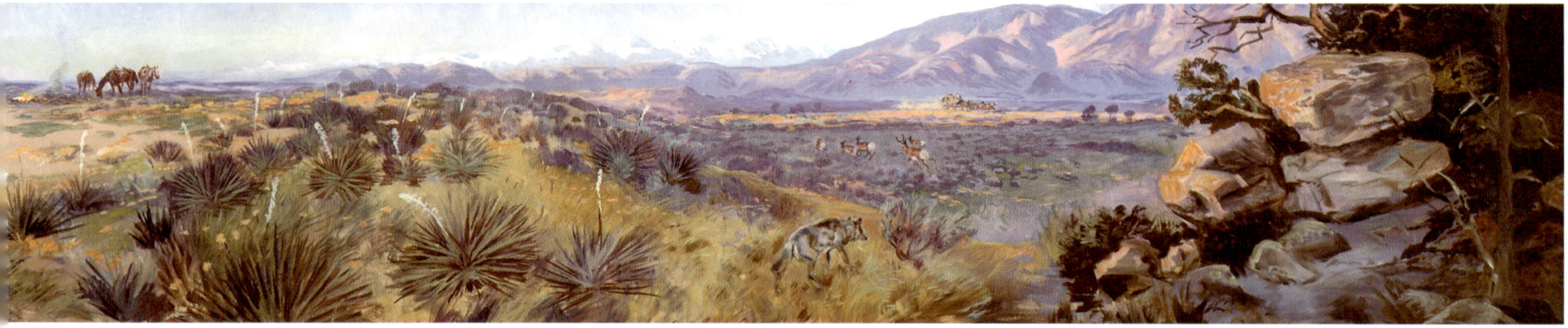

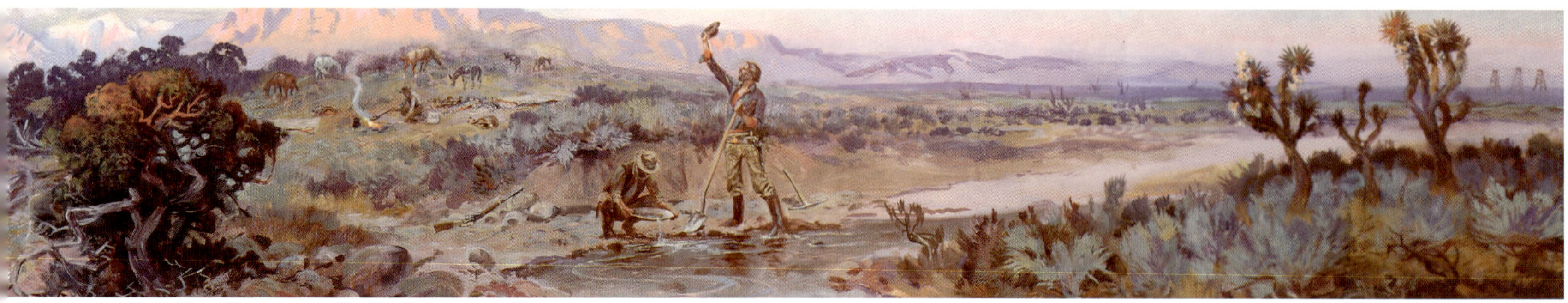

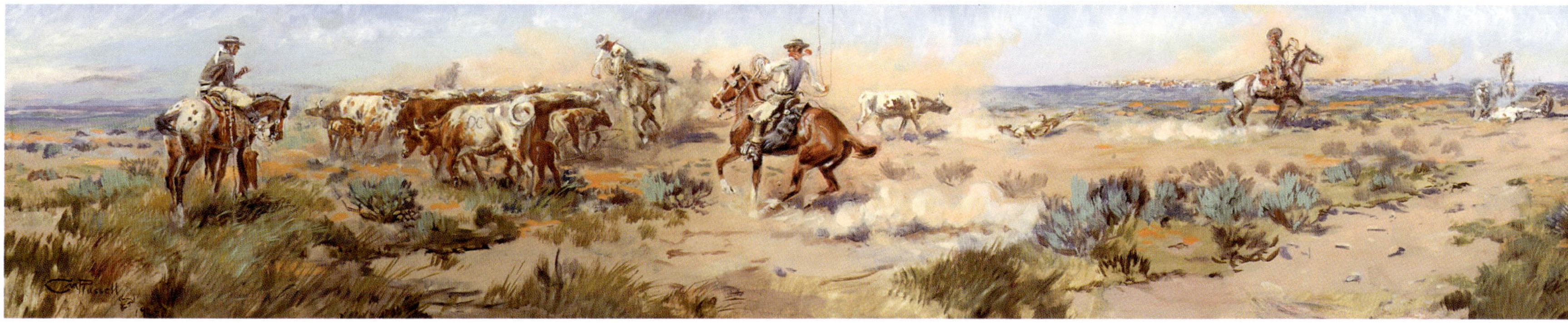

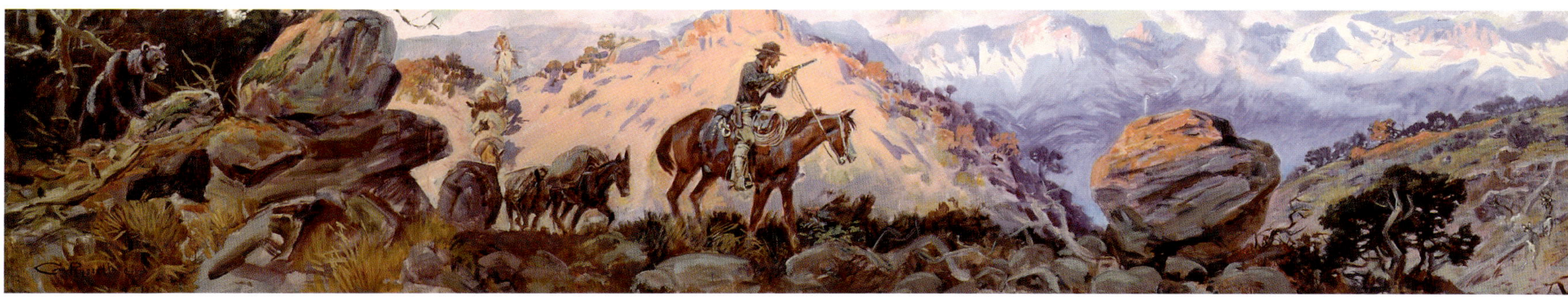

Russell as a Sculptor: A Brief Overview of His Bronzes

BY RUDOLF WUNDERLICH, GERALD PETERS AND KELLIE KETO

The recent publication by Rick Stewart, Charles M. Russell, Sculptor ushered in an unprecedented level of critical evaluation of the artist's sculptural works. Before Stewart's comprehensive evaluation, relatively little consideration was given to the specifics of Russell's casts. Following the disposition of Nancy Russell's estate in 1941, Homer Britzman conducted posthumous and highly questionable casting activity that that nearly doubled the number of bronzes attributed to the artist and obscured Russell's important contribution to American sculpture. Ironically, of Russell's forty-six bronze subjects, relatively few lifetime castings –numbering twenty or less per bronze –were produced during the Russell's lifetimes.

The genesis of Charlie Russell's career as a sculptor in bronze began in St. Louis, Missouri, where in October 1903, the artist and his wife traveled to visit his family. Nancy Russell had submitted some of her husband's paintings and watercolors for exhibition at the upcoming Saint Louis world's fair, which was titled the Louisiana Purchase Exposition and devoted to the theme of the American West in art. Some twenty million visitors over an eight-month period showed up to celebrate the centennial of the Louisiana Purchase. As an indication that America had finally accepted both sculpture as a legitimate art form, and the West as a legitimate part of America, sculpture of the American West was given special prominence in the vast fair grounds. A writer for the World's Fair Bulletin noted: "In studios and ateliers, in all parts of the United States, sculptors, the most famous in the land, are at work under contract on the 'scale models' which have been assigned to them to execute." [1]

Sculptor Karl Bitter had been named Chief of Sculpture for the Exposition, and under his guidance Alexander Stirling Calder, Daniel Chester French, Charles Grafly, Isidore Konti, Hermon Atkins MacNeil, Augustus Saint-Gaudens, John Quincy Adams Ward, and many others were commissioned to create major works for the grounds. Among the works inspired by cowboy, Indian, and wildlife themes were Adolph Weinman's melodramatic group titled *Destiny of the Red*

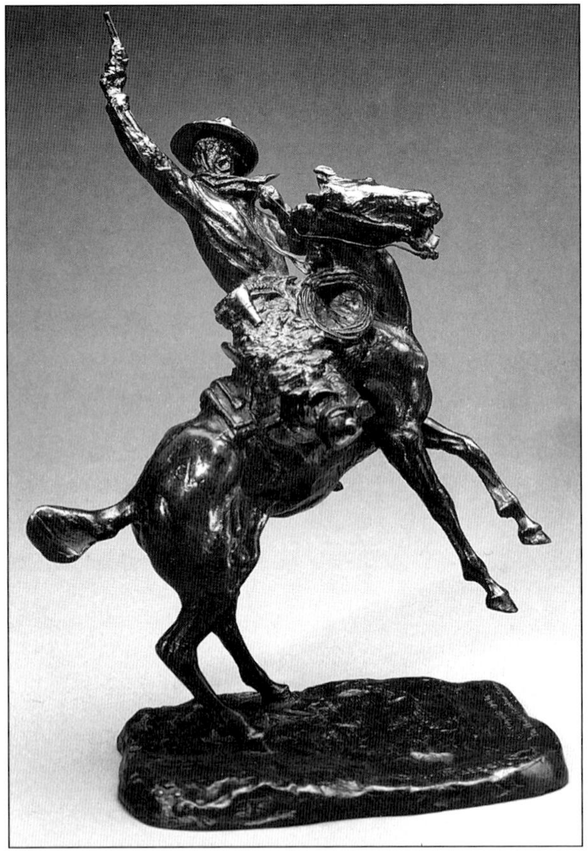

Smoking Up, No. 6, 1904, 12 1/2 x 9 5/8 x 6 3/8 inches

Man, Cyrus E. Dallin's equestrian statue of a Sioux chief, and Frederic Remington's *Cowboys on a Tear* from the bronze later copyrighted *Coming Through the Rye.* Solon H. Borglum, the young Nebraska sculptor whose background and interests were close to Russell's, created four oversized statues: *The Buffalo Dance*, *Cowboy at Rest*, *The Indian Sage*, and *A Peril on the Plains*.

In addition to the monumental sculptures on display, many of the bronzes were small in scale, utilitarian and less costly, reflecting a new trend in American sculpture. Such works, often finely detailed, obscured the boundaries between art and decoration. No doubt Russell was impressed by the many small sculptures depicting wildlife, particularly the fifteen bronzes exhibited by Edward Kemeys. Kemeys, largely self-taught, had spent much time in the West as a trapper and Indian scout. Active from the early 1870s, he was regarded as America's first sculptor of wildlife and endangered species in bronze. Though inspired by works of the French animaliers, Kemeys works were altogether devoid of academic conventions. Rather, he established a unique American style, rooted in realism and supported by a rising environmental movement initiated by sportsmen who feared the eventual extinction of these animals. Like Russell, Kemeys maintained that nature was his only teacher. He adopted a stylized wolf's head as part of his insignia and also wrote stories illustrated with his works.[2] His naturalistic bronzes exhibited great attention to detail as well as a freshness of execution that foreshadowed the animal models Russell executed a few years later.

The couple traveled on to New York where Russell executed his first bronze *Smoking Up* after previewing the world's fair exhibition. While in New York, Nancy became acquainted with the Roman Bronze Works foundry which had also cast works by Remington, Borglum and Schreyvogel. *Smoking Up* represents the only instance in Russell's sculptural oeuvre where the reproduction rights were conveyed to successive owners, thereby greatly complicating the casting history. While the inscription indicated the work was copyrighted in 1904 to the New York Cooperative Society, no copyright registration has been located in the Library of Congress. Having cast an initial order of around seven works at Roman Bronze Works between the years 1905-1907, The New York Cooperative Society sold the rights to the Arthur H. Harlow Company, a commercial art gallery in New York. Harlow acquired the rights to *Smoking Up* in order to produce the casts on demand.[3] Having produced at least twenty-one casts after Russell's death, Harlow then sold the rights to Walter Latendorf of the Mannados

Book Shop of New York who produced something in excess of 132 copies.[4]

Although the exact number of *Smoking Up* bronzes may never be known, the majority clearly are posthumous casts. A comparison of a posthumous cast formerly in the Homer Britzman collection, with number #6 featured as plate #37, is particularly revealing. The posthumous cast displays a marked loss of surface texture and detail. Elements such as the pistol, neckerchief, lariat, chaps, and saddle are faint echoes of the original. Surface details on the horse, such as the brand on the right rear hip, bridle on the head, overall skin texture, and general musculature are also indistinct. The rider and horse are tilted farther back on the posthumous cast and a small brace has been added at the base to the rearing animal's right back leg, a feature typical of all of the posthumous examples. Those casts produced after Russell's death, from a poorly maintained master model, are but pale echoes of the aritst's original intention.

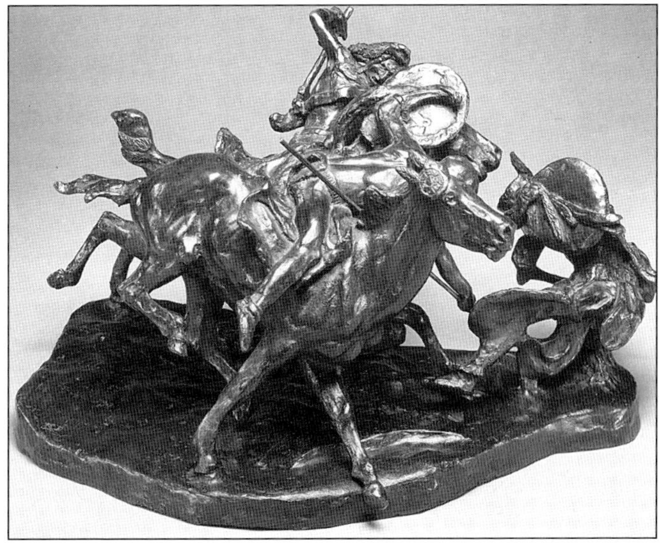

Counting Coup, 1905, 10 3/8 x 16 3/4 x 9 15/16 inches

As Russell increasingly focused on the production of his sculpture, his facility as a painter improved as a result. "By modeling one learns unconsciously to draw," William Ordway Partridge, a leading American sculptor, asserted in a treatise on sculpture techniques. "Modeling should be undertaken before drawing, as it is as useful to the painter almost as to the sculptor."[5] Throughout his career, Russell often relied on sculptural compositions to resolve particularly complex poses before painting on canvas. According to Russell's protègé Joe De Yong, the artist often used sculpture in the place of live models, a method learned from Russell's early days when few would pose for him. To work out problems of light and shadow he made "small, rough model-groups in beeswax, modeling clay, or plasticene, which nonetheless conveyed an unbelievably convincing feeling of action and vitality. These models he often set up under the direct light of a reading lamp on the living room table which he shifted for best arrangement of shadow, particularly."[6] One family member recounted that "Charlie used to keep a little hunk of plasticene on his painting stand, and when he'd get stuck on the painting of a face, he'd model the head and then paint from the little clay model-holding it in the position that would light it as he wanted it."[7] This was the case for his consummate drama on canvas, *When Blackfeet and Sioux Meet*, 1908, which relies heavily on his 1905 bronze *Counting Coup* (plate # 38), the second documented sculpture in Russell's oeuvre. The unified composition, the figural arrangement, and the narrative tension had all been worked out in wax and bronze prior to the execution of the painting.

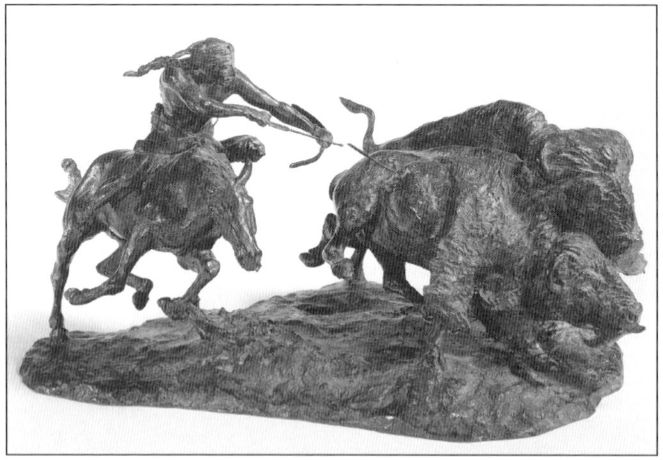

Buffalo Hunt, 1905, 10 x 18 1/4 x 12 1/2 inches

The Russells' second trip to New York City in 1905 must have been a particularly fruitful one, as two major sculptures, *Counting Coup* and *Buffalo Hunt*, were both modeled there. On March 4, 1905, Nancy Russell wrote her friend Josephine Trigg from New York City: "There are no amediate signs of home yet but I still have great hopes of getting there some time this spring. He {Russell} has his last group in wax don and it shure is a dandy I think he will have good success with this work we hope to have some returns after we go home but that is to be seen later on" [sic].[8] She was referring to the model of *Buffalo Hunt*, (plate # 40) which would be cast in bronze after their return to Montana.

Although Russell had painted and sketched the subject of a buffalo hunt many times, this was his first attempt to depict the action in three dimensions. A self supporting sculpture, Russell's innovative composition depicts the charging horse and wounded buffalo with all but one foot off the base. A tuft of grass supports one of the horse's front legs to provide two points of contact, while the injured buffalo is braced by the other animal against which it has fallen. Despite the aesthetic and technical success of this subject, various accounts recorded that only four bronzes were cast between 1905 and 1927 at Roman Bronze Works. Nancy Russell authorized additional casts after she registered a separate copyright for the work on July 31, 1928 under the title *Buffalo Runner*. A short time later the California Art Bronze Foundry produced at least two more casts.[9] Nancy's decision to change foundries was based on a series of defective casts she received from Roman Bronze Works that same year. The new foundry in Los Angeles, not far from her home in Pasadena, enabled better control over bronze production.

By 1911, Russell was receiving national acclaim for his naturalistic sculptures. In April, Russell's first one-man exhibition was held at the Folsom Galleries in New York. Titled "The West That Has Passed," the exhibition featured more than thirty of the artist's works, including A Bronc Twister which sold there for $250. The six-page catalogue contained an essay by the critic Arthur Hoeber, who placed Russell squarely in the path to succeed Remington as the premier artist of the American West. "Perhaps {Russell} is even more convincing in plastic form where he is untrammeled with color questions and where his feeling for action best manifests itself," Hoeber wrote in an expansion of his catalogue essay for the magazine World's Work.[10] Russell's innate ability to depict form in motion resulted in a spontaneous modeling style typical of some of the most avant-garde sculptors of the age. A comparison of the artist's *Bronc*

Twister (plate # 41) with a version modeled by Frederic Remington entitled *Bronco Buster* reveals how Russell's version as far more animated and naturalistic. It is as if Russell wanted to correct Remington's minor lapses of authenticity and surpass in the portrayal of arrested action as the horse leaps, in the artist's words "high, wide and crooked."[11] Comparing Russell's work to Remington's, the sculptor Gutzon Borglum observed: "In motive they show the same keen power of observation and ability to select the instant when the action is most complete and most expressive...Russell had not only the wit to see the dual situation attached to any great moment, but he had, and with an ability Remington had never shown, the power to portray animals, horses, cattlemen, in the mixed-up, tangled-up situations daily occurring in the wild unfenced West—situations no other artist has ever attempted.[12]

Despite Russell's rising fame, his larger, more elaborate bronzes such as *Counting Coup*, *Buffalo Hunt*, and *A Bronc Twister* did not do well with buyers. Nancy Russell's insistence on the relatively high prices for her husband's works resulted in sales far below her expectations. Having viewed the small wildlife sculptures at the St. Louis fair and being aware of the growing market for decorative sculpture at dealers like Tiffany's in New York, she no doubt saw an opportunity to capitalize on the small plaster models her husband had been giving away as gifts for many years. *Oh! Mother, What Is It?*, represents a departure for the artist as the first of a series of ashtray bronzes. Nancy Russell's copy of the Thurber Gallery exhibition catalogue, where the bronze was initially exhibited, reveals three of the pieces sold for $35.00 each, thus providing an inexpensive alternative to the artist's oils and watercolors.

Like Oh! Mother, What Is It?, all of Russell's early wildlife bronzes portrayed endangered species, such as the grizzly bear, the buffalo, and Rocky Mountain sheep to name a few. Indeed, Russell's choice of subjects was in line with the intellectual climate of the period when preservation issues were paramount. Respected critic Royal Cortissoz observed: "This and no other is emphatically the age of the animal sculptor, the one in which his true inspiration would seem to be positively in the air, energizing his art constantly in the simplest, most natural fashion."[13] At a time when artists were accused of creating overly sentimental, untruthful works, Russell was extolled for his highly accurate, sensitive observations. His familiarity with his subjects provided him with an uncommon understanding of animal behavior, enabling him to capture the

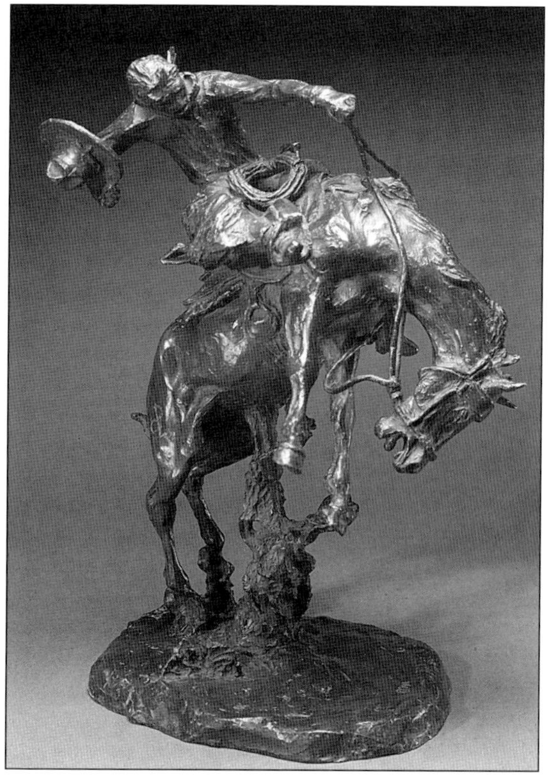

Bronc Twister, 1911, 18 1/8 x 12 3/4 x 9 inches

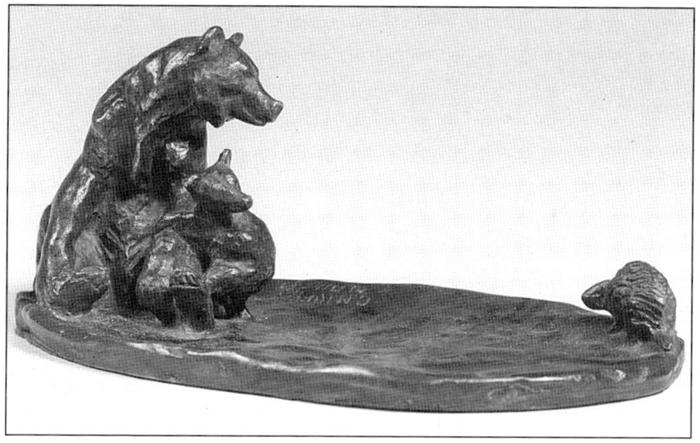

Oh! Mother, What Is It?, 1914, 4 x 8 5/8 x 4 3/8 inches

frolic-some inquisitiveness of grizzly cubs in their early months of life in the wild, for example.

Oh! Mother, What Is It? was copyrighted in April 1915, but it is not known exactly when the initial bronze casts were produced. In Charles M. Russell, Sculptor, Stewart calculates the number of lifetime casts at twenty, testifying to its popularity with collectors. Evidently, Nancy Russell had initially sent the plaster model to Benjamin Zoppo, who probably cast around twelve pieces by November 1, 1916.[14] When Zoppo ceased his casting activity in 1921, the model was transferred to Roman Bronze Works, where subsequent copies may have been produced. In January 1929, Roman Bronze Works sent the master model, apparently in rather poor condition, to Nancy Russell in California, and additional casts were made under her direction at the California Art Bronze Foundry in Los Angeles. Although the mold was destroyed by court order on December 5, 1941, according to the terms of Nancy Russell's will, Homer Britzman, purchased the estate, retained the plaster master model and had the Nelli Art Bronze Foundry make at least three additional casts in 1941-42.[15]

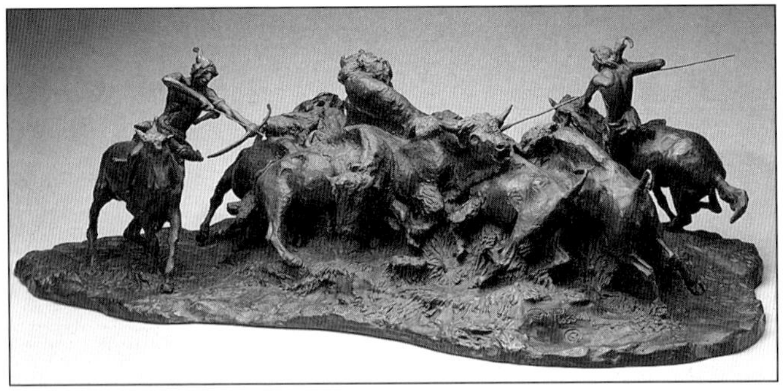

Meat For Wild Men, No. 1, 1924, 11 1/2 x 37 5/8 x 20 5/8 inches

Though *Oh! Mother, What is It?* was cast at Zoppo, Roman Bronze Works, California Art Bronze Foundry, and posthumously at Nelli Art Bronze Works, the Zoppo casts are superior in their overall surface modeling as well as the dull green patination that produced a rich, variegated surface (plate # 42). In contrast, the modeling on a later cast produced by the California Art Bronze Foundry is somewhat irregular and indistinct, as if a shoddy attempt to restore portions of the damaged master model had been made after it arrived from Roman Bronze Works. Stewart notes, "Some of the sculpture's appendages, such as the ears of the mother bear and the folds of skin under her lower jaw, have been altered with little regard for the accuracy of Russell's original. In the clumsy effort to recreate the mother bear's hind feet, the results look more human than ursine—a transformation that would have amused Russell who often depicted bears with anthropomorphic qualities."[16]

Testimony to Russell's greatness as an artist is the fact that he had little formal training, yet he mastered the art of modeling in three dimensions. In Meat for Wild Men, a highly complex composition with multiple viewpoints, Russell stabilized the action through the use of simplified forms that interact cohesively within the sculpture. Though Russell never witnessed a "surround," a type of buffalo hunt in which mounted warriors swooped down from several type of buffalo hunt in which mounted warriors swooped down from several directions forming a continuous fence around the herd and making them vulnerable to attack, he was familiar with descriptions by early writers and artists who had witnessed the spectacle. The subject of the buffalo hunt was one Russell explored repeatedly on canvas and in bronze throughout his prolific career. Such compositions had little to do with current Indian issues, but were popular themes extolling the romantic imagery he had successfully exploited in paintings such as *Buffalo Hunt No. 40*. (plate #26)

Meat for Wild Men, modeled in 1924, was originally commissioned by California oil man William W. Armstrong. Nancy Russell ordered two copies of the bronze version from Roman Bronze Works in September of 1924. The first cast, illustrated as plate #56, was sent to Armstrong. The second cast appeared the following year at an exhibition at the Arthur H. Harlow Galleries in New York. Due to the relatively large size and expense of Meat for Wild Men, only four casts of the piece were produced in the Russells' lifetimes. When Homer Britzman acquired the model in 1941, he arranged for Nelli Art Bronze Works to make a fifth cast. Guido Nelli, former proprietor of the California Art Bronze Foundry, was among those who noted how difficult the bronze had been to cast, reporting that the model had originally been divided into fifty-seven separate pieces for molding. After Britzman's death in 1953, representatives of his estate shipped the model to Roman Bronze Works, where another three posthumous copies were cast by 1956.[17] These bronzes most likely are marked "Roman Bronze Works Inc., N.Y.," since the firm had incorporated in 1947.

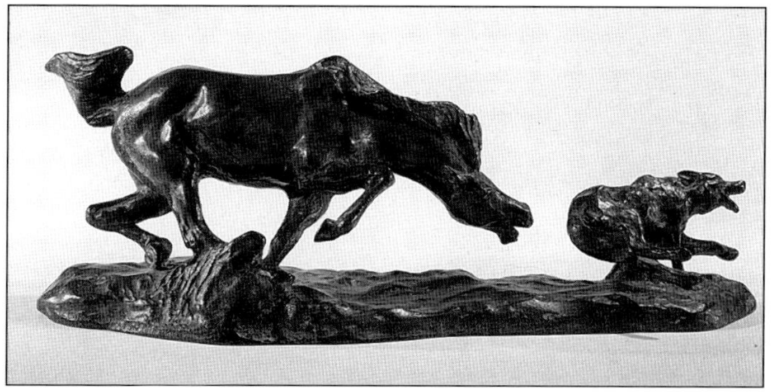

The Range Father, 1926, 5 1/2 x 15 x 5 inches

Despite Russell's failing health the year of his death, his facility as a sculptor was still in tact. *The Range Father* and *The Spirit of Winter*, both modeled in 1926, reveal a spontaneous execution and abstraction of form previously unattained. The allegorical work, *The Spirit of Winter* depicts a grisly figure surrounded by snarling wolves that embody torment, suffering, and death. Drawn from Blackfoot and Crow legends about starvation winters, its grimness seems to reflect Russell's personal struggle as much as Native American legend. It was one of Russell's last, major sculptures before his death October 24, 1926.

Historian J. Frank Dobie wrote about Russell: "Although barbed wire, population, the automobile, the airplane and World War I radically changed the West along with the rest of the world during Charles M. Russell's lifetime, he remained unchanged in his ways and allegiances." Russell's sculpture remains an accurate record of his considerable knowledge of that era in Western history to which he was a witness. He was a man who represented in his life, art, and philosophy the essence of the American West and its appeal.

NOTES

1. Stewart, Rick, Charles M. Russell, Sculptor, Amon Carter Museum, Fort Worth, Texas, 1994, (Distributed by Harry Abrams, Inc., New York), p. 32.

2. Stewart 37.

3. Stewart 143.

4. Stewart 144.

5. Stewart 24.

6. Stewart 25.

7. Stewart 25.

8. Stewart 39.

9. Stewart 158.

10. Stewart 55.

11. Stewart 57.

12. Stewart 57.

13. Stewart 61.

14. Stewart 198.

15. Stewart 198.

16. Stewart 198.

17. Stewart 287.

The Sculpture

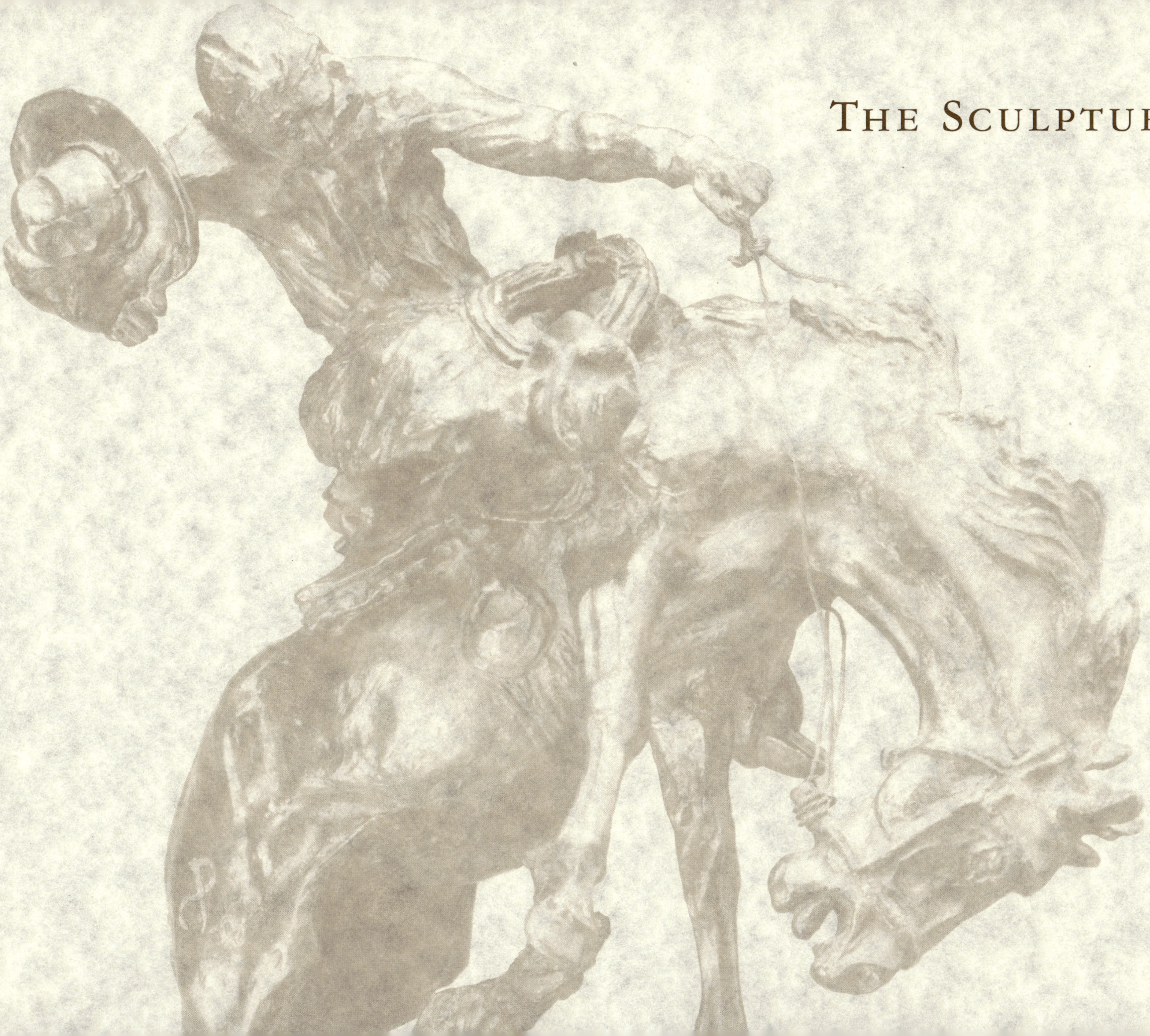

SCULPTURE PLATE LIST

Title / Year

38. Smoking Up, No.6
modeled 1904, cast *c.*1905
12 1/2 x 9 5/8 x 6 3/8 inches
foundry: Roman Bronze Works, New York
technique: lost wax cast
estimated number of lifetime casts: 14
incised: CM Russell/skull cipher

PROVENANCE: Private Collection; {Gerald Peters Gallery, Santa Fe, New Mexico}; Private Collection.

REFERENCE: Rick Stewart, Charles M. Russell, Sculptor, Amon Carter Museum, Fort Worth, Texas, 1994, pp. 142-146.

Smoking Up, Russell's first subject in bronze, was modeled during his initial visit to New York in 1904 while staying with illustrator and friend, John Marchand. The theme of 'cowboys on a tear' had already been exploited by Frederic Remington in his bronze *Coming Through the Rye*. Russell probably viewed Remington's sculpture at the Saint Louis World's Fair in 1903, and was inspired to create his own animated version a few months later.

The number of *Smoking Up* casts may never be known as it is the only instance where the Russell's sold the reproduction rights to an outside party. Rick Stewart greatly clarifies the complicated casting history in Charles M. Russell, Sculptor. Although the inscription bears the copyright to the New York Cooperative Society, no copyright registration has been located in the Library of Congress. Having cast an initial order of around seven works at Roman Bronze Works between the years 1905- 1907, The New York Cooperative Society sold the rights to a local gallery which produced casts on demand. While Stewart estimates approximately 14 casts were produced during the Russells' lifetimes, the great majority of casts –numbering around 132 –were posthumous bronzes ordered by successive owners of the model and its reproduction rights. (Stewart 144)

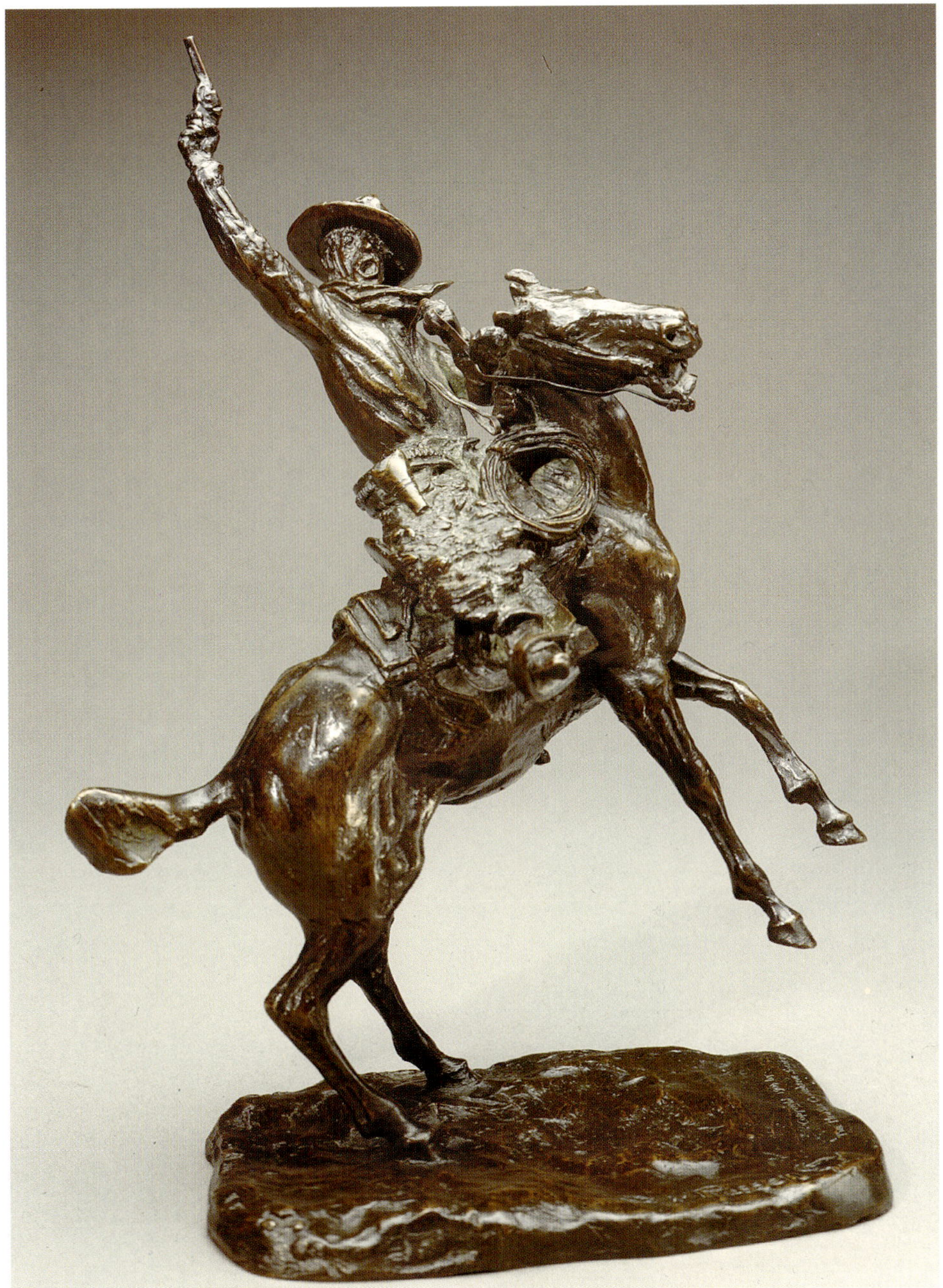

39. Counting Coup
modeled 1905, cast *c.*1925
10 3/8 x 16 3/4 x 9 15/16
foundry: Roman Bronze Works, New York
technique: lost wax cast
estimated number of lifetime casts: 9
incised: CM Russell/1907/skull cipher

PROVENANCE: Mr. Quail, Former Police Commissioner, New York, New York; Louis Liebson-Astor Galleries, New York; Private Collection, New York; Private collection, New Jersey; {Gerald Peters Gallery, Santa Fe, New Mexico}; Private Collection, California.

REFERENCES: Rick Stewart, Charles M. Russell, Sculptor, Amon Carter Museum, Fort Worth, Texas, 1994, pp. 147-152.

When Russell camped with the Blood Indians in the late 1880s, he met an old chief by the name of Medicine Whip who would become the subject of several of the artist's paintings, a short story and this bronze. The second documented sculpture in Russell's oeuvre, *Counting Coup* depicts a variation on Medicine Whip's original story. Here the Blood warrior has charged the Sioux wielding his lance against the downed Medicine Man, while a third figure, tomahawk raised, prepares to strike the thrusting Blood brave. Only nine lifetime casts were produced of this subject, and many major institutions with extensive Russell collections, including the Gilcrease Museum in Tulsa, do not own one.

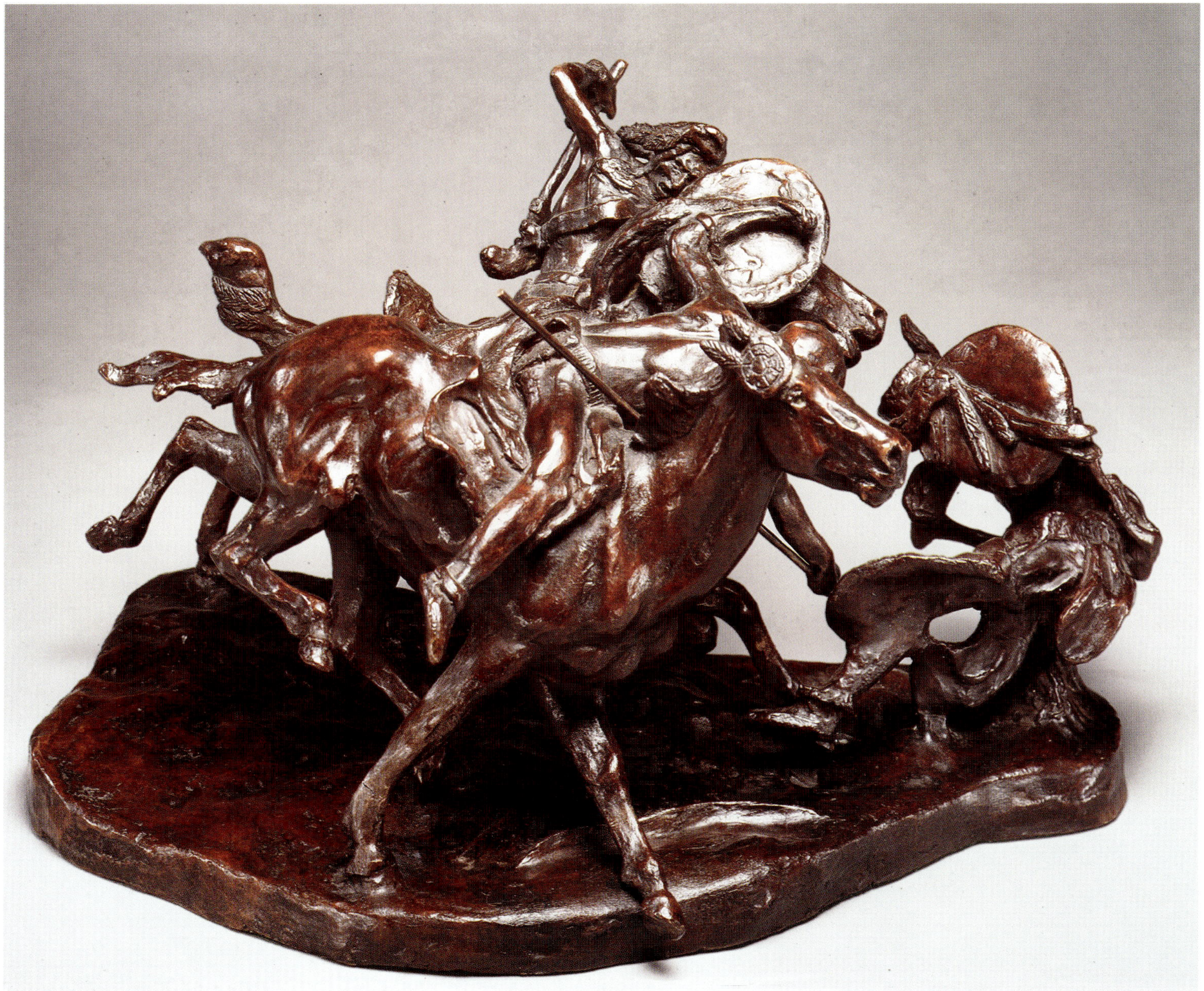

Photograph courtesy of The Amon Carter Museum. #1961.116

40. Buffalo Hunt or *Buffalo Runner*
modeled 1905, cast *c.*1928
10 x 18 1/4 x 12 1/2 x inches
foundry: Roman Bronze Works, New York
technique: lost wax cast
estimated number of lifetime casts: 9
incised: C.M Russell/skull cipher/1905/copyrighted

PROVENANCE: Private Collection, Ken Martin; {Gerald Peters Gallery, Santa Fe, New Mexico}; Private Collection, California.

REFERENCES: Rick Stewart, Charles M. Russell, Sculptor, Amon Carter Museum, Fort Worth, Texas, 1994, pp. 157-159.

The subject of the Indian buffalo hunt was a classic theme that Russell explored repeatedly on canvas and in bronze. In the manner of his contemporary Frederic Remington, he denied the forces of gravity by raising the figures off the base as much as possible. *Buffalo Hunt*, one of Russell's initial efforts in bronze, reveals a concern for a high degree of detail and naturalism, a style he would limit in favor of the simplified form of his later sculptures. The exact number of *Buffalo Hunt* casts produced during the Russell's lifetimes may never be known. Though Homer Britzman's inventory of the Russell Estate accounted for a total of nine casts, nearly twice that number have surfaced in public and private collections. (Stewart, page 157)

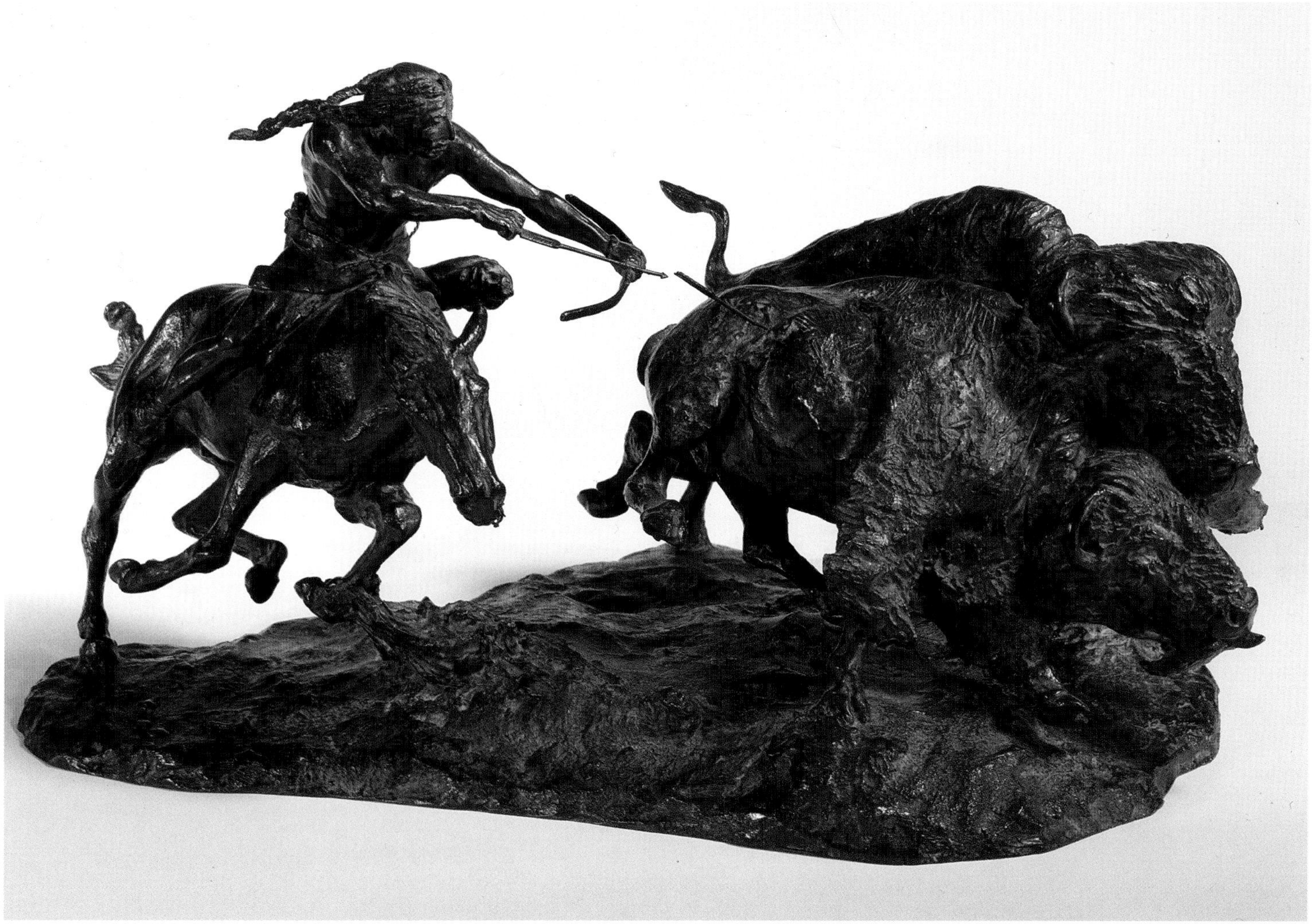

Photograph courtesy of The Amon Carter Museum. #1961.121

41. Bronc Twister
modeled and copyrighted 1911; cast *c.*1929-34
18 1/8 x 12 3/4 x 9 inches
foundry: California Art Bronze Foundry, Los Angeles CA
technique: lost wax cast
estimated number of lifetime casts: 14
incised: CM Russell/copyright/skull cipher

PROVENANCE: The Artist to Nancy Russell; Nancy Russell Estate; The Collection of Earl Adams; {Wunderlich and Peters Galleries}.

REFERENCES: Rick Stewart, Charles M. Russell, Sculptor, Amon Carter Museum, Fort Worth, Texas, 1994, pp. 178-185.

This sculpture, copyrighted July 12, 1911 as *The Weaver*, was the largest bronze Russell had cast at that time. The original title pertained to the bucking habits of a "particularly exasperating" type of horse that Ramon Adams described in his 1936 study, *Cowboy Lingo*. "His feet never struck the ground in a straight line. He had a peculiar weaving motion which was very disconcerting to a man who had not the firmest of seats in the saddle." The subject of a weaving horse in bronze was one several major Western artists had attempted, including Frederic Remington. Russell's version was much more animated and naturalistic in the portrayal of arrested action as the horse's back arches high in the air pitching the ill-fated rider side to side. (Stewart 179)

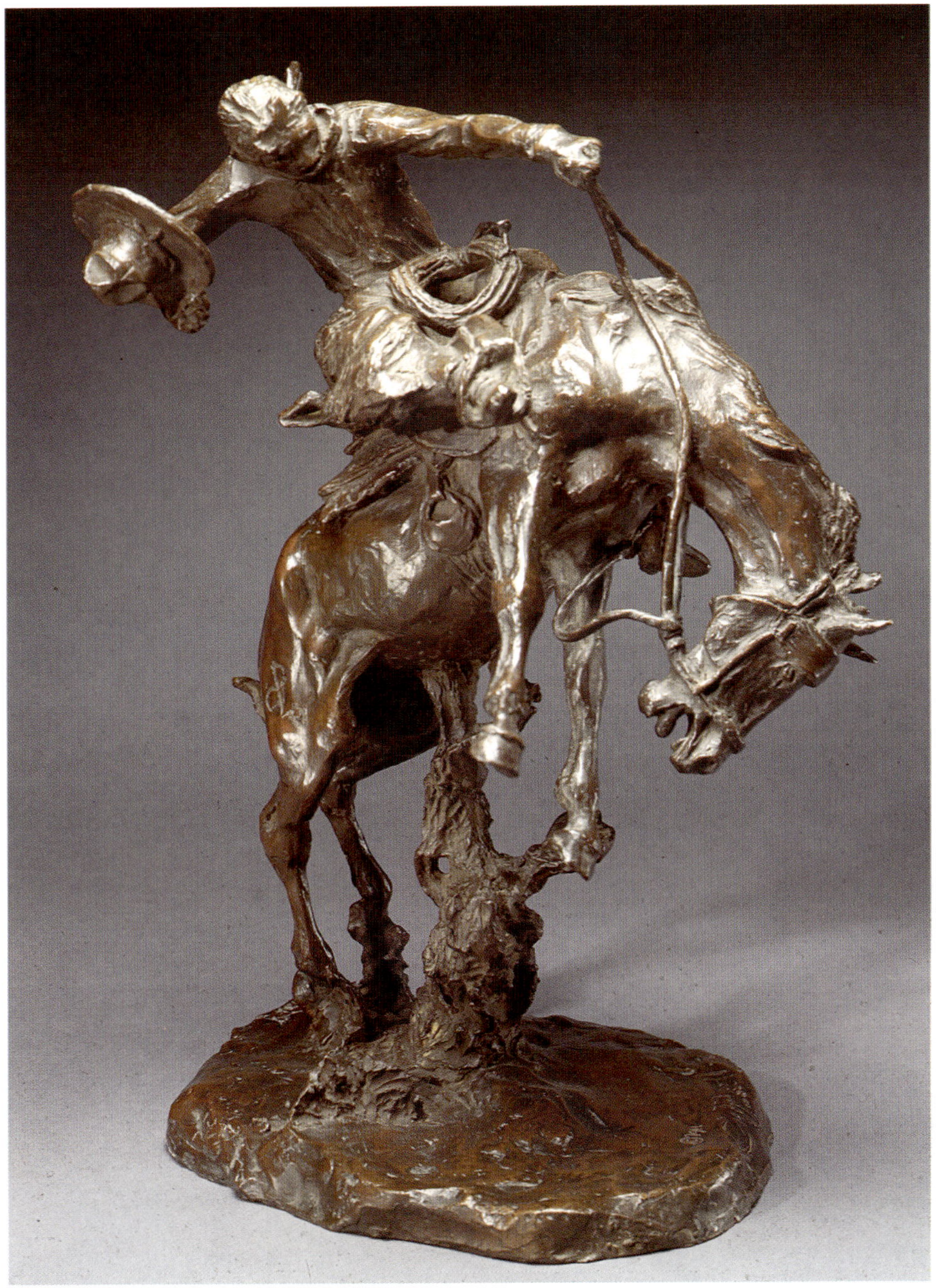

42. Oh! Mother, What Is It?
modeled 1914, cast *c.*1916
4 x 8 5/8 x 4 3/8 inches
foundry: Benjamin Zoppo Foundry, New York
technique: lost wax cast
estimated number of lifetime casts: 20
incised: CM Russell/copyright/1914

PROVENANCE: Kennedy Galleries, New York, New York; L. Brown, Denver, Colorado; {Gerald Peters Gallery, Santa Fe, New Mexico}; Private Collection, Texas.

REFERENCES: Rick Stewart, Charles M. Russell, Sculptor, Amon Carter Museum, Fort Worth, Texas, pp. 197-200.

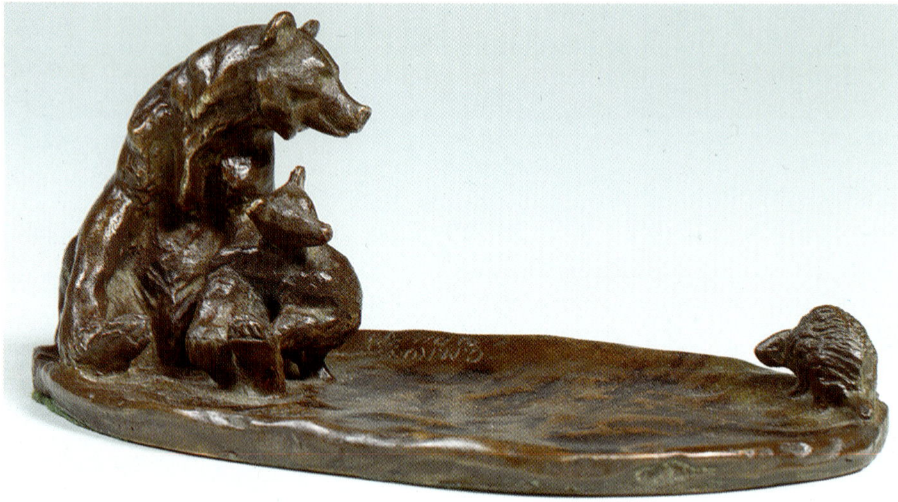

43. Smoking with the Spirit of the Buffalo
modeled 1914, cast *c.*1916
4 1/2 x 8 1/8 x 5 3/8 inches
foundry: Benjamin Zoppo Foundry, New York
technique: lost wax cast
estimated number of lifetime casts: 18
incised: CM Russell/copyright 1914/skull cipher

PROVENANCE: The Artist; Claude E. Lanstrom, Great Falls, Montana, circa 1916-1920; Mrs. Claude E. Lanstrom; E.E. MacGilvra, Butte, Montana, 1955; A.T. Seymour, III, Fort Worth, Texas, 1978; {Gerald Peters Gallery, Santa Fe, New Mexico}; Private Collection, Texas.

REFERENCES: Rick Stewart, Charles M. Russell, Sculptor, Amon Carter Museum, Fort Worth, Texas, 1994, pp. 201-207.

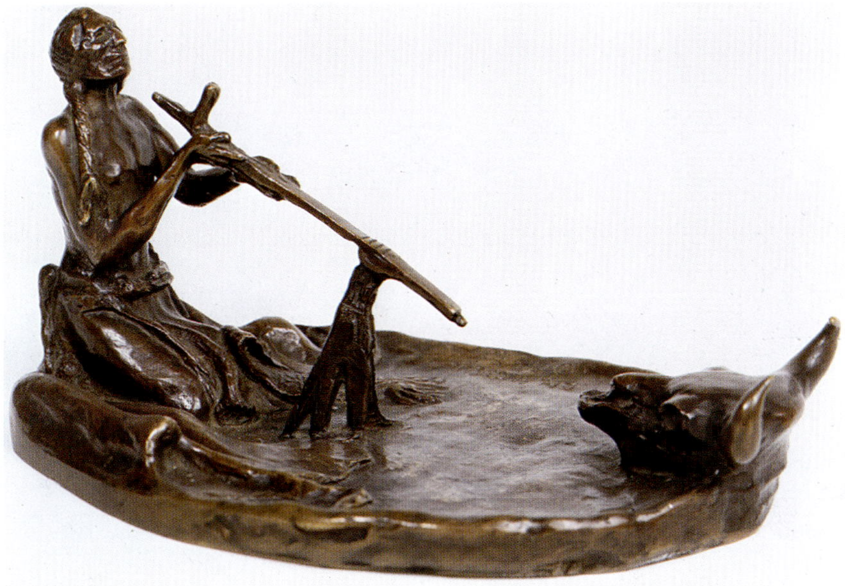

Russell's exposure to works by distinguished American sculptors such as Solon Borglum, Cyrus Dallin, and Alexander Phimister Procter at the 1903 World's Fair no doubt spurred his interest in small-scale, utilitarian sculpture. Such works often finely detailed, blurred the boundaries between art and decoration. In 1916, Russell had conceived of several minor bronzes, in the form of ashtrays, to be exhibited in his one-man show "The West that Has Passed." Though recognized American sculptors had capitalized on the demand for functional sculpture, few artists had produced ashtrays at that time. Nancy Russell, having realized the marketing opportunities involving the more affordable bronzes, encouraged her husband's production of these works. Among the initial ashtray bronzes Russell featured were wildlife and Indian themes such as *Oh! Mother, What Is It?* and *Smoking with the Spirit of the Buffalo.*

44. Snake Priest
modeled 1914, cast *c.*1916-1918
4 1/16 x 8 1/2 x 4 inches
foundry: Benjamin Zoppo Foundry, New York
technique: lost wax cast
estimated number of lifetime casts: 10
incised: CM Russell/copyright/CMR/skull cipher

PROVENANCE: Private Collection; {Wunderlich and Peters Galleries}.

REFERENCES: Rick Stewart, Charles M. Russell, Sculptor, Amon Carter Museum, Fort Worth, Texas, 1994, pp. 208-211.

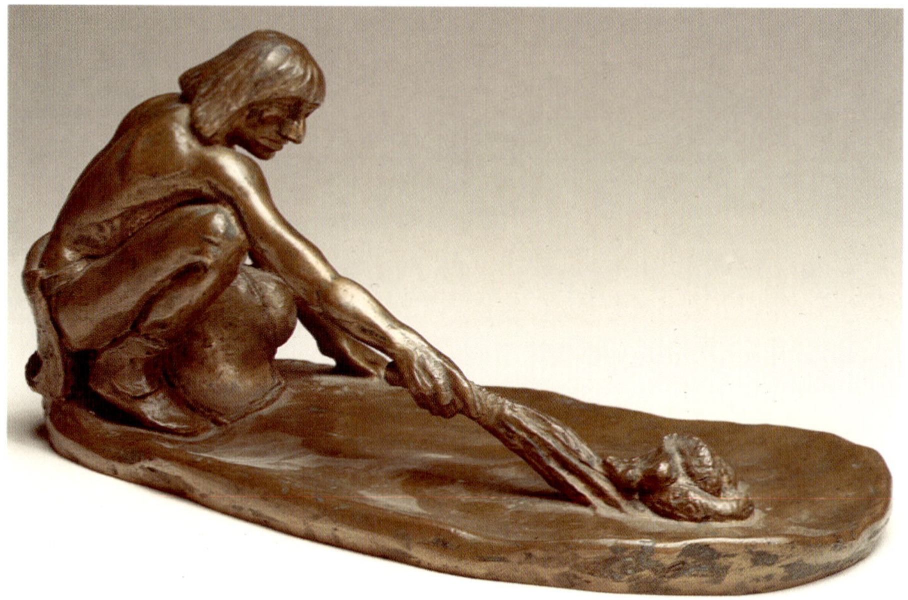

45. Scalp Dancer
modeled 1914, cast *c.*1916
6 1/4 x 8 1/4 x 5 1/4 inches
foundry: Benjamin Zoppo Foundry, New York
technique: lost wax cast
estimated number of lifetime casts: 10
incised: CM Russell/copyright 1914/skull cipher

PROVENANCE: The Artist; George Sack; Penelope Potter (daughter of George Sack); {Gerald Peters Gallery, Santa Fe, New Mexico}; Private Collection, Texas.

REFERENCES: Rick Stewart, Charles M. Russell, Sculptor, Amon Carter Museum, Fort Worth, Texas, 1994, pp. 212-215.

In a letter dated March 22, 1916, Nancy Russell contracted with Benjamin Zoppo in New York to cast nine of her husband's subjects in bronze including *Snake Priest* and *Scalp Dancer*. Though Roman Bronze and California Art Bronze foundries cast some of these subjects, those cast by the Zoppo Foundry are among the finest for the dull green patination that produced a rich, variegated surface.

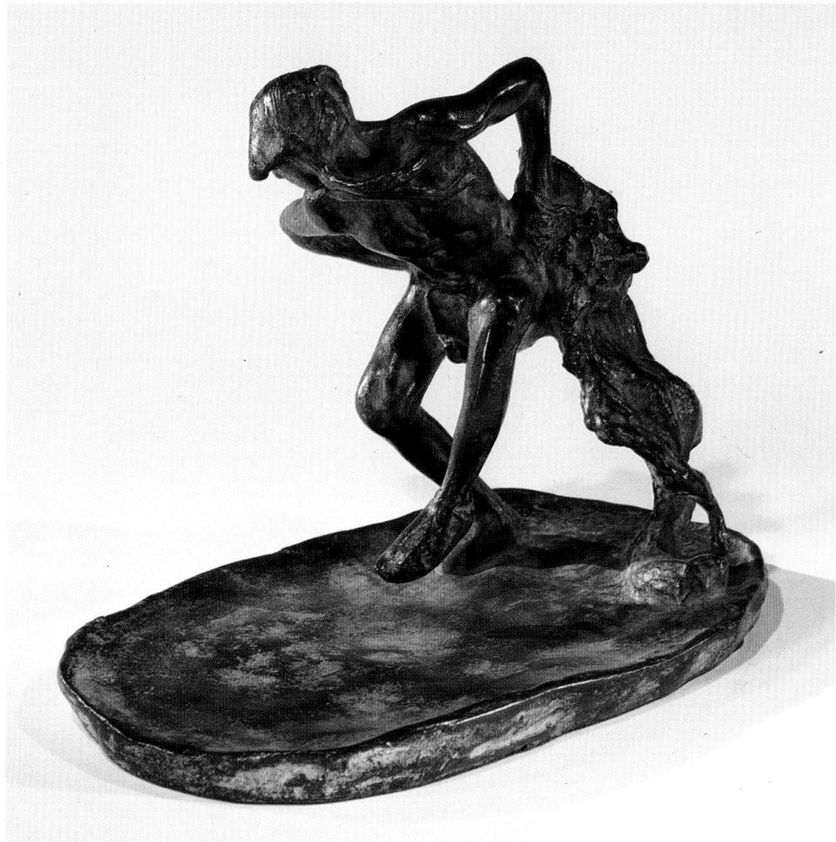

Photograph courtesy of The Amon Carter Museum. #1961.118

46. The Last Laugh
modeled 1916, cast *c.*1922
4 3/8 x 7 7/8 x 5 1/4 inches
foundry: Roman Bronze Works, New York
technique: lost wax cast
estimated number of lifetime casts: 10
incised: CM Russell/skull cipher/copyright 1916

PROVENANCE: Private Collection; {Gerald Peters Gallery, Santa Fe, New Mexico}; Private Collection, Texas.

REFERENCES: Rick Stewart, Charles M. Russell, Sculptor, Amon Carter Museum, Fort Worth, Texas, 1994, pp. 222-225.

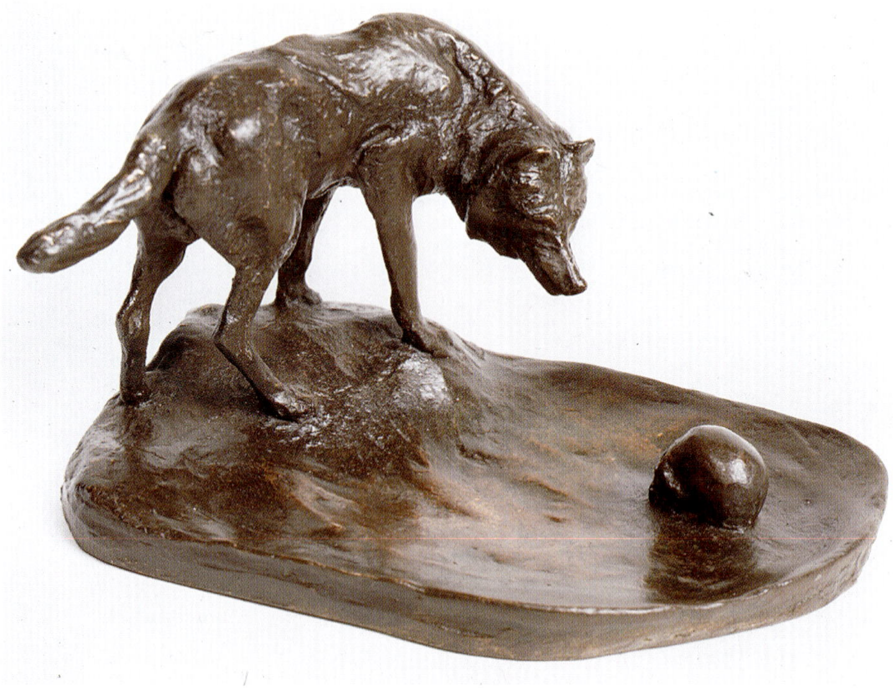

47. To Noses that Read, A Smell that Spells Man
modeled 1920, cast *c.*1929-34
4 5/8 x 8 1/4 x 7 5/8 inches
foundry: California Art Bronze Foundry, Los Angeles
technique: lost wax cast
estimated number of lifetime casts: 12
incised: CM Russell/copyright/skull cipher/To Noses That Read/A Smell That Spells Man

PROVENANCE: The Artist; Private Collection; Private Collection, Oklahoma.

REFERENCES: Rick Stewart, Charles M. Russell, Sculptor, Amon Carter Museum, Fort Worth, Texas, 1994, pp. 245-248.

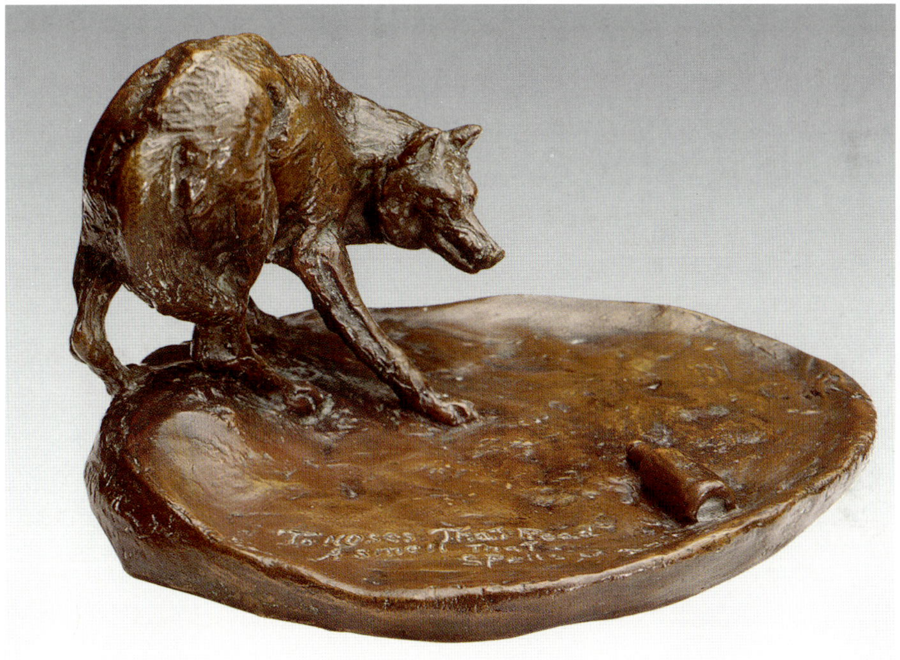

Author and naturalist, Ernest Thompson Seton helped form Russell's thinking about nature and wildlife, particularly with regard to his sculpture. Seton was an active member of the growing movement to preserve western lands for the benefit of wildlife, an issue Russell embraced fully around the turn of the century. The author, whom Russell met at least once, wrote in 1907: "The wolves seem more cunning and wary each year. They have learned how to live in spite of all that can be done to destroy them." Both works portray the contentious relationship between rancher and wolf as the suspicious animal recoils from the symbols of man, represented as the flask and human skull. (Stewart 245)

*Note: Many of the bronzes represented on the following pages were cast after Charles Russell's death in 1926. However, since Nancy Russell was so integral in the bronze production from 1904 forward, lifetime casts are denoted until her death in 1940.

48. Weapons of the Weak
modeled 1921, cast *c.*1922-28
5 3/4 x 5 7/8 x 5 1/2 inches
foundry: Roman Bronze Works, New York
technique: lost wax cast
estimated number of lifetime casts: 7
incised: CM Russell/skull cipher

PROVENANCE: Jim Phillips, Pittsburgh, Pennsylvania; Private Collection, Denver, Colorado.

REFERENCES: Rick Stewart, Charles M. Russell, Sculptor, Amon Carter Museum, Fort Worth, Texas, 1994, pp. 226-229.

Having developed a better understanding of mass and form, Russell reworked two earlier sculptures resulting in the production of *Weapons of the Weak* and *An Enemy that Warns.* Unlike the ashtray bronzes that had been cast by the Zoppo foundry five years earlier, the new works were not obviously utilitarian in form, though they still could be employed in a decorative manner. The maturation of Russell's sculpture is apparent in the integration of the base as an element of the overall composition, and a minimization of painstaking detail for a more reductive style.

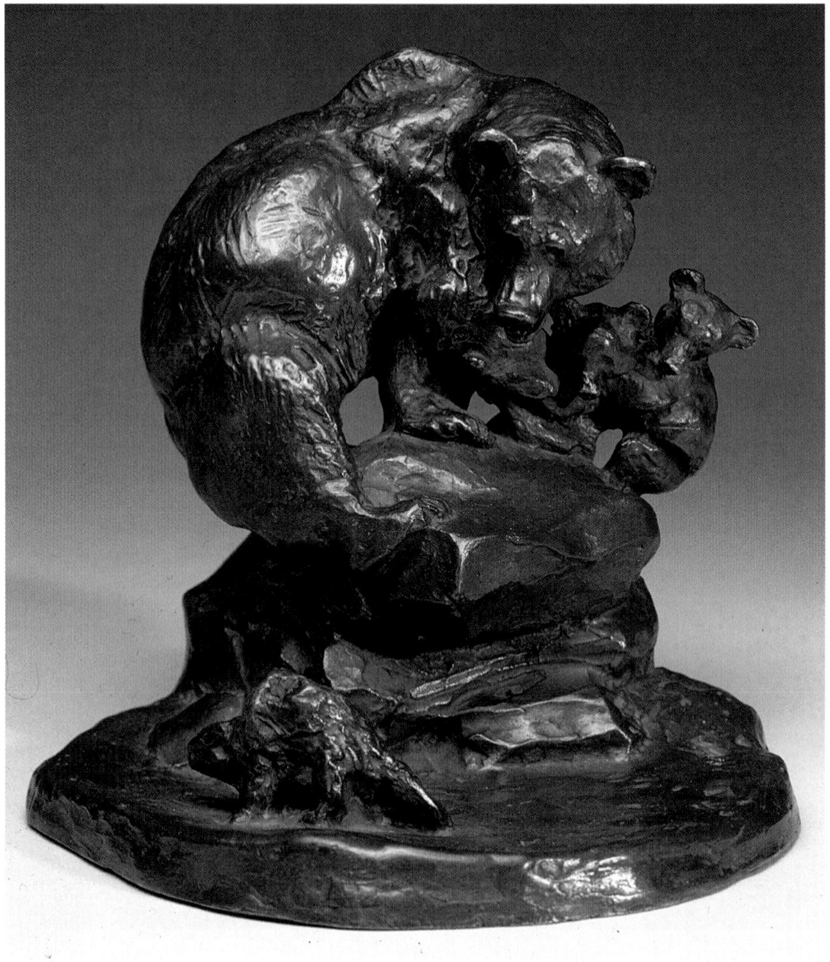

49. An Enemy That Warns
modeled 1921, cast *c.*1922-28
5 x 8 x 6 inches
foundry: Roman Bronze Works, New York
technique: lost wax cast
estimated number of lifetime casts: 10
incised: CM Russell/skull cipher

PROVENANCE: Walter Bimson, Paradise Valley, Arizona; Private Collection, Denver, Colorado; {Gerald Peters Gallery, Santa Fe, New Mexico}; Private Collection, Texas.

REFERENCE: Rick Stewart, Charles M. Russell, Sculptor, Amon Carter Museum, Fort Worth, Texas, 1994, pp. 230-233.

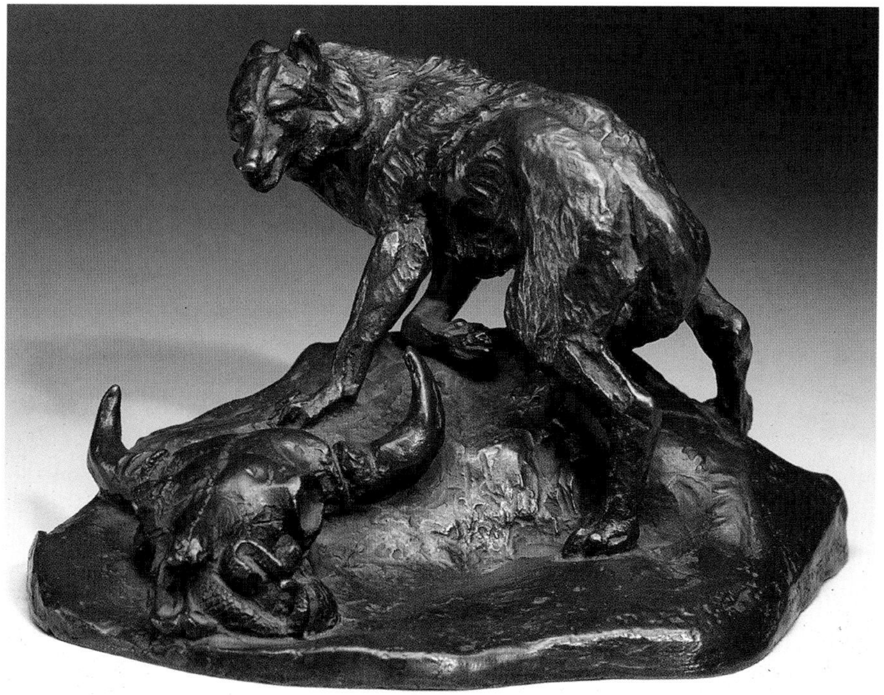

50. *Where the Best of Riders Quit*
modeled 1921-22, cast *c.*1929
14 1/2 x 7 13/16 x 8 1/2 inches
foundry: California Art Bronze Foundry, Los Angeles
technique: lost wax cast
estimated number of lifetime casts: 15
incised: CM Russell/skull cipher

PROVENANCE: Private Collection, New York; {Gerald Peters Gallery, Santa Fe, New Mexico}; Private Collection, Texas; Private Collection, California.

REFERENCES: Rick Stewart, Charles M. Russell, Sculptor, Amon Carter Museum, Fort Worth, Texas, 1994, pp. 234-239.

Where the Best of Riders Quit, one of around fifteen lifetime casts, a relatively large edition for Russell, attested to the success and popularity of this bronze. As with all of the artist's major equestrian sculptures, the spirited bronc is the object of admiration. The "throwback," another type of bucking horse, was apt to intentionally hurl himself backward crushing and sometimes even killing the rider. Here, Russell achieves his delicate balance of spontaneous creation and critical details while challenging the traditional means of support. An innovative composition aesthetically and technically, the mass of horse and rider balances almost weightlessly over the bronc's hind legs and tail.

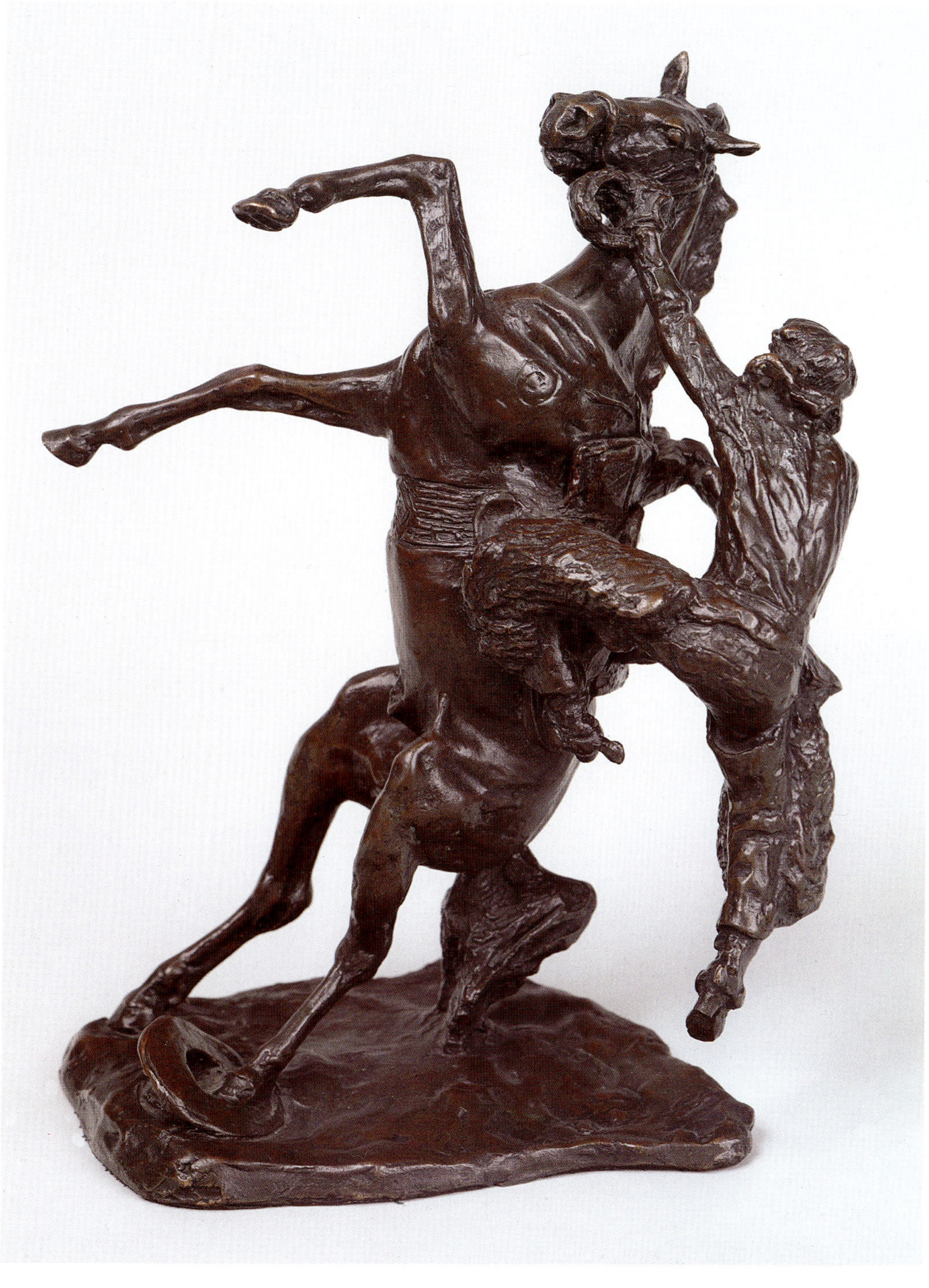

51. The Medicine Man
modeled 1920, cast *c.*1922
7 1/16 x 5 7/8 x 5 1/4 inches
foundry: Roman Bronze Works, New York
technique: lost wax cast
estimated number of lifetime casts: 20
incised: CM Russell/skull cipher

PROVENANCE: Walter Bimson; Private Collection; {Gerald Peters Gallery, Santa Fe, New Mexico}; Private Collection, California.

REFERENCES: Rick Stewart, Charles M. Russell, Sculptor, Amon Carter Museum, Fort Worth, Texas, 1994, pp. 240-244.

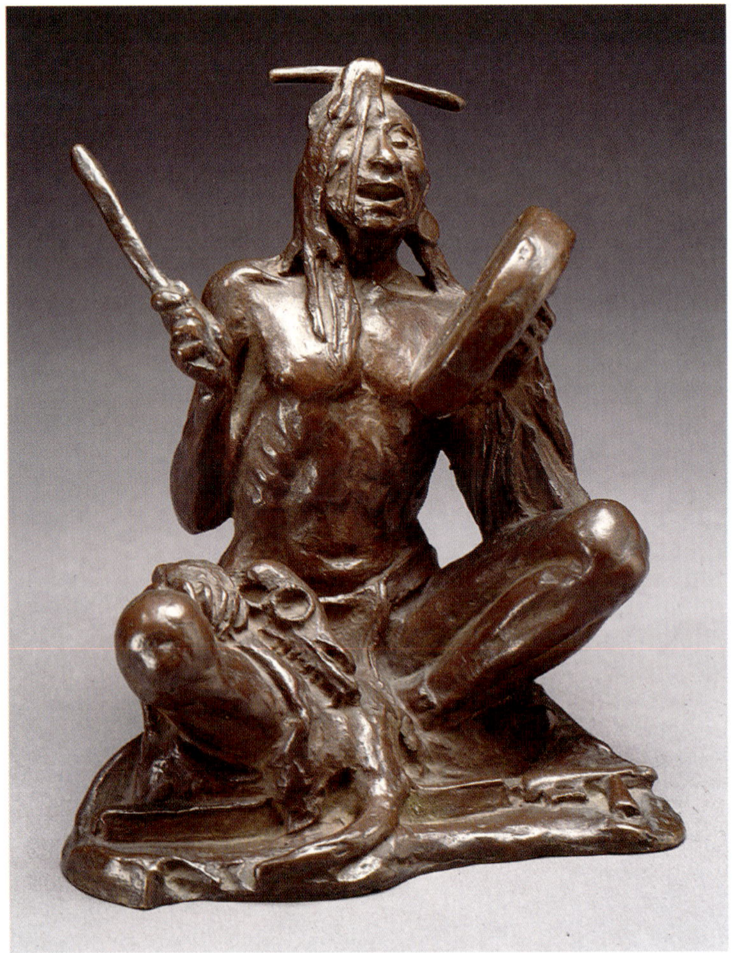

52. Buffalo Rubbing Rock
modeled 1921, cast *c.*1922-28
7 1/8 x 7 x 3 7/8 inches
foundry: Roman Bronze Works, New York
technique: lost wax cast
estimated number of lifetime casts: 18 (9 pairs)
incised: CM Russell/skull cipher/1921

PROVENANCE: Private Collection, Arizona; {Gerald Peters Gallery, Santa Fe, New Mexico}; Private Collection, Texas.

REFERENCE: Rick Stewart, Charles M. Russell, Sculptor, Amon Carter Museum, Fort Worth, Texas, 1994, pp. 259-263.

The Medicine Man and *Buffalo Rubbing Rock*, two sensitive portrayals of their subjects, were produced as bookends and proved quite popular among buyers. The works were probably two of six that Charlie completed in early 1921 during the Russells' first visit to Southern California. Roman Bronze Works cast the initial examples for a 1922 exhibition at the Kanst Art Galleries in Los Angeles.

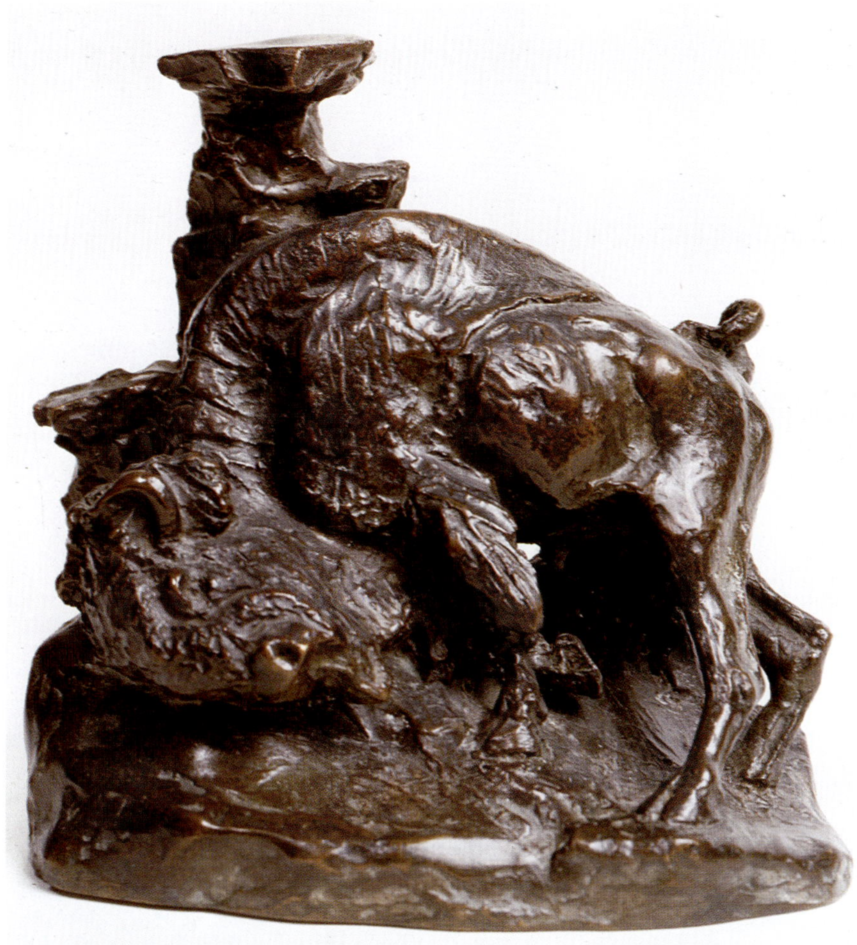

53. *The Enemy's Tracks*
modeled 1920, cast *c.*1929
12 3/4 x 8 3/8 x 5 1/2 inches
foundry: California Art Bronze Foundry, Los Angeles
technique: lost wax cast
estimated number of lifetime casts: 16
incised: CM Russell/copyright/skull cipher

PROVENANCE: Nancy Russell, Pasedena, California; Charles S. Jones, Chairman of the Board, Richfield Oil; National Cowboy Hall of Fame, Oklahoma City, Oklahoma; Private Collection, Texas.

REFERENCES: Rick Stewart, Charles M. Russell, Sculptor, Amon Carter Museum, Fort Worth, Texas, 1994, pp. 230-233.

By 1929, Nancy Russell had severed her relationship with the Roman Bronze Works in New York in favor of the California Art Bronze Foundry, operated by Guido Nelli in Los Angeles. In a letter to John Erickson, the governor of Montana, Mrs. Russell wrote of the foundry, "There is a bronze foundry here that is doing all of Charlie's bronze now...The owner himself does the work and is one of the best in the United States and would do the work as reasonably as anyone else and take twice the interest than most bronze foundries do." (Stewart 103) This piece was likely one of three casts Nelli produced that summer.

Russell's understanding of human and equine anatomy is apparent in the subtle modulation of muscle and bone. Indeed, the horse is an exceptional example of the wiry-framed mustang prevalent throughout the Plains Indian culture. The attention to the warrior's trappings, such as the fringed beaded bag, and carefully coiffed hair, derived from Russell's fascination with the relics of the passing West.

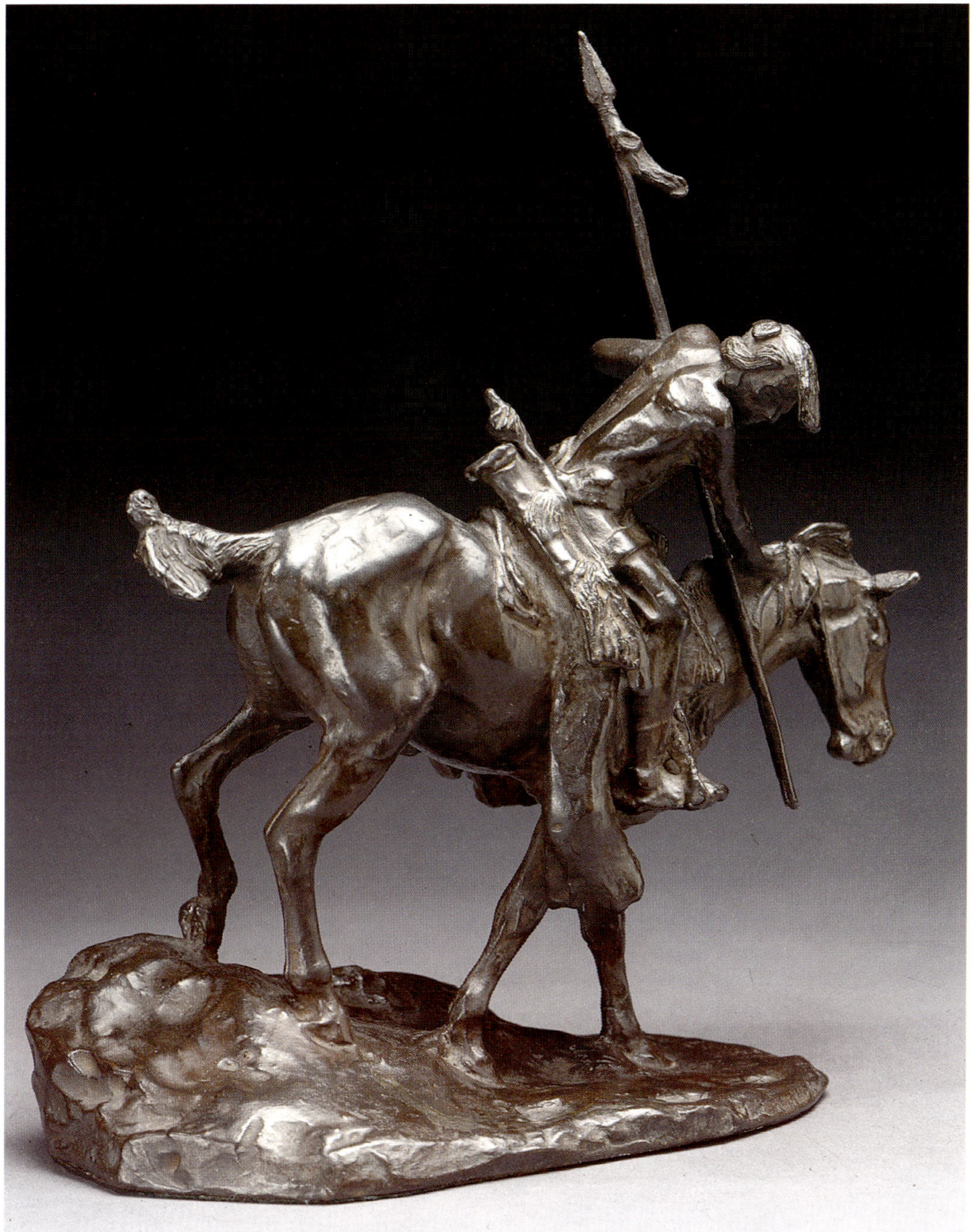

54. The Bucker and the Buckeroo
modeled 1923-24; cast *c.*1929-34
15 1/4 x 9 13/16 x 7 1/8 inches
foundry: California Art Bronze Foundry, Los Angeles
technique: lost wax cast
estimated number of lifetime casts: 19 unnumbered
incised: CM Russell/copyright/skull cipher

PROVENANCE: Art Institute of Chicago, Chicago, Illinois; {Gerald Peters Gallery, Santa Fe, New Mexico}; Private Collection, Texas.

REFERENCE: Amon Carter Museum of Western Art, Catalogue of the Collection: 1972 (1972), No. 669; Rick Stewart, Charles M. Russell, Sculptor, Amon Carter Museum Fort Worth, Texas, pp. 80-81, 268-273.

The Bucker and the Buckeroo faithfully delineates the action of a horse known to experienced riders as "sunfishing." According to Ramon Adams, "'Sunfishing' was a term used when a horse twisted his body into a crescent...or, in other words, when he seemed to try to touch the ground with first one shoulder and then the other, letting the sunlight hit his belly." (Stewart 269) In comparing Russell's work to Remington's, the sculptor Gutzon Borglum noted, "In motive they show the same keen power of observation and ability to select the instant when the action is most complete and most expressive...Russell had not only the wit to see the dual situation attached to any great moment, but he had, and with an ability Remington had never shown, the power to draw animals, horses, cattlemen, in the mixed-up, tangled up situations daily occurring in the wild unfenced West –situations no other artist has ever attempted." (Stewart 81)

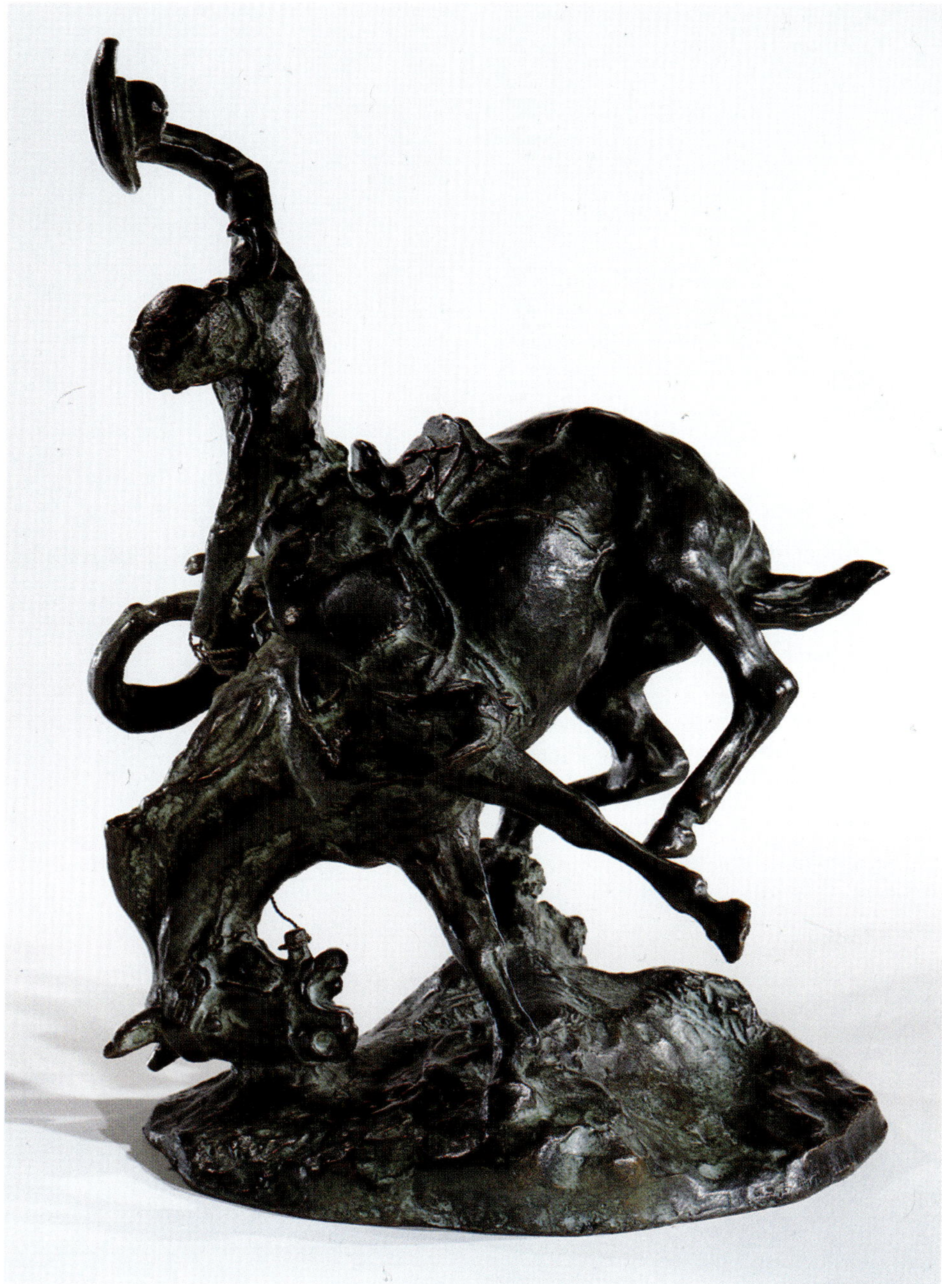

Photograph courtesy of The Amon Carter Museum. #1961.32

55. *The Horse Wrangler*
modeled 1924, cast *c.*1926
13 1/2 x 13 1/8 x 7 3/4 inches
foundry: Roman Bronze Works, New York
technique: lost wax cast
estimated number of lifetime casts: 9
incised: CM Russell

PROVENANCE: Museum of Western Art, Denver, Colorado; {Gerald Peters Gallery, Santa Fe, New Mexico}; Private Collection, California.

REFERENCES: Rick Stewart, Charles M. Russell, Sculptor, Amon Carter Museum, Fort Worth, Texas, 1994, pp. 281-285.

In his later years, Russell yearned for the freedom he enjoyed on the range as a youth. *The Horse Wrangler*, a testament to those years, portrays a youthful Russell astride one of his favorite horses, Redbird. Simple and direct, the sculpture seems a poignant characterization of how the artist wished to be remembered.

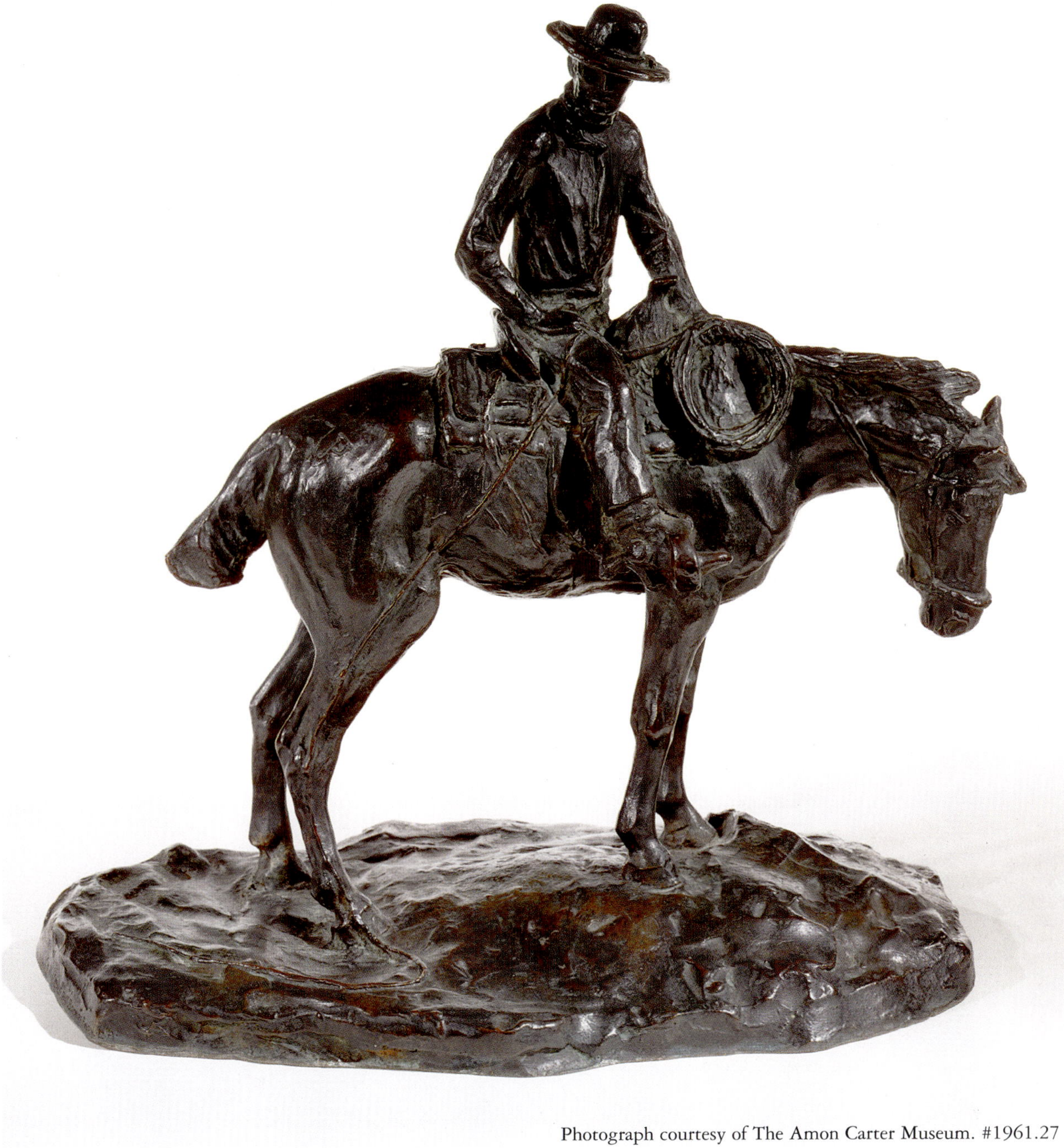

Photograph courtesy of The Amon Carter Museum. #1961.27

56. *Meat for Wild Men No. 1*
modeled 1924, cast *c.*1926-27
11 1/2 x 37 5/8 x 20 5/8 inches
foundry: Roman Bronze Works, New York
technique: lost wax cast
estimated number of lifetime casts: 4
incised: CM Russell/copyright/skull cipher/1924

PROVENANCE: The Artist; William W. Armstrong; Private Collection.

REFERENCES: Rick Stewart, Charles M. Russell, Sculptor, Amon Carter Museum, Fort Worth, Texas, 1994, pp. 286-290.

Meat for Wild Men, number one of only four casts, represents the pinnacle of Russell's work as a sculptor. As in his paintings, scenes of dramatic and narrative action interested Russell with regard to his sculpture, and allowed him to fully exploit the technical challenges of the medium. Guido Nelli, the owner of the California Art Bronze Foundry, was among those who noted how difficult this bronze had been to produce, reporting that the model originally had been cut into fifty-seven pieces for molding. (Stewart 287) Although a highly complex composition with multiple viewpoints, Russell stabilized the action through the use of simplified forms that interact cohesively within the sculpture. *Meat for Wild Men* closely resembles two of Russell's major buffalo hunt canvases, *The Surround* (plate #16) and *Buffalo Hunt, No. 40* (plate #27), and may well have inspired this ambitious subject in bronze.

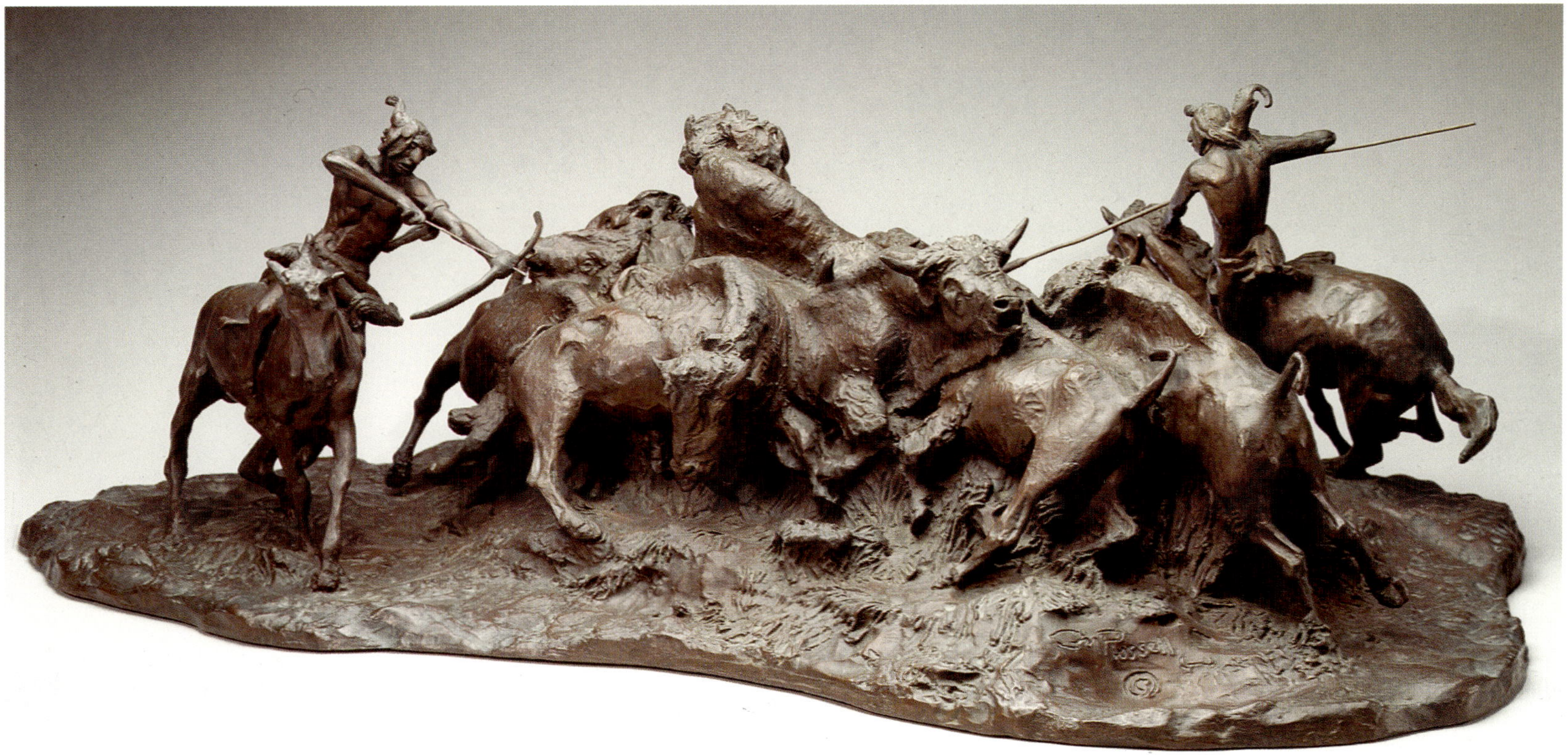

57. *Will Rogers*
modeled 1926, cast *c.* 1928
10 1/2 x 9 3/8 x 4 7/8 inches
foundry: Roman Bronze Works, New York
technique: Lost wax cast
estimated number of lifetime casts: 9
incised: CM Russell/skull cipher

PROVENANCE: Private Collection; {Gerald Peters Gallery, Santa Fe, New Mexico;} Private Collection, California.

REFERENCES: Rick Stewart, Charles M. Russell, Sculptor, Amon Carter Museum, Fort Worth, Texas, pp. 318-324.

Russell shared a long friendship with Will Rogers, the most beloved cowboy performer on the American scene. Rogers had become famous traveling in western shows, commenting on politics in his usual drawl while spinning rope. The two men had initially met in New York City in 1904. "Charlie Russell was trying to sell a few paintings and I was trying to sell a few jokes when I first met him years ago," Rogers once wrote. Russell modeled this image of Rogers on horseback with the intention of having it cast in bronze during his last visit to California in March-April 1926.

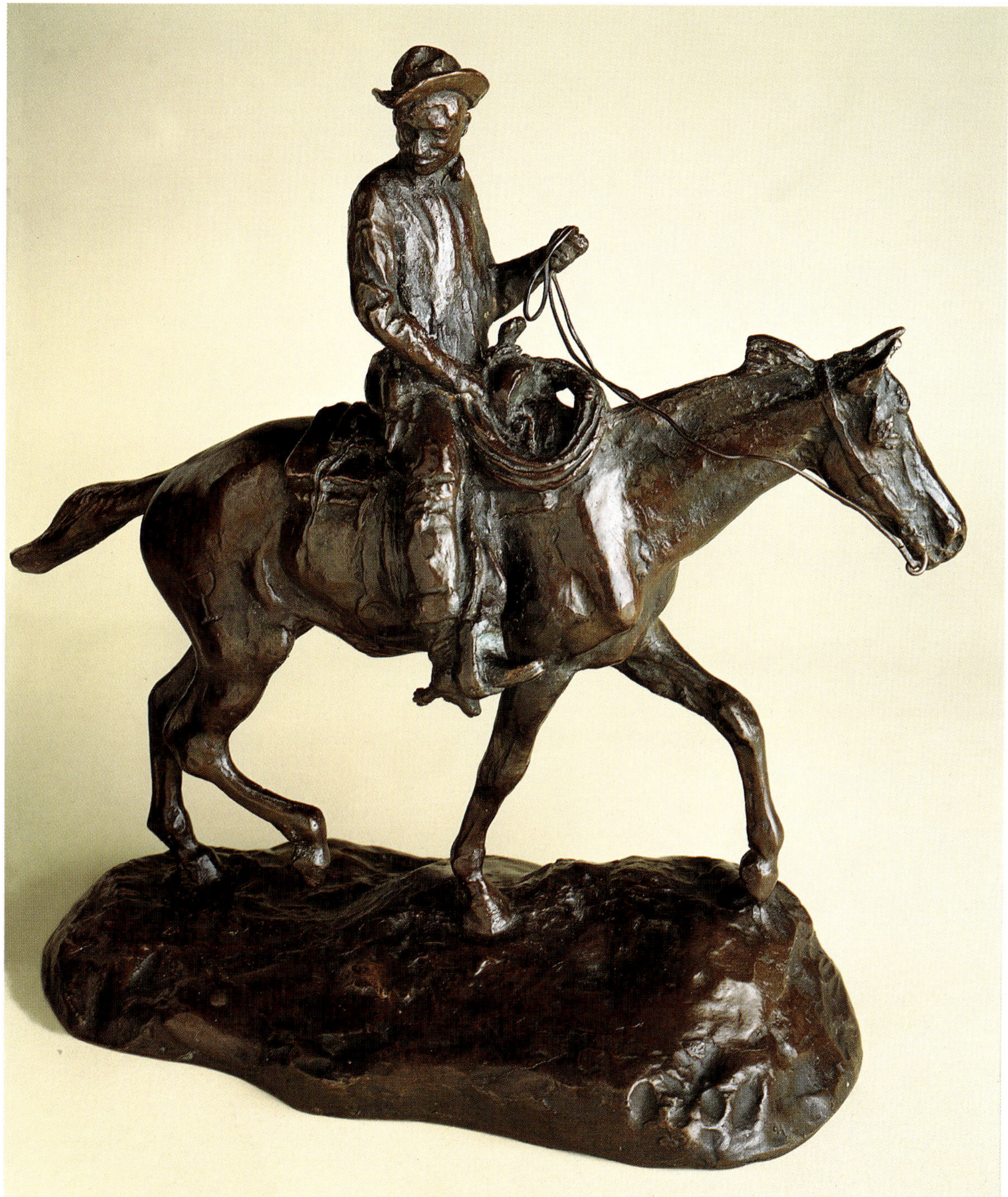

58. Piegan Squaw
modeled 1902, cast *c.*1927-28
6 1/2 x 4 5/8 x 3 1/2 inches
foundry: California Art Bronze Foundry, Los Angeles
technique: lost wax cast
estimated number of lifetime casts: 15
incised: CM Russell/copyright/skull cipher

PROVENANCE: The Artist; Private Collection; Private Collection, Oklahoma.

REFERENCES: Rick Stewart, Charles M. Russell, Sculptor, Amon Carter Museum, Fort Worth, Texas, 1994, pp. 331-335.

During the 1890s, Russell was interested in realistic depictions of domestic Indian life and left a faithful record of the customs and dress of Indian women. It is supposed the *Piegan Squaw* subject was inspired by a fictional character from a story by William Bleasdell Cameron. Russell portrayed the Blackfoot heroine Keeoma in an illustration for Western Field and Stream, which published Cameron's story in July, 1897. (Stewart 331) Russell created the original painted plaster model of *Piegan Squaw* in 1902, just a few years after Cameron's article appeared.

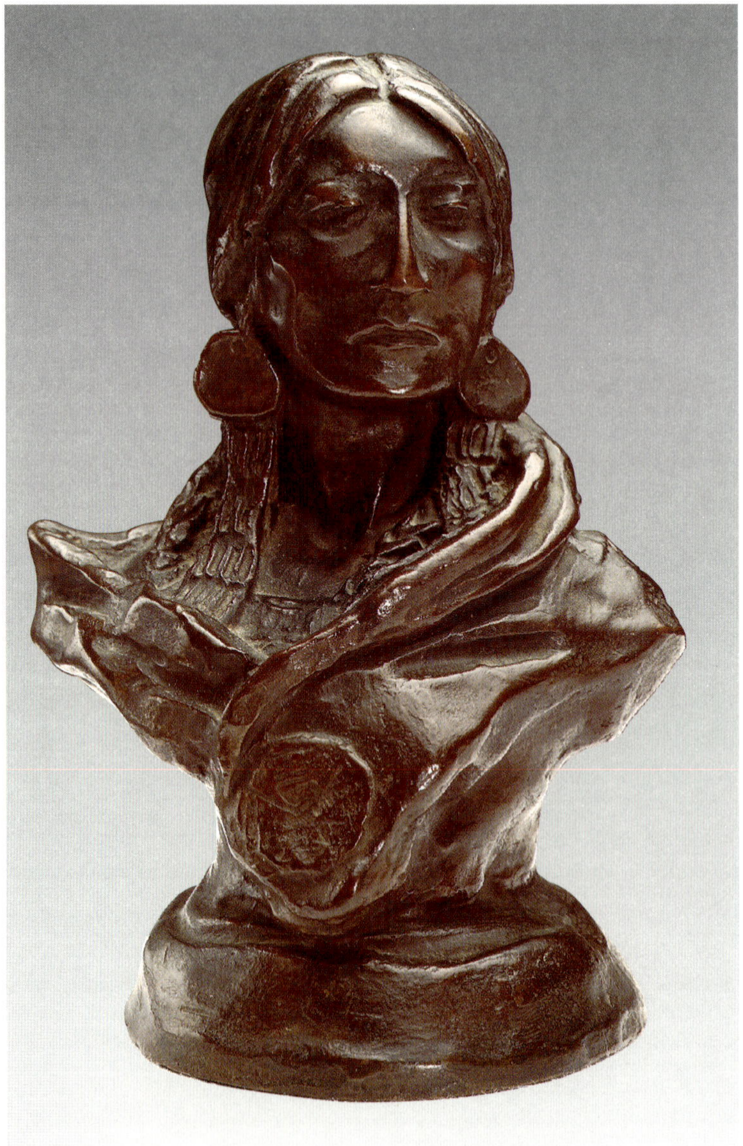

59. The Texas Steer
modeled 1925, cast *c.* 1927
5 x 6 5/8 x 3 1/2 inches
foundry: Roman Bronze Works, New York
technique: lost wax cast
estimated number of lifetime casts: 9
incised: CMR/skull cipher

PROVENANCE: Private Collection; {Mongerson and Peters Galleries}; Private Collection, Texas.

REFERENCES: Rick Stewart, Charles M. Russell, Sculptor, Amon Carter Museum, Fort Worth, Texas, 1994, pp. 353-357.

Russell had firsthand experience with the rangy Texas longhorns from his stint as a night wrangler for the Davis, Hauser, Stuart ranch. The wild longhorns had evolved from Andalusian stock into a rugged animal capable of roaming barren mesas for long periods of time with little water or feed. The Texas longhorn gets its name from its most prominent feature: its tremendous horns could measure over seven feet long. The longhorn populated the Montana ranges that Russell knew as a young man. Unfortunately, like the bison and the grizzly, it became the victim of progress. By the end of the century, the longhorn had been replaced by hybrid animals more suited to fenced-in ranges and regulated growth. Although Texas Steer depicts the animal lying down and chewing its cud, it has the unmistakable physical characteristics that many people in Russell's day termed "all leg and horns", high shoulders, flat ribs, long length, and a big-boned frame with a prominent backbone. (Stewart 81)

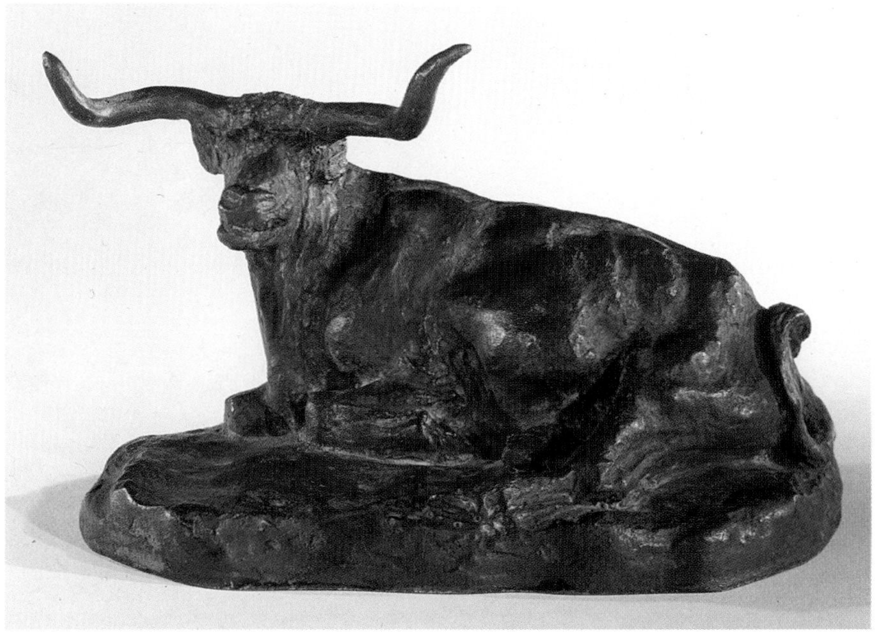

Photograph courtesy of The Amon Carter Museum. #1961.109

60. The Range Father
modeled 1926, cast *c.*1929-34
5 1/2 x 15 x 5 inches
foundry: California Art Bronze Foundry, Los Angeles
technique: lost wax cast
estimated number of lifetime casts: 8
incised: CM Russell/ skull cipher/ copyright

PROVENANCE: Private Collection, Denver, Colorado; {Gerald Peters Gallery, Santa Fe, New Mexico}; Private Collection

REFERENCES: Rick Stewart, Charles M. Russell, Sculptor, Amon Carter Museum, Fort Worth, Texas, 1994, pp. 298-302.

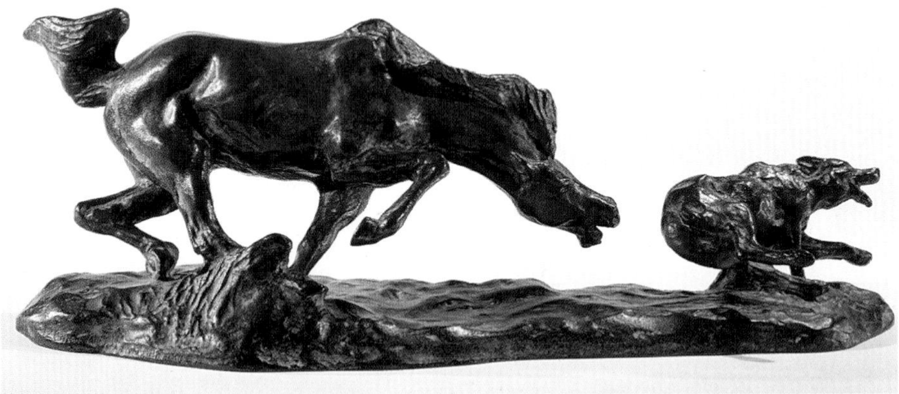
Photograph courtesy of The Amon Carter Museum. #1961.95

The Range Father, modeled just six months before Russell's death, reveals a spontaneous execution and abstraction of form previously unattained. This bronze may well have been his most impressionistic, depicting the wild stallion and maurauding wolf in the moment of utmost exertion. Russell's considerable knowledge and increased technical ability facilitated the spare, sinuous forms that transcended the comparatively static compositions of his contemporaries.

Critics continually praised the accuracy of his observations and the animated naturalism of his subjects. His longtime friend Frank Bird Linderman selected *The Range Father* as one of two works reproduced in an appreciative eulogy in the April 1927 issue of Outlook. Linderman commented, "His horses are alive, and his bronzes are so full of lively action that they seem fairly to move." (Stewart 299)

61. The Cryer
modeled 1926, cast *c.*1929-34
10 3/8 x 6 x 8 inches
foundry: California Art Bronze Foundry, Los Angeles
technique: lost wax cast
estimated number of lifetime casts: 6
incised: CM Russell/skull cipher/copyright

PROVENANCE: Private Collection; {Mongerson Wunderlich Gallery, Chicago, Illinois}; Private Collection, Denver, Colorado.

REFERENCES: Rick Stewart, Charles M. Russell, Sculptor, Amon Carter Museum, Fort Worth, Texas, 1994, pp. 358-361.

The bronze figure of an Indian with a raised tomahawk on a rearing horse titled *The Cryer* did not exist in bronze prior to 1929. The original model, which the artist apparently completed shortly before his death, must have been extensively damaged before it could be cast into bronze. Nancy Russell wrote a letter to George Sack, Russell's primary bronze collector regarding the piece in February 1929. "Now about 'The Cryer.' That is our Indian on the rearing horse that has been restored to such a degree that I don't believe anyone would know that Charlie hadn't put it back together. Joe De Yong used the best of his ability and so did Charlie Beil, who I've just told you of. Between them, I feel the model is really nearly perfect and Charlie would chuckle over the way they put together the bits of his composition and have it now in a perfect whole." (Stewart 359)

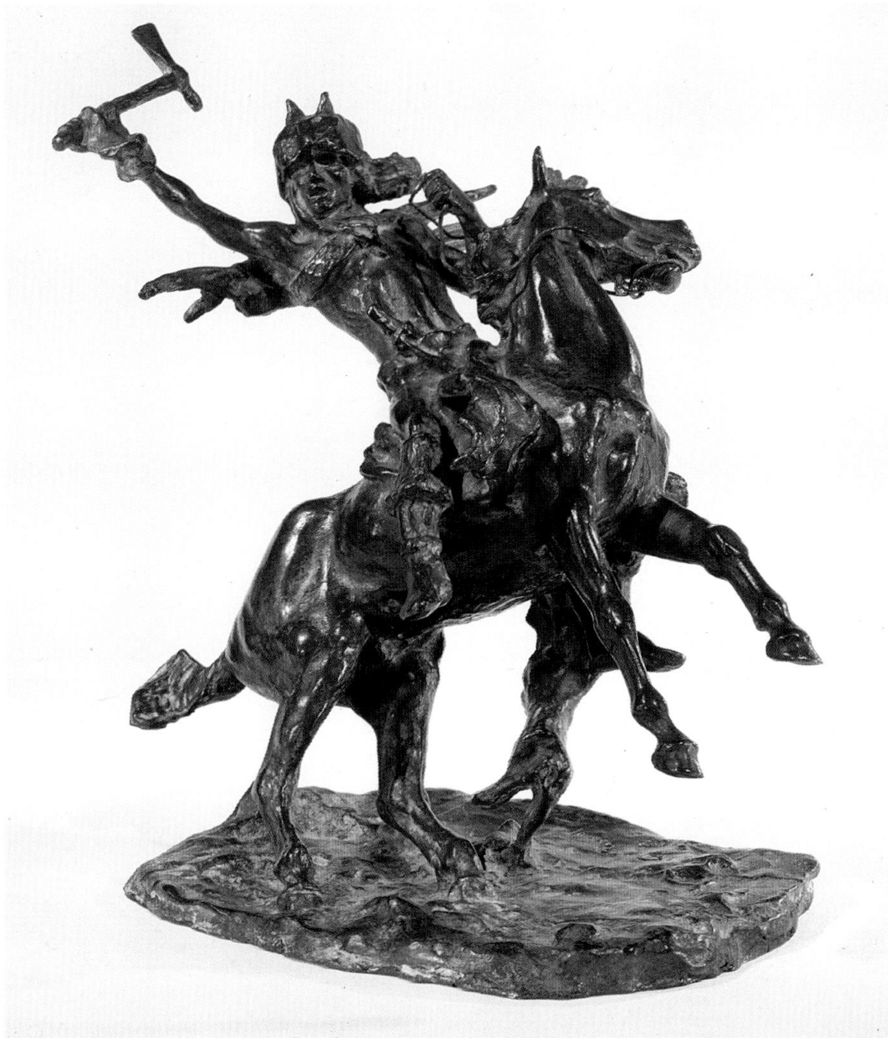

Photograph courtesy of The Amon Carter Museum. #1961.81

62. *Wolf with Bone*

modeled *c.* 1901
plaster model
5 3/4 x 9 x 5 3/8 inches
signed: C.M. Russell / skull cipher

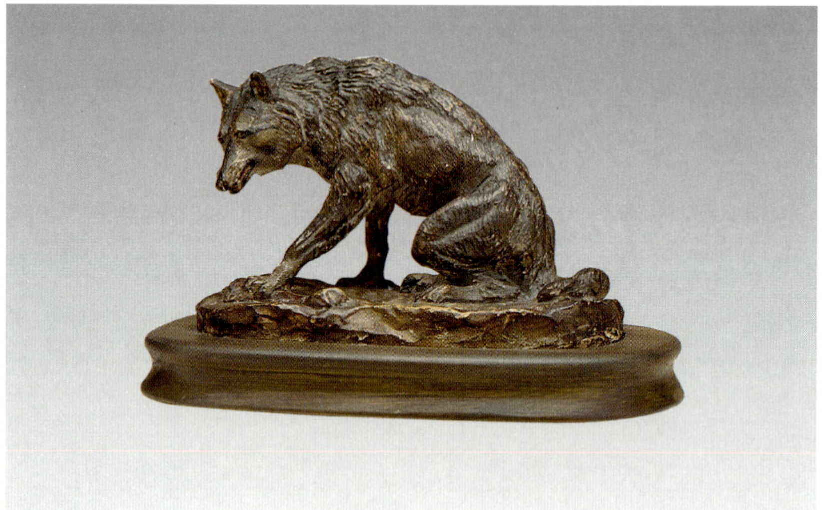

PROVENANCE: Alexander Gallery, Kennedy Gallery, New York, New York; Private Collection, Denver, Colorado.

REFERENCE: Rick Stewart, Charles M. Russell, Sculptor, Amon Carter Museum, Fort Worth, Texas, 1994, pp. 42, 345-348.

Years after Russell's death, people still remembered the informal yet extraordinary wax sculptures of animals the artist made to amuse himself and his friends. Nancy Russell in particular received a great many of them for her birthday, their wedding anniversary, or as Christmas presents. The artist was also fond of creating centerpieces for special occasions, arranging miniature models in naturalistic tableaux. One early photograph in the Britzman Collection shows an Arab rider and camel set against a painted desert backdrop with clay boulders strewn on the ground. (Stewart 42) The plaster model of *Wolf with Bone* was copyrighted as *Lone Wolf* in 1928, and cast either in the last few months of Russell's life or in the months immediately following his death. Approximately nine casts of *Lone Wolf* have been identified and bear the Roman Bronze Works foundry notice.

63. Arab Camel Rider
hand painted wax model
3 3/8 x 2 3/4 x 3 1/4 inches
signed: CMR/skull cipher

PROVENANCE: M. Knoedler & Company, New York; Glenn Nielsen, Wyoming, 1958; {Mongerson Wunderlich Gallery, Chicago, Illinois, 1987}.

REFERENCES: Rick Stewart, Charles M. Russell, Sculptor, Amon Carter Museum, Fort Worth, Texas, 1994, p. 42.

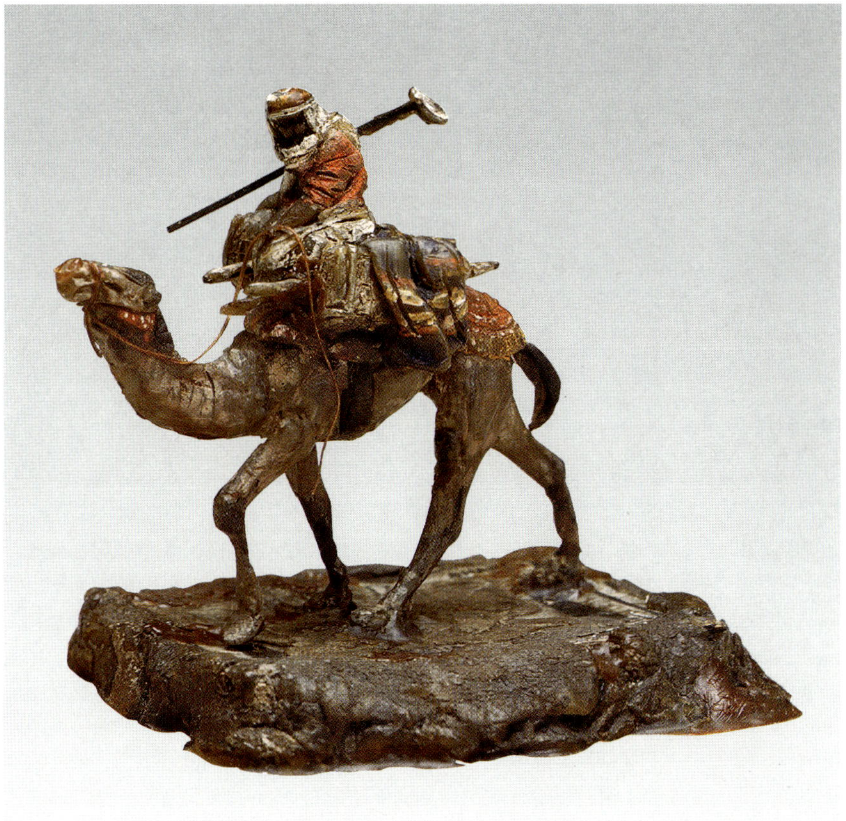

64. Chief Crowfoot
hand painted plaster cast
modeled 1901
7 1/4 x 6 3/4 x 4 3/4 inches
unsigned

PROVENANCE: Private Collection; {Gerald Peters Gallery, Santa Fe, New Mexico}.

REFERENCE: Rick Stewart, Charles M. Russell, Sculptor, Amon Carter Museum, Fort Worth, Texas, 1994, pp.340-343.

This plaster bust, modeled in 1901, was later copyrighted and cast as *Sleeping Thunder* in 1927. According to various accounts, the model was based on a fictional warrior from one of Russell's stories. The character of *Sleeping Thunder* may have been fashioned after a Blackfoot chief or a Blood Indian name Apskinas, both of whom Russell had spent time with a young man. Whatever the source, this sculpture reveals the penetrating character of Russell's strong warrior types.

Joe DeYong's 1941 inventory of the Russell estate listed no fewer than nine plaster copies of this work. When Homer Britzman later acquired the estate and divided the works among he and his partners, the models slipped into obscurity. For the exception of this example and the one housed at the CM Russell Museum, the remaining seven models have yet to be located. (Stewart 342)

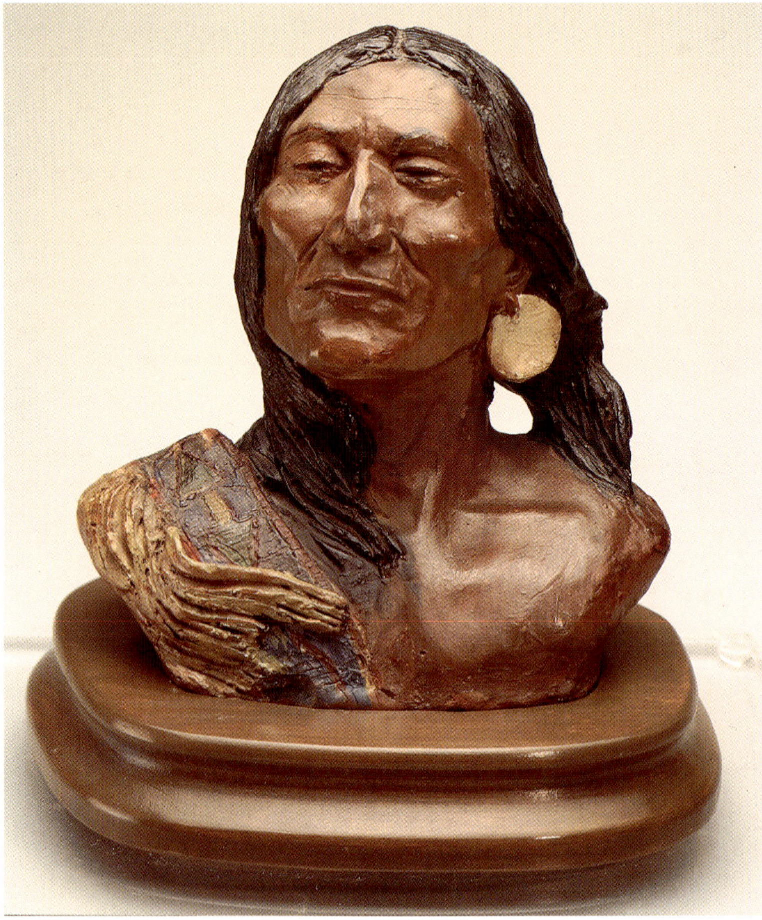

65. *Blackfoot War Chief*
modeled 1911, cast 1961
10 5/8 x 4 1/4 x 9 3/4 inches
foundry: Roman Bronze Works, New York
number of casts: edition of 25

PROVENANCE: Private Collection, New York, New York; Frederic Renner, Paradise Valley, Arizona; Historical Society of Montana, Helena, Montana; {Gerald Peters Gallery, Santa Fe, New Mexico}; Private Collection, Texas.

Note: This bronze is a posthumous casting of a model copyrighted by Russell in 1911 by the same title. Frederic Renner presented it to the Historical Society of Montana who had it cast in 1961 in an edition of 25.

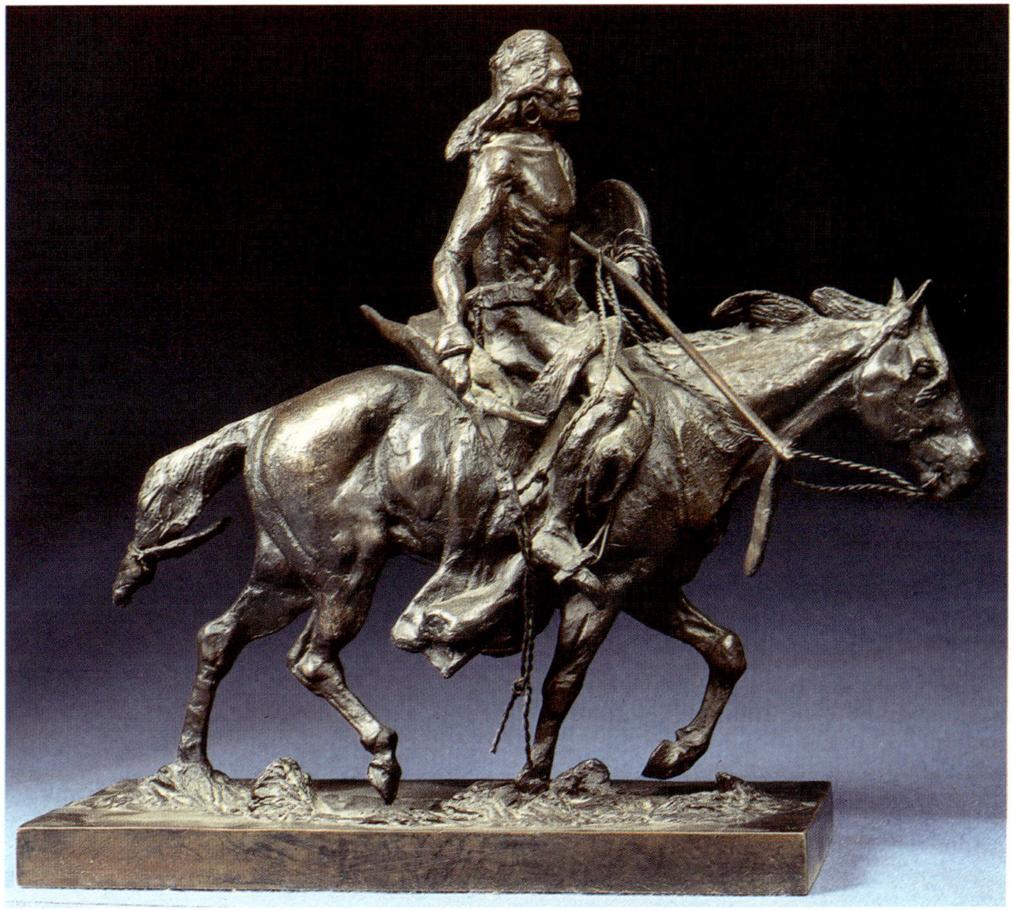

Charles M. Russell: The Art of the Letter

BY BRIAN DIPPIE

He wore the same expression painting and whenever he sat down to write a letter--jaw jutted out, mouth grimly set, eyes firmly fixed in front of him. But when it came to "paper talk," as Charlie Russell called it, there was more desperation than farsightedness in his gaze.

Russell began sending illustrated letters--actually, illustrated communications with minimal commentary--to his folks back home in Saint Louis and to Montana friends in the 1880s. His aversion to writing was pronounced, and evident in the few examples from the period that survive. A letter to Ben Roberts (here in its entirety) describing his now legendary trip to southern Alberta in 1888 indicates how grudgingly the words came to the young Cowboy Artist:

> "I have reached my stoping place I am s[t]aying at a cattle ranch on high rive[r] I am not doing aney thing now as I got here to late for the roundup I like the county pritty well so far there is lots of Indians here they visit us nearly every day
>
> I give my bst regards to Mrs Ro [crossed out]
>
> give my bst regards to Mrs. Roberts and eveybody."[1]

It was a long reach from the painful recording of such basic information to lines like "I m mighty lame with a pen an this same limping makes me slow writing" and "if the old west had of been as tough as the moov[i]es make it thay d be runing buffalo yet on the Great Falls flat."

By the time Russell scrawled those sentiments he was a national celebrity, and what he wrote was treasured. The demand on him for letters grew constantly. Old friends wanted him to keep in touch while he was traveling, and traveling brought new friends to write when he was home. He made common cause with men like Montana writer Frank B. Linderman, a champion of Indian rights, and his fame brought other famous folk like the Sage of Paducah, humorist Irvin S. Cobb, into his orbit. But Russell never forgot his oldest friends --cowboy pals like Patrick T. "Tommy" Tucker (who told whoppers about their youthful antics in his 1933 memoirs "Riding the High Country, but was not stretching the truth when he recalled roping a buffalo in 1883) and Harry T. "Tom" Duckett (who in July 1901 was priveledged with a multi-paged letter breezily recounting the fates of such rangeland acquaintences as Panhandle Jack, Merit Flanigan and Pat Rily). Russell liked to exchange gripes about progress with Montana oldtimers like Harry P. Stanford, a Kalispel taxidermist. And he never forgot his Great Falls crowd. A letter to one of the Central Avenue barkeeps, cigar store merchants or gamblers would be displayed and savored by the entire downtown "bunch." Social friends who had Nancy's seal of approval like Paris Gibson, Chris Dickinson, Edgar I. Holland and Frank Brown were not neglected either. Paper talk was always work for Russell, but he became a genius at saying something warm and amusing and often sentimental in a few lines. The flaws that had inhibited his writing in his youth--spelling, punctuation, grammatical structure--only made his mature prose the more delightful. It was Russell himself who spoke from the page.

Russell letters and Christmas greetings (perhaps his very favorite art form) are treasured to this day for their sketches, of course, often featuring Charlie himself as all-purpose comic foil. They are treasured as well for their decency and good humor, their homespun philosophy, and their abiding loyalty to the Old West. Charlie Russell has been dead almost seventy years now, but he still speaks through his paper talk, and people still like to hear what he has to say.

NOTES

1. C. M. Russell to Ben R. Roberts, {June 1888}, in Brian W. Dippie, ed., Charles M. Russell, Word Painter: Letters 1887-1926 (Fort Worth: Amon Carter Museum, in association with Harry N. Abrams, New York, 1993), pp. 14-15.

THE LETTERS

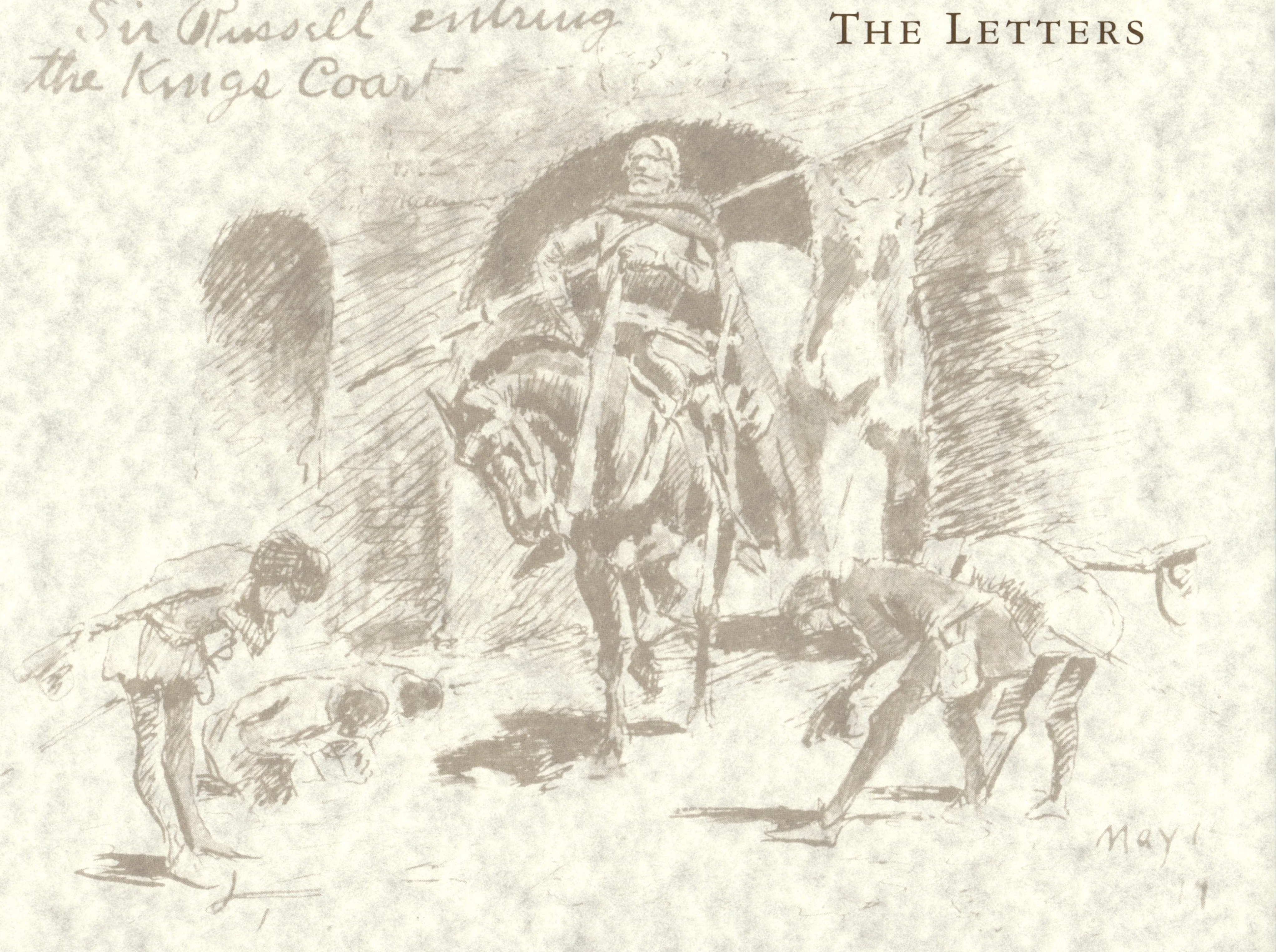

LETTER PLATE LIST

Title / Year

66. *Panhandle Jack/Merit Flanigan/Pat Rily,* (Three pages of a letter to Harry Duckett), July 1901
watercolor, ink on paper

PROVENANCE: P.P. Johnson; Collection of William John Upjohn; {Gerald Peters Gallery, Santa Fe, New Mexico}; Private Collection, Oklahoma.

RELATED LITERATURE: Good Medicine, The Illustrated Letters of Charles M. Russell with Introduction by Will Rogers and Biographical Note by Nancy Russell, Doubleday, Doran & Company, Inc., Garden City, New York, 1929 pp.106 & 121; Karl Yost and Frederic G. Renner, A Bibliography of Published Works by Charles M. Russell, University of Nebraska Press, Lincoln, NB, 1971, pp. 24, 128, & 134; Brian W. Dippie, Charles M. Russell, Word Painter, Amon Carter Museum, Fort Worth, Texas, 1993, pp. 44, 412.

Russell met Harry T. "Tom" Duckett during his job as a night herder for a large cattle operation in the Judith Basin around the early 1880s. They both retired from the range in 1892; Duckett left to pursue journalism and Russell went on to pursue his art. Duckett wrote Russell in the late nineties, inquiring after other rangeland acquaintances. Charlie replied in July 1901 with a unique letter of more than a dozen pages, each devoted to a single individual. (Dippie 44)

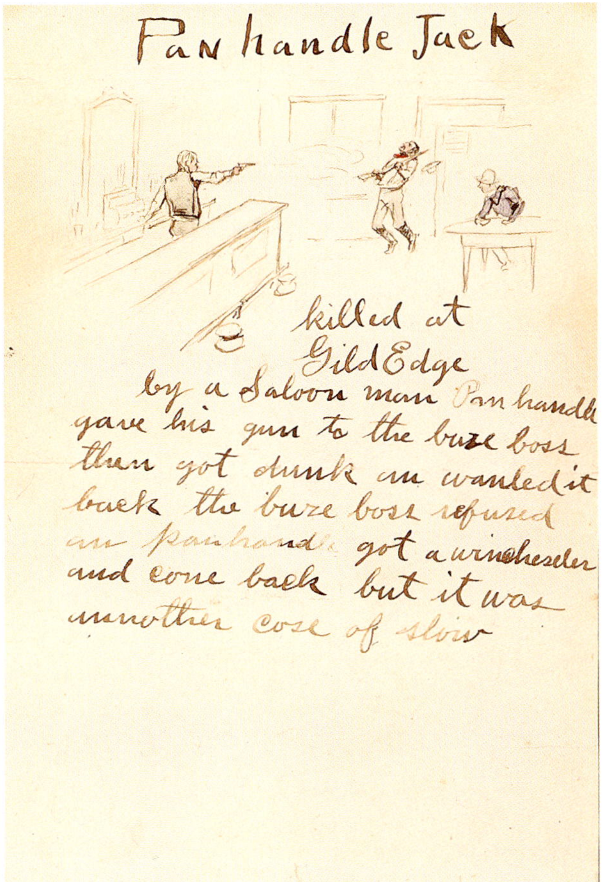
Pan handle Jack
killed at
Gild Edge
by a Saloon man Pan handle
gave his gun to the buze boss
then got drunk an wanted it
back the buze boss refused
an panhandle got a winchester
and come back but it was
annother case of slow

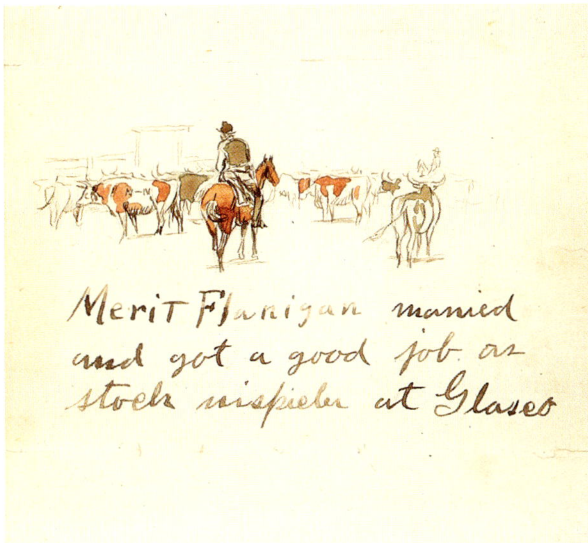
Merit Flanigan married
and got a good job as
stock inspector at Glasco

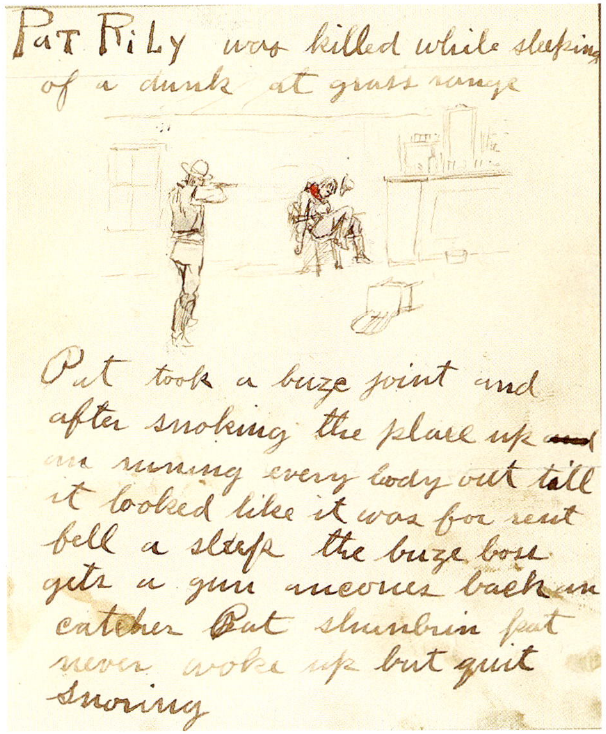
Pat Rily was killed while sleeping
of a drunk at grass range
Pat took a buze joint and
after smoking the place up and
an running every body out till
it looked like it was for rent
fell a sleep the buze boss
gets a gun an comes back an
catches Pat slumbrin pat
never woke up but quit
snoring

67. *Her's How Senitor,* {to Paris Gibson} July 1, 1906
watercolor, ink on paper

PROVENANCE: Private Collection, Oklahoma; {Gerald Peters Gallery, Santa Fe, New Mexico}; Private Collection, California; Private Collection.
REFERENCES: Brian W. Dippie, Charles M. Russell, Word Painter, Amon Carter Museum, Fort Worth, Texas, 1993, p.77, 413.

Paris Gisbson was Great Falls' grand old man. Though his vision was as forward-looking and progressive as Russell's was backward-looking and nostalgic, Charlie was quick to sing his praises. In 1883, in partnership with railroad magnate James J. Hill, Gibson surveyed and platted the city and became its first mayor when it was formally incorporated five years later. When fifty friends gathered at the Park Hotel on July 1, 1906, to celebrate Gibson's seventy-sixth birthday, Charlie was on hand. In lieu of a spoken toast, he presented the senator with this watercolor greeting. (Dippie 77)

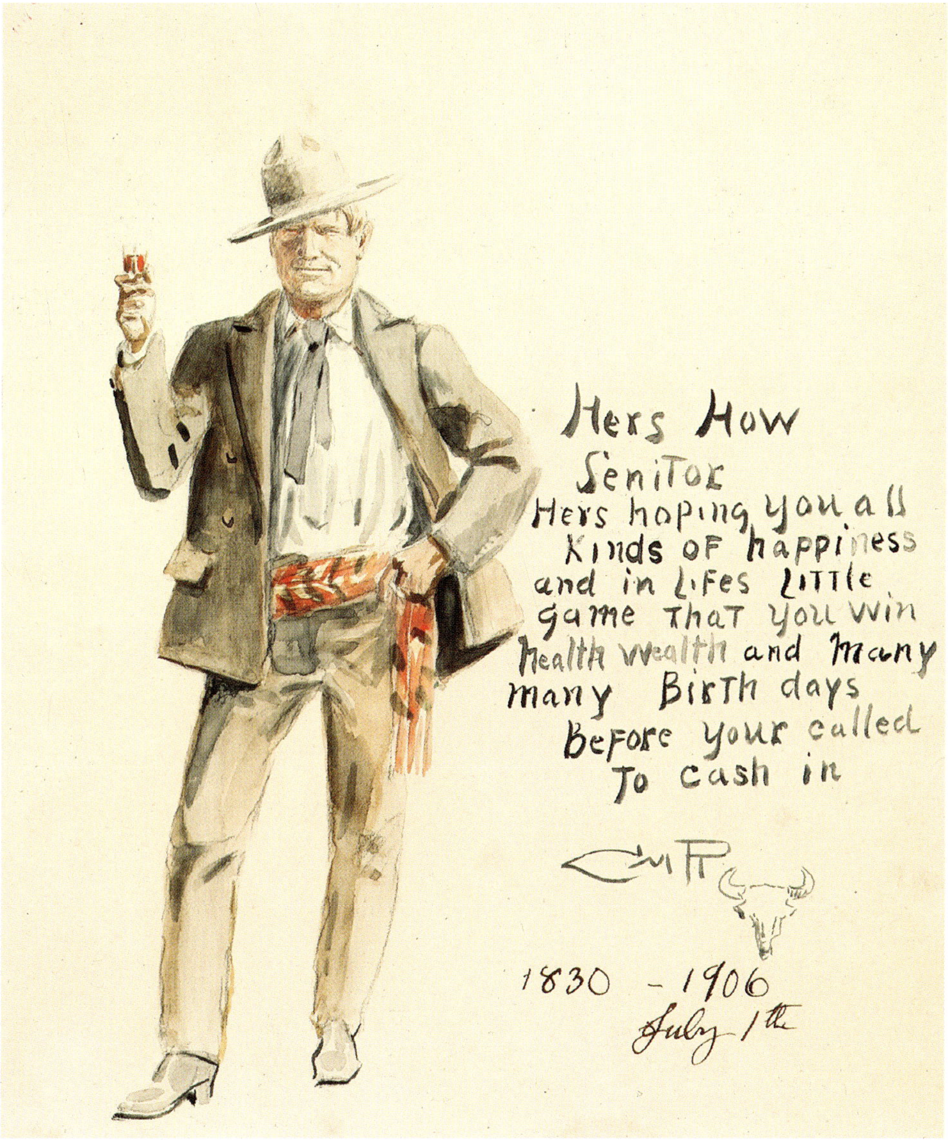
Hers How
Senitor
Hers hoping you all
Kinds of happiness
and in Lifes Little
game that you win
Health wealth and many
many Birth days
Before your called
To cash in
CMR
1830 - 1906
July 1th

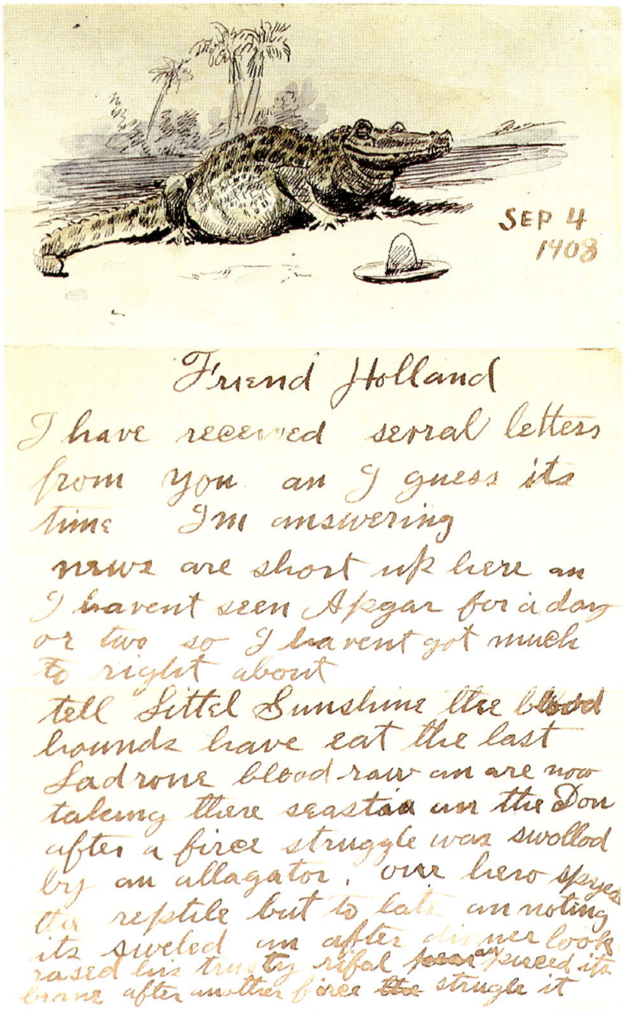

SEP 4 1908

Friend Holland

I have received serral letters from you an I guess its time Im answering

news are short up here an I havent seen Apgar for a day or two so I havent got much to right about

tell Littel Sunshine the ~~blood~~ hounds have eat the last Ladrone blood-raw an are now takeing there seastia in the Don after a firce struggle was swollod by an allagator. our hero sprged the reptile but to late an noting its sweled un after dinner look rased his trusty rifal ~~fear~~ pierced its brane after nother firce ~~the~~ strugle it

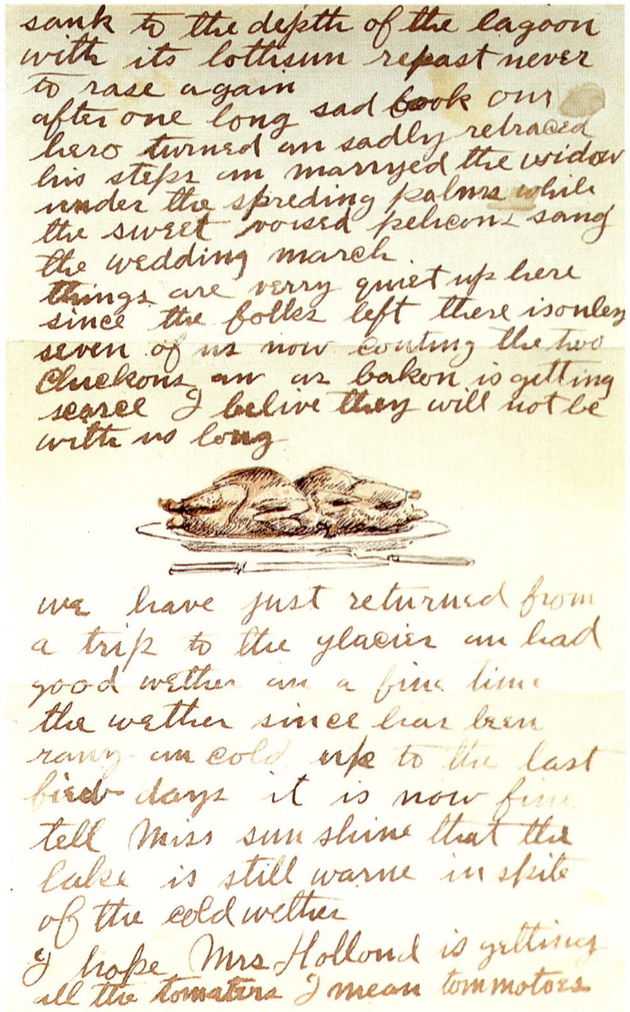

sank to the depth of the lagoon with its lottisum repast never to rase again after one long sad look our hero turned an sadly retraced his steps an marryed the widow under the spreding palms while the sweet voised pelicons sang the wedding march.

things are verry quiet up here since the folks left there is onley seven of us now counting the two chickons an as bakon is getting scarce I belive they will not be with us long

we have just returned from a trip to the glacier an had good wether an a fine time the wether since has been rany an cold up to the last fiew days it is now fine tell Miss sun shine that the cake is still warme in spite of the cold wether I hope Mrs Hollond is getting all the tomaters I mean tommotors

68. *Friend Holland,* {Edgar I. Holland}, September 4, 1908
watercolor, ink on paper (four pages)

PROVENANCE: The Artist; E. I. Holland, Los Angeles, California; (to his daughter) Virginia Holland Wilcox, California; {Gerald Peters Gallery, Santa Fe, New Mexico}; Private Collection, California; Private Collection.

REFERENCES: Brian W. Dippie, Charles M. Russell, Word Painter, Amon Carter Museum, Fort Worth, Texas, 1993, pp. 106-107; Good Medicine, The Illustrated Letters of Charles M. Russell, with Introduction by Will Rogers and Biographical Note by Nancy Russell, Doubleday, Doran & Co. Inc., Garden City, New York, 1929, pp. 72-73, 414.

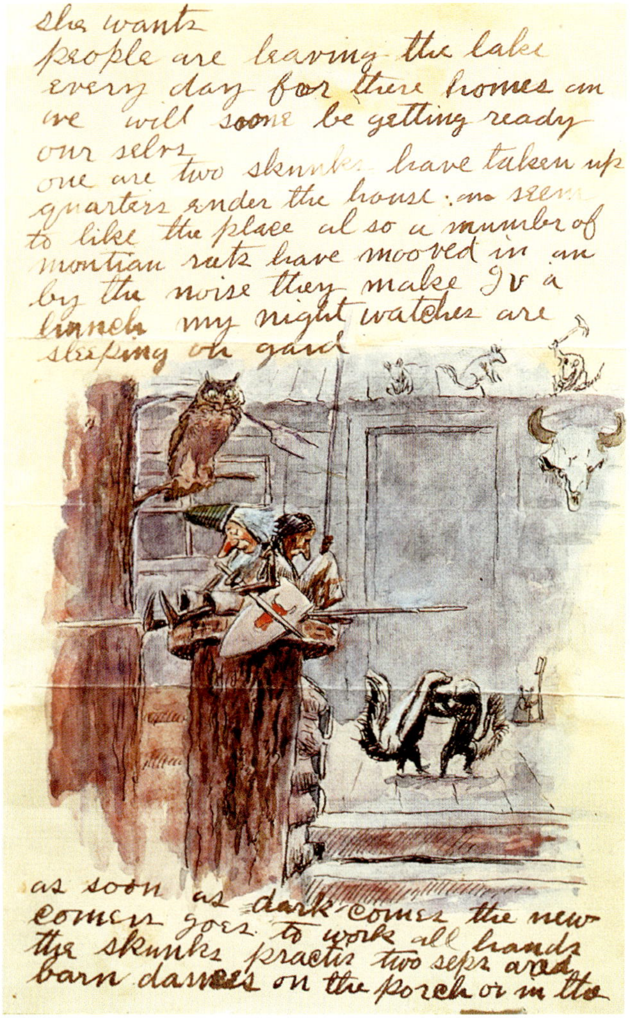

she wants
people are leaving the lake
every day for there homes an
we will soone be getting ready
our selvs
one are two skunks have taken up
quarters under the house an seem
to like the place al so a number of
montian rats have mooved in an
by the noise they make Iv a
hunch my night watches are
sleeping on gard

as soon as dark comes the new
comers goes to work all hands
the skunks practis two seps an
barn dances on the porch or in the

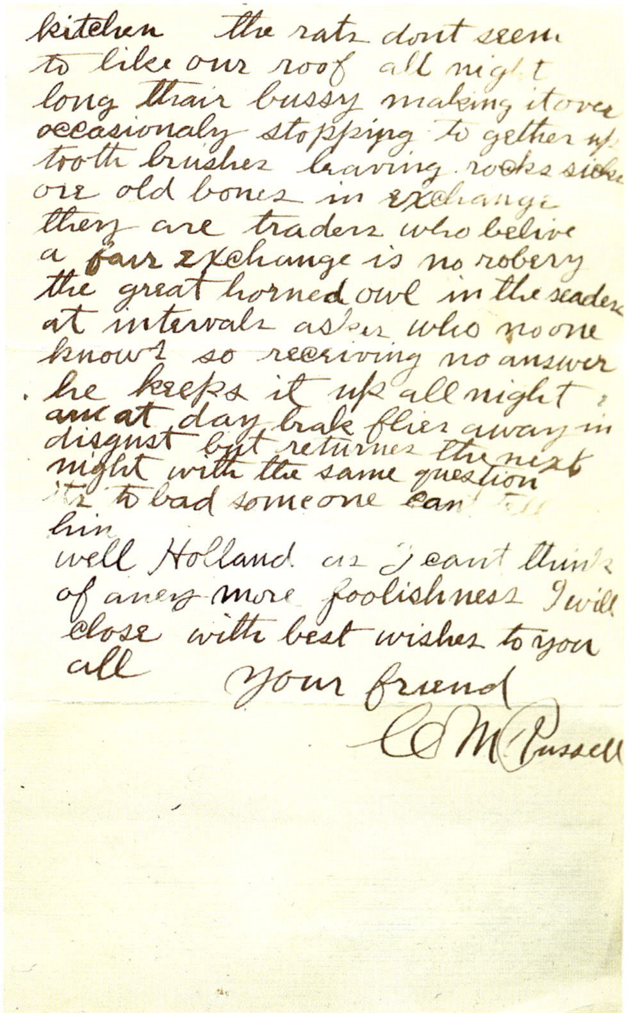

kitchen the rats dont seem
to like our roof all night
long thair bussy making it over
occasionaly stopping to gether up
tooth brushes leaving rocks sticks
ore old bones in exchange
they are traders who belive
a fair exchange is no robery
the great horned owl in the seader
at intervals askes who noone
knows so receiving no answer
he keeps it up all night
an at day brake flies away in
disgust but returnes the next
night with the same question
its to bad someone cant tell
him
well Holland as I cant think
of aney more foolishness I will
close with best wishes to you
all
your friend
C M Russell

The Russells spent many summers at their cabin on Lake McDonald within the area that was to become Glacier National Park. Their cabin, named Bull Head Lodge, served as a refuge for the artist. It was here that he was able to spend time close to nature, where the geography, flora, and fauna served to remind him of the untamed world he had once known. This four page letter addressed E.I. Holland, was written when Charlie was vacationing at Bull Head Lodge during the summer of 1908. The Hollands had stayed with the Russells at Lake McDonald earlier in the summer, and they periodically received reports on the doings there. "Not much was happening," Charlie wrote, though the pack rats that had invaded Bull Head Lodge were busy rearranging their new home. He kidded Virgina Holland about the correct pronunciation of "tommotoes", their daughter Marion (Little Sunshine) about her taste in literature, and let the "sweetness and strength of character" that Holland cherished in him shine through in this gentle letter. (Dippie 73)

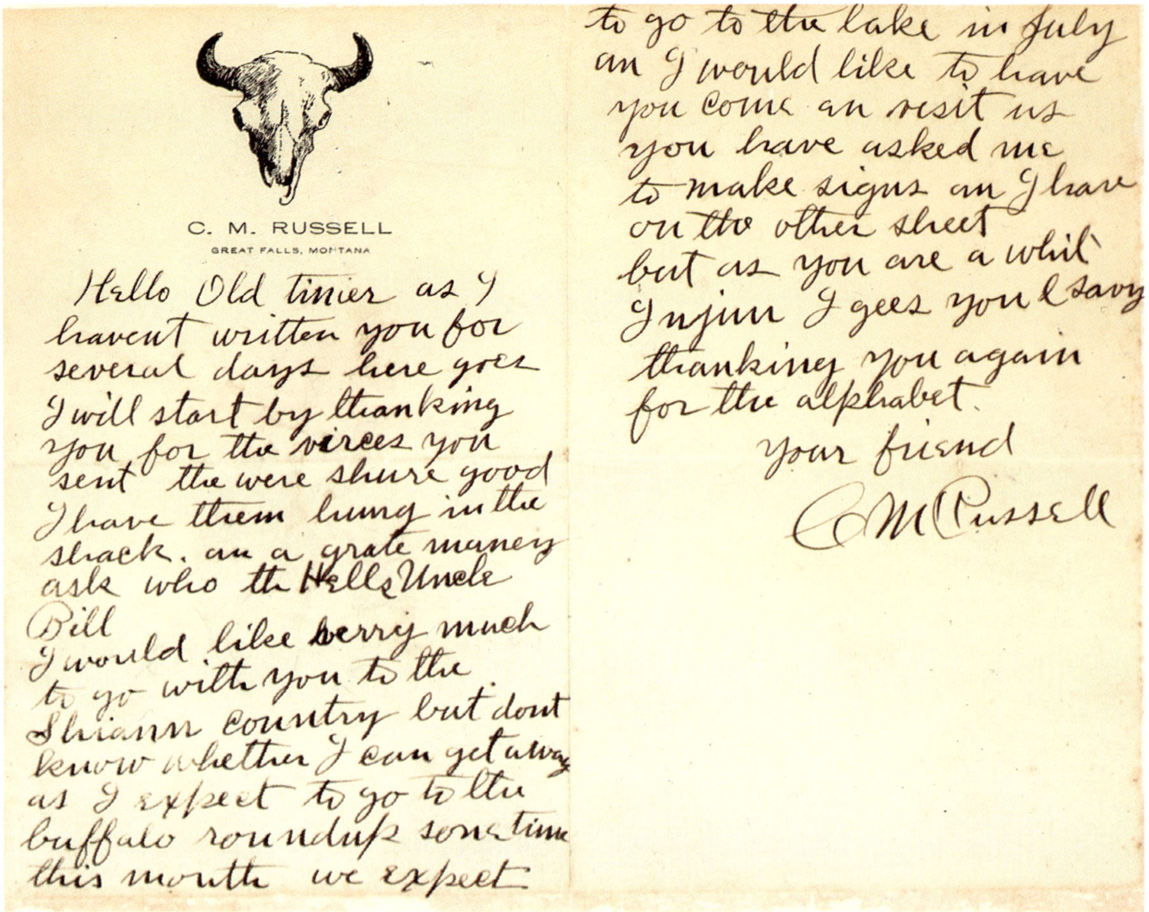

C. M. RUSSELL
GREAT FALLS, MONTANA

Hello Old timer as I
havent written you for
several days here goes
I will start by thanking
you for the verces you
sent the were shure good
I have them hung in the
shack. an a grate maney
ask who the Hells Uncle
Bill
I would like berry much
to go with you to the
Shianne country but dont
know whether I can get away
as I expect to go to the
buffalo roundup sometime
this month we expect
to go to the lake in July
an I would like to have
you come an visit us
you have asked me
to make signs an I have
on the other sheet
but as you are a whit
Injun I gees you savy
thanking you again
for the alphabet.
Your friend
CMRussell

69. *Hello Old Timer,* {Frank B. Linderman} May 12, 1909
watercolor, ink on paper

PROVENANCE: Thomas Nygard; {Gerald Peters Gallery, Santa Fe, New Mexico}; Private Collection, Colorado.

REFERENCES: Brian W. Dippie, Charles M. Russell, Word Painter, Amon Carter Museum, Fort Worth, Texas, 1993, pp. 117, 414.

The friendship between Frank Bird Linderman and Charles Russell seemed predestined. They were both veteran outdoorsmen, lovers of wildlife and wild country, students of native customs and tales, and defenders of Indian rights. On April 15, 1909, Linderman wrote Russell to invite him on a trip through Cheyenne country in southeastern Montana, and at the same time implored Charlie to consider a hunt with him that fall on the north and south forks of the Flathead River. He also enclosed copies of some verse, aphorisms that he printed on cards as the sayings of an old prospector called Uncle Billy and the Cree alphabet. Russell's elaborate thank-you (plate #5) was meant to imitate the Cree syllabary. (Dippie 414)

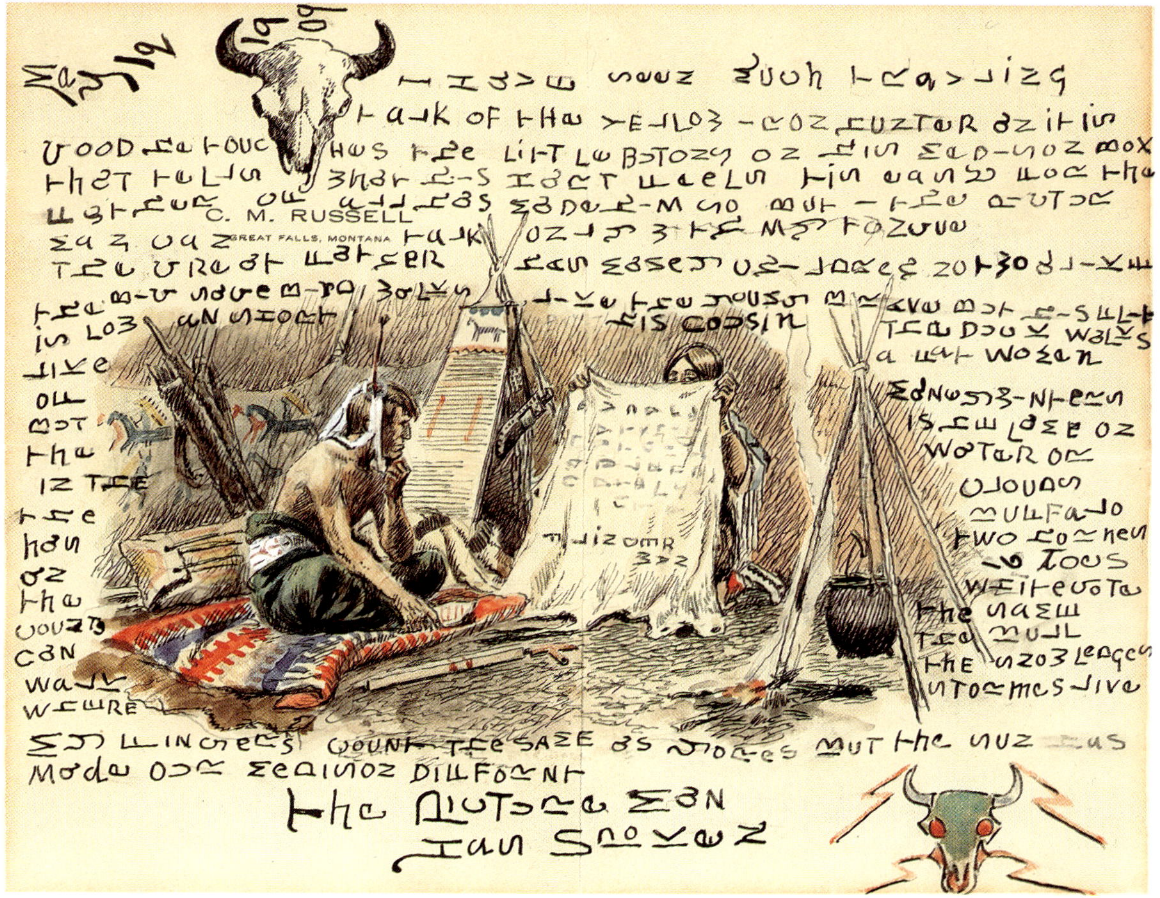

70. *The Picture Man Has Spoken,* {Frank B. Linderman}, May 19, 1909
watercolor, ink on paper

PROVENANCE: Thomas Nygard; {Gerald Peters Gallery, Santa Fe, New Mexico}; Private Collection, Colorado.

REFERENCES: Brian W. Dippie, Charles M. Russell, Word Painter, Amon Carter Museum, Fort Worth, Texas, 1993, p. 118, 414-415.

71. *Friend Frank,* {Frank B. Linderman}, September 14, 1912
watercolor, ink on paper

PROVENANCE: Linderman Family, Courtesy of J.N. Bartfield Galleries, New York, New York.

REFERENCES: Brian W. Dippie, Charles M. Russell, Word Painter, Amon Carter Museum, Fort Worth, Texas, 1993, p. 169, 416.

The July 4th, 1912, celebration on the Blackfeet Reservation near Browning attracted a number of artists and writers, including Russell, Percy Raban, Frank Tenney Johnson, and Philadelphia-born artist Bill Krieghoff. Frank Linderman was an honored guest of the Blackfeet tribe, and he erected a buffalo hide tipi to house his party. Linderman arranged a feast for the group inside his lodge, and his friend Crooked Horn told of the old days. Russell communicated with the old Blackfeet in sign language, and the events made for a stirring experience. When Russell wrote in September, it was to thank Linderman for the part he played in the summer celebration, and to accept his invitation to bring Bill Krieghoff along for a fall hunt. (Dippie, 169)

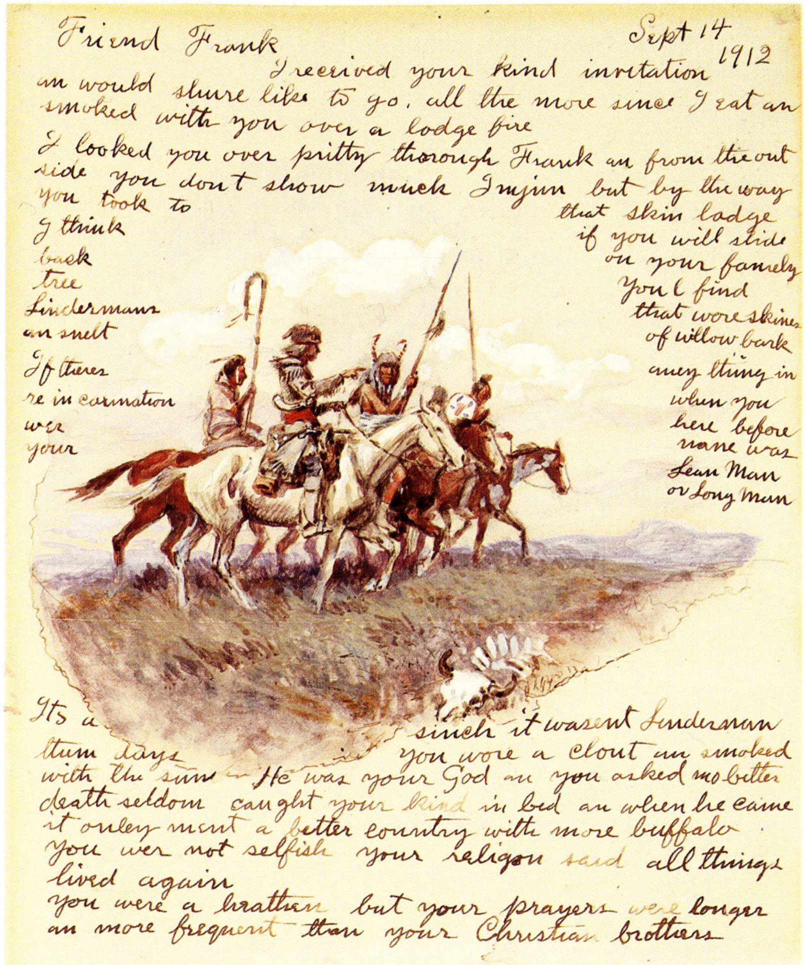

Friend Frank Sept 14 1912

I received your kind invitation an would shure like to go. all the more since I eat an smoked with you over a lodge fire

I looked you over pritty thorough Frank an from the out side you dont show much Injun but by the way you took to that skin lodge I think if you will slide back on your famely tree You'l find Lindermans that wore skines an smelt of willow bark

If theres any thing in re incarnation when you wer here before your name was Lean Man or Long Man

Its a sinch it wasent Linderman them days you wore a clout an smoked with the sun He was your God an you asked no better death seldom caught your kind in bed an when he came it onley ment a better country with more buffalo

You wer not selfish your religon said all things lived again

You were a heathen but your prayers were longer an more frequent than your Christian brothers

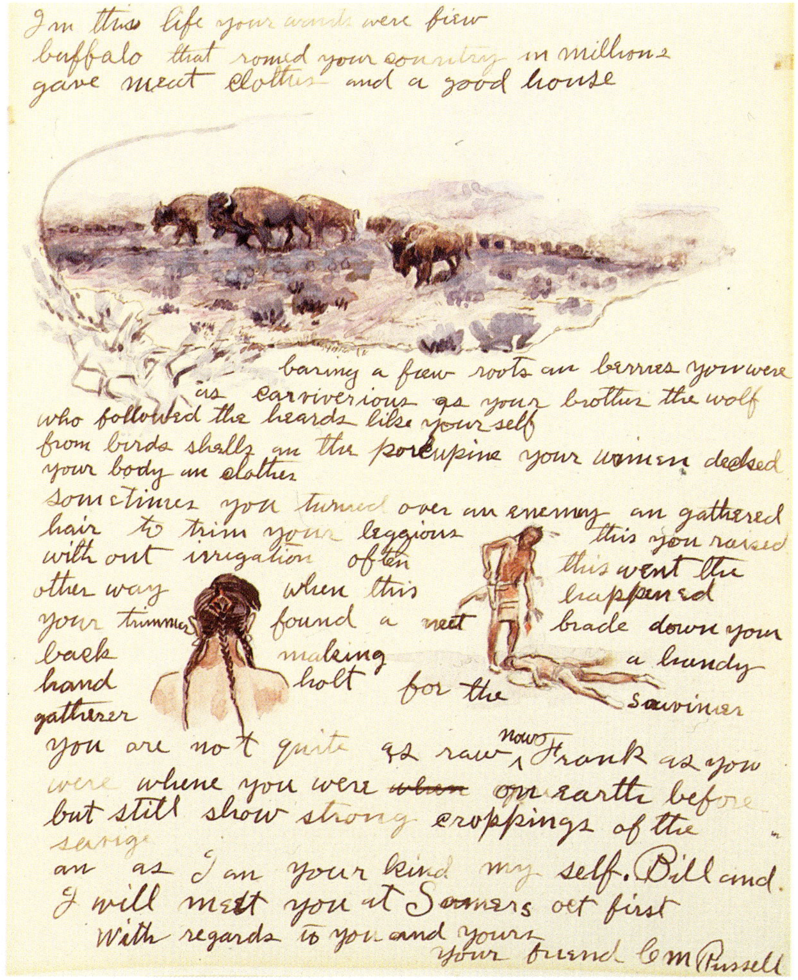

In this life your wants were few buffalo that romed your country in millions gave meat clothes and a good house

baring a few roots an berries you were as carnivorious as your brother the wolf who followed the heards like your self from birds shells an the porcupine your women decked your body an clothes

sometimes you turned over an enemy an gathered hair to trim your leggions this you raised with out irrigation often this went the other way when this happened your trimmer found a neet blade down your back making a handy hand holt for the sauvineer gatherer

You are not quite as raw now Frank as you were when you were ~~when~~ on earth before but still show strong croppings of the savige an as I am your kind my self. Bill and I will meet you at Somers oct first

With regards to you and yours

Your friend CM Russell

72. *Friend Holland,* {Edgar I. Holland}, May 14, 1914
watercolor, ink on paper (2 pages)

PROVENANCE: The Artist; E. I. Holland, Los Angeles, California; (to his daughter) Virginia Holland Wilcox, California; {Gerald Peters Gallery, Santa Fe, New Mexico}; Private Collection, California; Private Collection.

REFERENCES: Good Medicine, The Illustrated Letters of Charles M. Russell ,with Introduction by Will Rogers and Biographical Note by Nancy Russell, Doubleday, Doran & Co., Inc., Garden City, New York, 1929, p. 81.; Brian W. Dippie, Charles M. Russell, Word Painter, Amon Carter Museum, Fort Worth, Texas, 1993, pp. 203, 417.

Russell's first international exhibition at the Doré Galleries in London took him to England in 1914. His old friend and Great Falls neighbor Edgar Holland, received one of Charlie's most amusing accounts of Old England. Charlie's inquiries into English history revealed that the Russells were entitled to claim noble lineage. According to Charlie's sources, being of the nobility meant the honor of having had an ancestor beheaded, and on that basis Charlie was ready to claim noble blood. (Dippie 203)

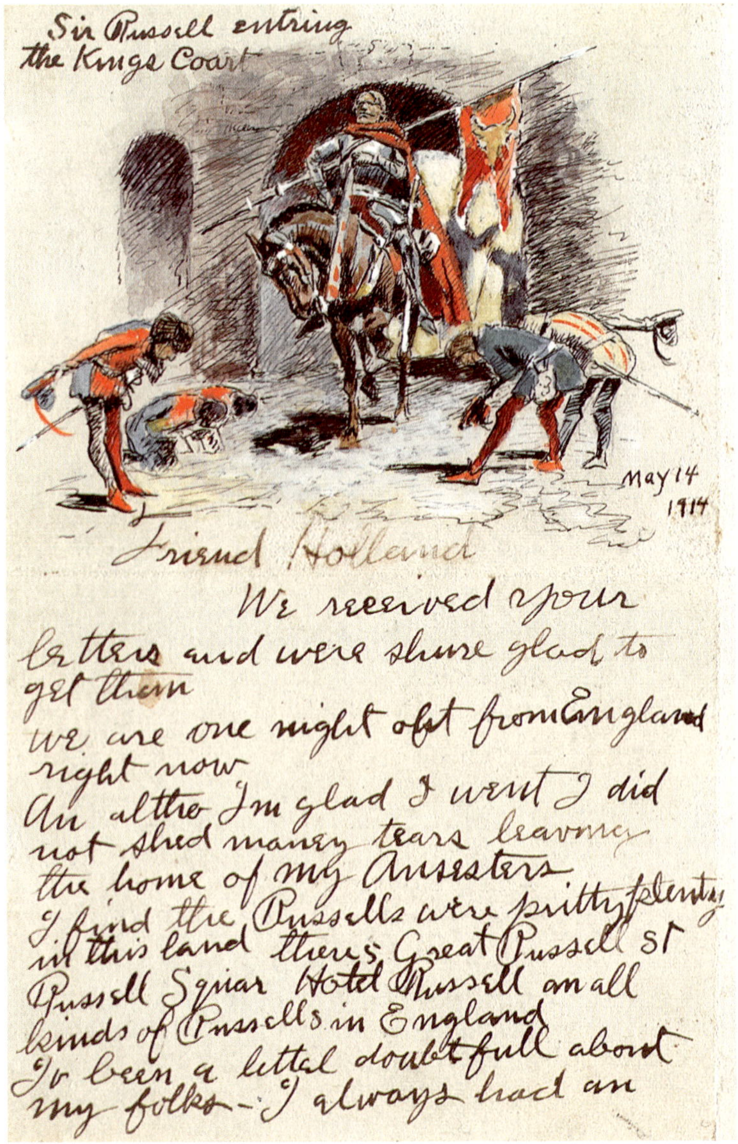
Sir Russell entring
the Kings Coart

May 14
1914

Friend Holland
We received your
letters and were shure glad to
get them
we are one night oft from England
right now
An altho Im glad I went I did
not shed maney tears leaving
the home of my ansesters
I find the Russells were pritty plenty
in this land theres Great Russell St
Russell Squar Hotel Russell an all
kinds of Russells in England
Iv been a littal doubtfull about
my folks - I always had an

I das that the Russell tree was
a scrub.
but the other day I was told that
Sir Sombody Russell was led to the
block an had the upper end of his
back bone removed by the Kings
ax man who was a bussyer man
them days
than Fred Piper ever was on sater
day night.
this loping off of Sir Russells Head
makes it sinch he was a Nobel
man, as in those dayes
scrubs mostley cashed in in
bed. A verry unrefined way of
quitten
So Holland if I happen to pass
you on the street an you feel
a chill like an ice wagon had
[illegible] dont blame me its
the blood of the Nobility I got
in me
It might pay you to com over
an round up this Historical range
but as you clame I belive Scotch
blood you'd have to work the coun
try further north
where I dont doubt you'd find
Hollands Onery enough to mix
with the Kings an as near

as I can make from history
If a man was a fighter
an could count enough notches
he was Be Knighted by the King
or Be Headed. eather way his
pedigree was safe an all those
to whome he left his name which
was generly all he had to leave
were of noble blood
so now Holland if you can scare
up a record like this I will
speak to you as an equal
with best wishes
to you and Yors
from your friend
C M Russell

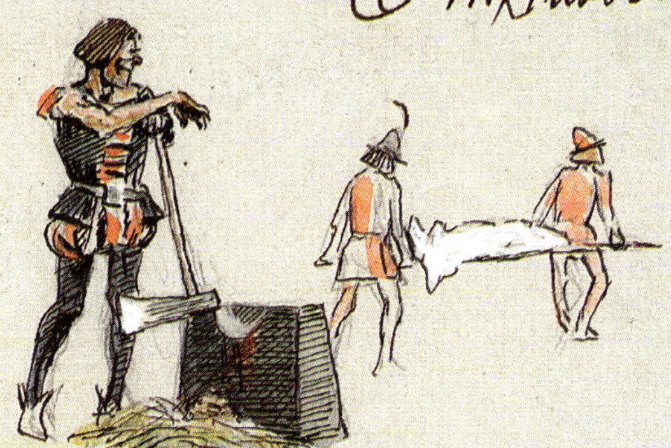

Sir Russells Departure

73. *Friend Chris,* {C.N. Dickinson}, July 12, 1917
watercolor, ink on paper

PROVENANCE: Harry and Connie Lockwood, Midwestern Galleries, Cincinnati, Ohio.

REFERENCES: Brian W. Dippie, Paper Talk, Illustrated Letters of Charles M. Russell, Amon Carter Museum, Fort Worth, Texas, 1962, p. 75; Brian W. Dippie, Charles M. Russell, Word Painter, Amon Carter Museum, Fort Worth, Texas, 1993, p. 239, 419.

In 1917, Russell decided to find a suitable place to pasture one of his favorite horses, Neenah. Acquired from a Cree Indian boy in 1900, Neenah was the last of his treasured saddle horses. He asked Chris Dickinson, a Great Falls neighbor and founder of the Great Falls Meat Company, if he could put Neenah out on Hans' Field on the south side of town. This was where the company grazed some of its livestock on the short, nutritious buffalo grass. Chris was pleased to accommodate his friend and telephoned Russell for his brand so that Neenah could be brought in upon request. This letter was Charlie's reply. (Word Painter 239)

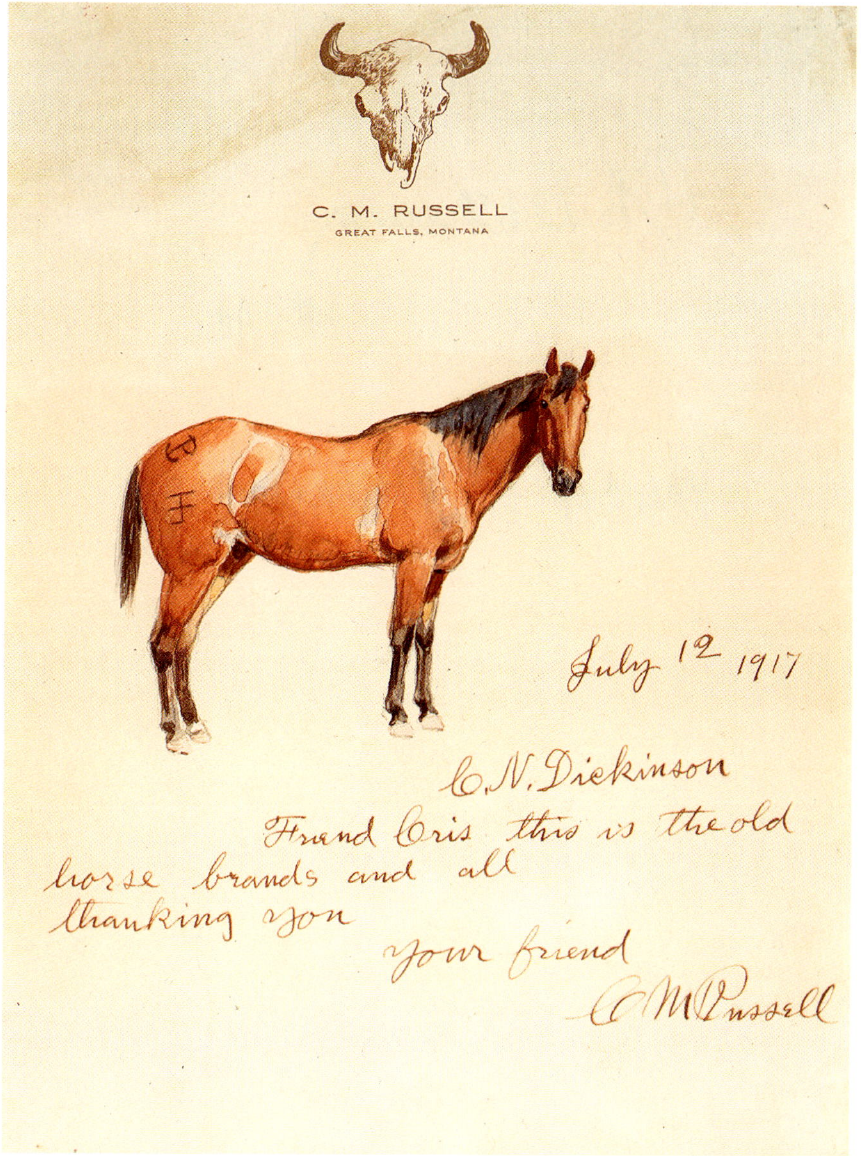

C. M. RUSSELL
GREAT FALLS, MONTANA

July 12 1917

C.N. Dickinson
Frend Cris this is the old horse brands and all thanking you
your friend
C M Russell

74. *Friend Frank,* {Frank B. Linderman}, January, 18, 1919
watercolor, ink on paper

PROVENANCE: Linderman Family, Courtesy of J.N. Barfield Galleries, New York, New York.

REFERENCES: Brian W. Dippie, Charles M. Russell, Word Painter, Amon Carter Museum, Fort Worth, Texas, 1993, p. 269, 420.

In 1917, Frank Linderman moved into a log house on Goose Bay, Flathead Lake where he pursued a career as a writer. A fellow student of Indian lore, he had contacted Russell for comments on a series of tribal tales. Russell's advice mirrored his artistic manifesto. "Sinch you saddle on romance hes a high headed hoss with plenty of blemishes but keep him moovn an theres fiew that can call the leg he limpps on and most folks like prancers." Through experience Russell had learned that stark facts were no substitute for emotion, whether the task at hand was a painting or a book. (Dippie 269)

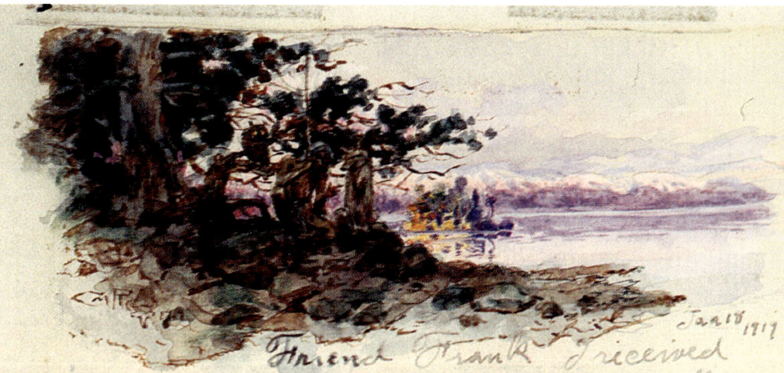

Jan 18 1917

Friend Frank I received
your letter allso storyes and red them all
and they were not dull reading
I think you might have made that Steam boat
Story longer an pushed in som romance
they were all good but the Crew of the
Tuscan was my choise
The Throw away is realy called a Give away
dance it was a small hunting camp
when the dancers went to sleep little Bird
cut all the ponys looz and drove them
way from the lodges holding out one she
had saddled for her self
she Stole her mans gun an crouching in
the door of the lodge she threw som
buffalo fat on the fire and when it
lit up after calling hubby a few names
like louse maggot and rotten hart she
drove a trade ball through him sending
him to the sand hills
these are the onley storyes in the batch
that dont suite my taste to an all spice

in at that making their letter the way you
handled them I will let miss Trigg look
them over
those Na Pa Wolfer and mining stories you
speak of sound good to me and I will
be glad to do what I can with them
Your in a good country to get Na Pa stories
that old gent aint been seen for a long time
but I belive he's still hang round your camp
any how his tracks is mighty plane
when you start those wolfer and miners
~~for~~ sinch your saddle on romance hes a
high headed hoss with plenty of blemishes
but keep him moovin an theres few that can
call the leg he limps on and most folks
like prancers

with best wishes
to you all from we three
your friend
C M Russell

75. *My Dear Mr. Cobb,* {Irvin S. Cobb}, March 6, 1919
(three pages)
watercolor, ink on paper

PROVENANCE: Robert Adams; {Mongerson Wunderlich Galleries, Chicago, Illinois}; Private Collection, Chicago, Illinois.

REFERENCES: Brian W. Dippie, Charles M. Russell, Word Painter, Amon Carter Museum, Fort Worth, Texas, 1993, pp.275-276, 420.

Irving S. Cobb of Paducah, Kentucky, was already an American icon when he wrote a fan letter to Charles Russell on Febuary 23, 1919. "I'd rather meet you than almost any man in this country...America owes you a lot for putting down on canvas the life of the West that is going so fast." he said. As Russell had heard Cobb speak, read his stories and enjoyed his musings, he did not wait to become acquainted and responded with this letter on March 6th.

In 1925, Cobb took up Charlie's invitation to spend a summer on Lake McDonald. Though Cobb was in national demand as an after-dinner speaker, he concluded that nobody could rival Charlie as a storyteller. Cobb wrote, "He hunkered on his heels and let wisdom seep out of the squeezed corner of his lips like sugar dripping from a sugar tree." (Dippie 275)

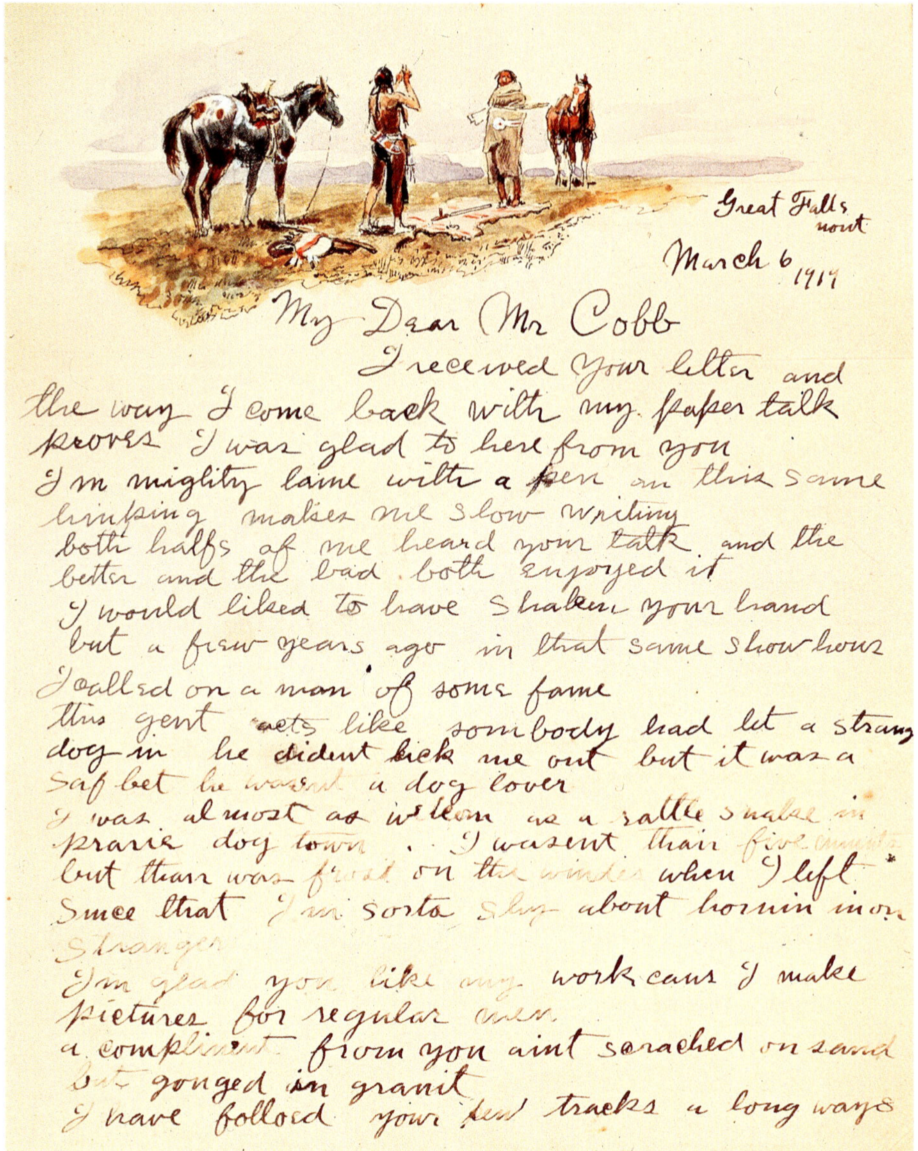

Great Falls
mont
March 6 1919

My Dear Mr Cobb
I received your letter and
the way I come back with my paper talk
proves I was glad to here from you
I'm mighty lame with a pen an this same
limping makes me slow writing
both halfs of me heard your talk and the
better and the bad both enjoyed it
I would liked to have shaken your hand
but a few years ago in that same show hous
I called on a man of some fame
this gent acts like sombody had let a strang
dog in he didnt kick me out but it was a
safe bet he wasent a dog lover
I was almost as welcom as a rattle snake in
prarie dog town. I wasent thair five minuts
but thair was frost on the windes when I left
Since that I'm sorta shy about hornin in on
strangers
I'm glad you like my work caus I make
pictures for regular men.
a compliment from you aint scratched on sand
but gonged in granit
I have folloed your pen tracks a long ways

2

and know you travle with your eyes and
ears open
this old world has picture painters and picture
writers
I think a good pen pusher has a brush man
skinned to the dew claws an your a skinner
I just red your talk on [illegible] and Im
with you all the way
C M R never was long on looks in the last
frew years Old dad Time has been trading me
tooth akes for teeth an hes mighty liberal
with rinkles but if I was allowed to cheat a
little I might hide some of the blemishes

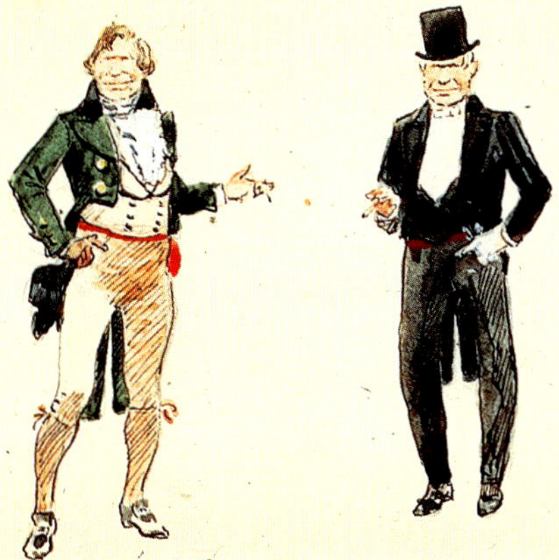

Maby I wouldent look aney better but its a sinch I couldent
look worse if they'd shed to Eves garments
I know ladyes that would stampeed town broke horses
but see them at a party and they loom up like
a Brazilian butterfly and hubby at his side looks
like a road ranch bed bug
if the shes wont play squar why cant the hes
deal off the bottom

The sketch on the frount page showes the meeting
of a pair of my red brothers
they may be strangers and not of the same
towng often they went wide of one another but
if one of them slid from his pony and spred
his robe this was the same as offering a stranger
a chair and ment lets talk if the pipe lay
with stem tords the one invited yust it ment
will you smoke the answer was generly yes
and when they had each taken a long drow
they both felt safe it is the wild mans oath
of friendship
So Mr Cobb the next time you come near
me my robe will be spread and my
pipe lay stem tords you
I forgot to say the man in the sketch that
offers the pipe is making the sign of friends

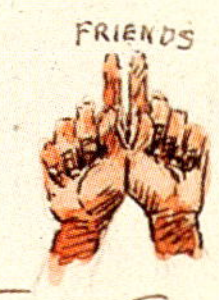

if you ever hit the
Glacier National Park in your drifting
you are welcome at
my camp my wife boy and I live
thair parte of the summer

with best whishes
your I cant say friend cause we
aint smoked yet
CM Russell

76. *P.T. Tucker/Friend Tommy,* {Patrick T. "Tommy" Tucker}, October 27, 1921
watercolor, ink on paper

PROVENANCE: Private Collection, California.

REFERENCES: Brian W. Dippie, Charles M. Russell, Word Painter, Amon Carter Museum, Fort Worth, Texas, 1993, pp. 318, 422.

Tommy Tucker and Charlie Russell had been acquainted since their days cowpunching in the Judith Basin. Years later, Tucker capitalized on their acquaintance in a series of stories about their rangeland escapdes, published in his memoirs Riding High Country (1933). One of Tucker's tales relays an incident that took place when he and Russell were working the Cottonwood Creek range and spotted a small of herd of buffalo in the distance. About twenty cowboys decided to round up the buffalo and mix them in with the cattle herd. Russell's vivid illustration recounts Tucker overtaking the herd after a two-mile chase. (Dippie 318)

C. M. RUSSELL

GREAT FALLS, MONTANA

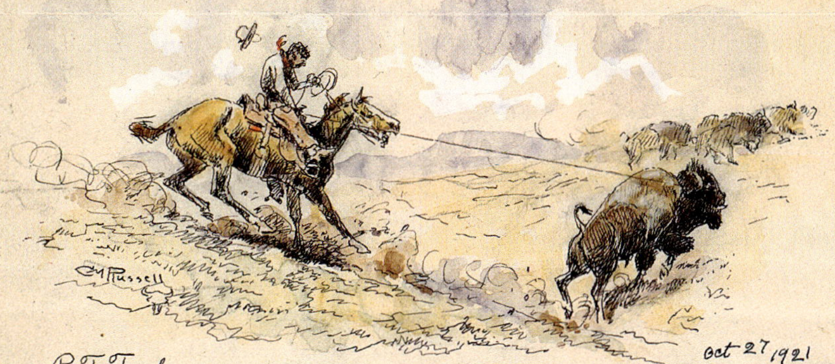

Oct 27 1921

P T Tucker

Friend Tommy I'm a long time answering your letter but that dont mean Iv forgotten you You daughter cam to see me and I was glad to meet her and I want to thank her for the photografs she sent among them was one of you and a bull that bull was some size but hed look puny compared to the one you droped your loop on thirty seven years ago. If I rember right he got one for foot through the loop and the hondue lay in frount of his hump and judging from the way he traveled you and Bunky wasent even a good rough lock he started for Texas like he didnt mean to make many stops but you and Bunky dident want to go that far so you through of your dallyes and made him a present of your raw hide Those were good old days Tom we were kids then the buffalo went long ago the wild cows we knew and the cow hosses have joined them and most of the cow punchers of our time have crossed the big devide we usto know every body but time has made us strangers but we got no licence to kick we got the cream let these com lattys have the skim milk If ever I get down on your range Il round you up and I want you to do the same

with best whishes to you and your big fambly from me and my small one

your friend CMRussell

77. *Letter to Frank Brown,* April 4, 1922 (one page with envelope postmarked April 4, 1923)
watercolor, ink on paper

PROVENANCE: Tucker Dorn; Private Collection, Colorado.

Charles Russell was one of the original cowboys. In April of 1922, Russell visited a recreation of the Wild West, by way of a movie set, to see his former lifestyle played out in a movie. In this letter to Frank Brown, he comments on how "thair are more two gun men here than the history of the west from north to south ever knew." On a studio trip, he saw the filming of a dance hall scene that made "Chicago Joes look like a Kindergarden." He joked that it would have been easier to get along with some of the West's toughest riders than "these hair-trigger moovie gunfighters."

C. M. RUSSELL
GREAT FALLS, MONTANA

SANTA BARBARA CALIF.
APR 4
1923

Frank Brown
Great Falls Meat Co
Great Falls
Montana

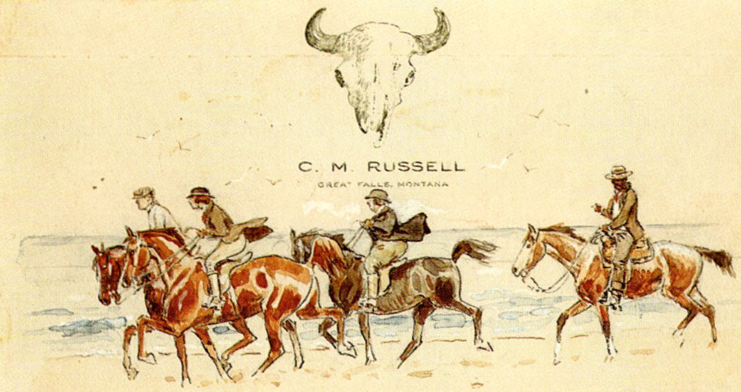

Apral 4 1922

Frank Brown

Friend Frank I receaved your letter and was glad to here from you. thair is not much to write about down here so Il make my letter mostly picture The sketch will show you some of the folks that pass my camp this kind ride the beaches of Calif Its hard to size up folks in this country but Im betting the he in the lead can get an ace of the bottom hes probably an Oil man from Wyoming or a high class burgelar from New York. The shes are wife and daughter of a well to do Bootleger from Kansas coming from that state of corse maws strong for dry barrel that she uses around the house and the size drink she takes would make Bill Rance grinde his teeth both the henna haired daughter and her maw smoke privetly in Kansas but wide open in Cal Maw aint riding caus she loves horses but her Dock told her it would remove leaf lard. the man in the drag cant be classed among the idle rich he can count his coin with out taking it out of his pocket socially he aint got much to say him nor the hoss under him dont savy much but Spanish. thair boath native sons Pedro maby thats his name dont know his fambly tree but its a safe bet his mother was a pyute and his dad maby a Spanish Gentelman who gathed his coin from the rode in the old Stage coach day but compared to the hold up gents here to day Pedros dad was in the kinder garden class but this party woulde be out of luck with out Pedro hes like a packer with a pack trane puts them on and takes them off if a pack slips hes thair to set it up and see that it stays his horse dont wast time pranceing but can run rings around his high stepping cousins

Frank Linderman and I tuck in a Rotery dinner they dident have custard pie and I was glad of it your shure spoilt that speaces of pastry for me They told us all about this City and how foolish a man was that wanted to live aneywhere elce but thairs quite a fiew foolish left and Im glad Im one of them we expect to start home about the first of May Frank Linderman and fambly who are our nabors leave in a fiew days

With best whishes to You and Yours
from the Russells

Your friend CM Russell

78. *Friend Frank*, {Frank B. Linderman}, April 24, 1924
watercolor, ink on paper

PROVENANCE: J.N. Bartfield Galleries, New York, New York

REFERENCE: Brian W. Dippie, Charles M. Russell, Word Painter, Amon Carter Museum, Fort Worth, Texas, 1993, p. 347, 423.

From 1920 on, the Russells spent much of their time in California, where Nancy was actively promoting Charlie's career. Though a thriving art community, Charlie was not accustomed to the hustle and bustle of city streets. In this charming letter to friend Frank, Russell joked about recuperating from an auto accident while in Los Angeles. Linderman had sent him a poem, "If I Were a Medicine-man," advocating a potion of buck-berries. Charlie relayed that the medicine verse had worked and filled Linderman in on his recent visit with Ed Borein in Santa Barbara. (Dippie 347)

April 24 1924

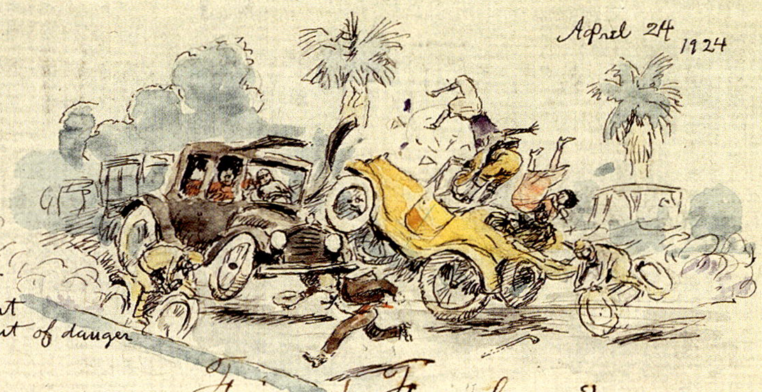

I have quit the Sticks but am not out of danger yet

Friend Frank I am
answering your many letters
because I did not answer them all
dont mean that I did not appreaeate them
but the pen to me is the same as a pick
it's work and I'm one of the men that
sweats when I write
the medicen virs you sent worked
I have shed the sticks
I am still a littel sprung in the nees
an I dont have to blow a horn to warn the trafick
a slice of hart from a friend some times
is better and always easier to take than the
branes of a docter
your medicon came from the hart and
wase sounitaps
the Doctors showed me the wagon roads but
my Friends cleared the trail for me

we went to Santa Barbra a few days ago
and saw the bunch the all sent regards to
you and yours
Borien has a fine doby house and to make it
look real Mexico he banght a burrow
but they had to git rid of him caus he wouldent
stay in one place only long enough to grase off
a flower bed and when he got the hole nabor
hood looking like an over stocked sheep range
he starts standing on his hind legs triming
the clothe lines union suits and lingerie
was good pickings but he balked on corsits

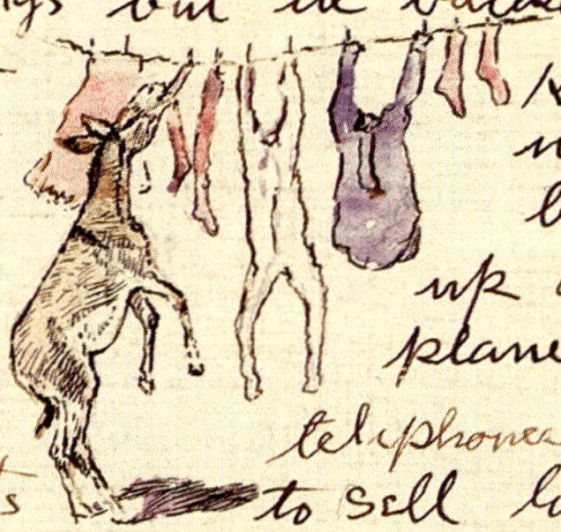

the ladys dident kick much
caus they dont use many
clothes these days but the lies of the
naborhood put up a rore that
could be herd plane at San Pedro
then a kid telephones wantin to
know if Ed wants to sell long ears
and Eward sells for reasonable prices
well Frank as I'm out of paper talk I'l
close with best whishes to you and yours
the same gose to all friends

your friend C M Russell

PS I told Ed if hed send a burrow
hide to Kalispell that Harry Stanford would
build him a burrow that would stay in
one place regards to Harry

Adress 1323 3rd av Los Angeles Cal

79. *Friend Harry,* {Harry Stanford} May 8, 1925
watercolor, ink on paper
8 1/2 x 11 inches

PROVENANCE: Harry Stanford, Kalispell, Montana; Private Collection, Denver, Colorado; Private Collection, New York.

REFERENCES: Good Medicine, The Illustrated Letters of Charles M. Russell with Introduction by Will Rogers and Biographical note by Nancy Russell, Doubleday, Doran & Company, Inc., Garden City, New York, 1929, p. 53.

Harry P. Stanford, a native of Halifax, Nova Scotia, arrived in Fort Benton by steamboat in 1879 and ended up in Kalispell, Montana in 1891. There he served as the first chief of police, but made his living as a taxidermist –the best in Montana, according to Russell. As a taxidermist, history buff, and authority on Indian lore, Stanford and Russell shared much in common. This letter, a thank-you for an Indian headdress Russell received, was also an excuse to reminisce about the old days "when the only real American wore fashions stolen from the animals and the birds he knew."

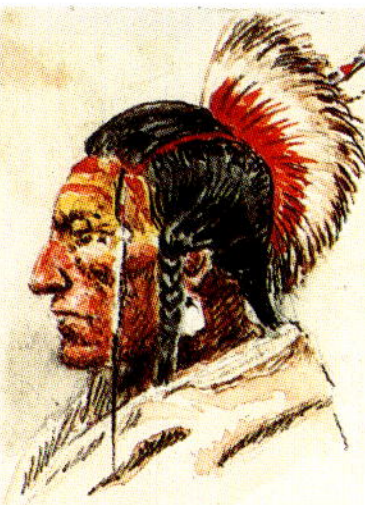

C. M. RUSSELL
GREAT FALLS, MONTANA

May 8 1925

Friend Harry

I'm a long time thanking you for the Head dress you sent. but I never was fast an old Dad time aint changed my gate

the Head dress is a good one it is certanly a wild mans Crest.

I think our red brother stole his fashion from animals and birds he knew he saw the Sage Cock dance and spred his tail fethers thats where Mr Injun got his dance bussel

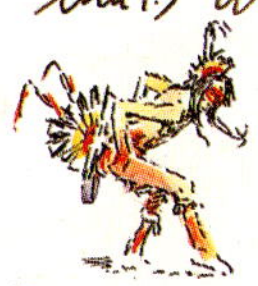

he liked the war bonnet that the Canadian Jay and the King Fisher wore so he made himself one.

but the only real American dont use much stile any more Unkle Sam lets him play Injun once a year and he dances under the flag that made a farmer out of him

once nature gave him everything he wanted. now the agent gives him bib overalls hooks his hands around plow handles and tell him its a good thing push it along

maby it is but thair having a hell of a time

C. M. RUSSELL
GREAT FALLS, MONTANA

prooving it. to people who since time began never don aney thing harder than pull a bow string ore push a shining knife

nature was not always kind to these people but she never lied to them

the red Skined wilde men are all moste gone now Harry but if fine clothes and fancy ones means Saviges we got lots of sheones now and moste of them set traps for men

thanking you again for the head dress

good medicine to you and yours

Your friend Ah wah Cous

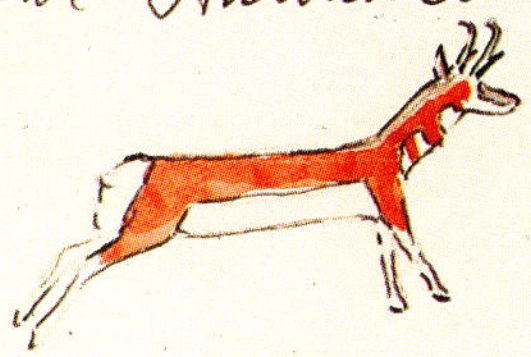

80. *Friend Borg,* {Carl Borg}, August 29, 1925
watercolor, ink on paper

PROVENANCE: Earl C. Adams Collection; Collection of Wiley T. Buchanan III.

EXHIBITIONS: In "The West Remembered: Artists and Images 1837-1973", mention is made of the letter, which is listed as lot #111. The works listed were from the collection of Earl Adams. The catalogue is dated June 16-September 15, 1973.

REFERENCES: Brian W. Dippie, Charles M. Russell, Word Painter, Amon Carter Museum, Fort Worth, Texas, 1993, pp. 379, 424.

Carl Oscar Borg was a renowned landscape painter who also specialized in portrayals of Navajo and Hopi life. He and Russell shared many mutual friends, such as Charles F. Lummis, Edward Borein, and Frank Bird Linderman. In this letter, Russell quips about being "Dr. Russell," as the University of Montana had just awarded him an honorary Doctor of Laws degree for the "greatest historic accomplishment in an artistic way of any person in the state." This was only the fourth awarded in history, and Russell was moved by the distinction. He also jokes about the latest ladies fashions. "Short hair and britches lookes good on some ladyes but sometimes its hard telling Ma from Paw." His satiric sense of humor was evident in all his letters and made them all the more enjoyable to his friends.

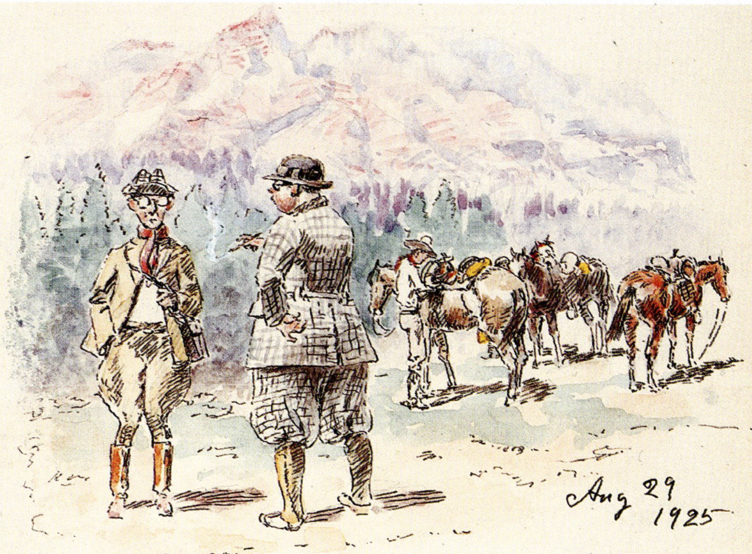

Aug 29 1925

Carl Borg

Friend Borg

Im a long time saying so but I got your letter and was glad to here from you
were still camped in the big hills
the Mountians still ware the same old clothes
but Humans dont
Short hair and britches looks good on some ladyes
but some times its hard telling Ma from Paw
the above sketch will show what I mean
I herd the one on the left call the meaty one Violet they say thair are He and She flowers
maby this is a he one
but if this is a Violet Im a Forget me not
shes almost as Lady like as Ed Borinz
I asked the Guide what the small one was
he said he dident know but it acted scart like it belonged to Violet
well Borg how is every body in the oringe belt
it was tough on the Borinzs and Hoffmans that Shake up but I hope it wasent as bad as we herd
I aint worring about Ed if he dont run out of Bull Durham hes all right
Mrs Leighton and her son ~~left~~ here last night they all spent several month here and seemed to enjoy it Mr Leighton fishing and his wife ~~took~~ made lots of good pictures
I wish you all would come up sometime
I think the Leightons are coming next summer
they are nice people and here in the mountians is where you find out
well Borg thair is no news here so I will close
with best wishes to every body
incuden your self and Wife
your friend CM Russell

My Wife sends the Same

if you ever get sick you know Im
Dr Russell

81. Merry Christmas, Mrs. C.A. Macrum, 1904 (illustrated envelope)
watercolor, ink on paper
11 x 14 inches

PROVENANCE: Harry and Connie Lockwood, Midwestern Galleries, Cincinnati, Ohio.

82. Indian Head, Tell'Um
watercolor, ink on paper
4 x 5 inches

PROVENANCE: Private Collection, Oklahoma.

REFERENCES: Brian W. Dippie, Paper Talk: Illustrated Letters of Charles M. Russell, Amon Carter Museum, Fort Worth, Texas, 1962, p. 76; Karl Yost and Frederic Renner, A Bibliography of the Published Works of Charles M. Russell, University of Nebraska Press, Lincoln, NB, 1971, pp. 36, 114.

Russell, though not a particularly religious man, often used Christmas as an excuse to celebrate his valued friendships. Many received individualized poems, and illustrated cards such as this Indian head caricature that was sent to Maynard Dixon. Sometimes he even illustrated the envelopes as in Merry Christmas, Mrs. Macrum. This envelope is one of the few examples of Nancy Russell's artistry, represented in the portait of her husband on the left.

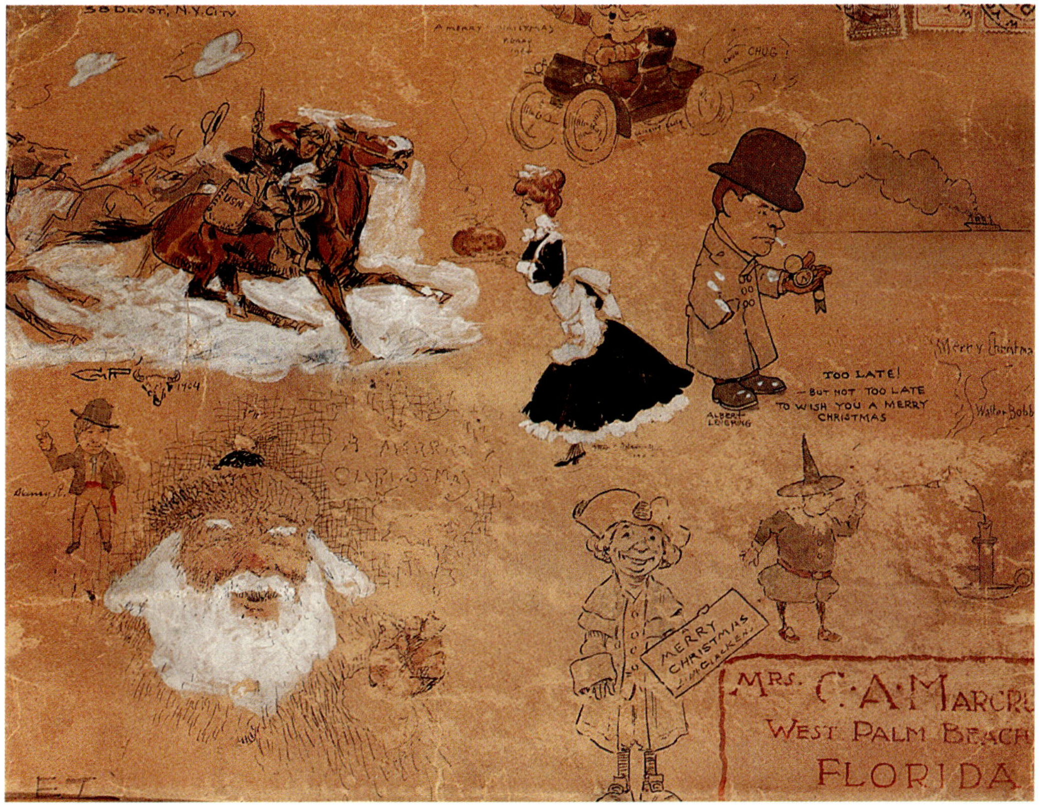
TOO LATE!
—BUT NOT TOO LATE
TO WISH YOU A MERRY
CHRISTMAS
MERRY
CHRISTMAS
FLORIDA

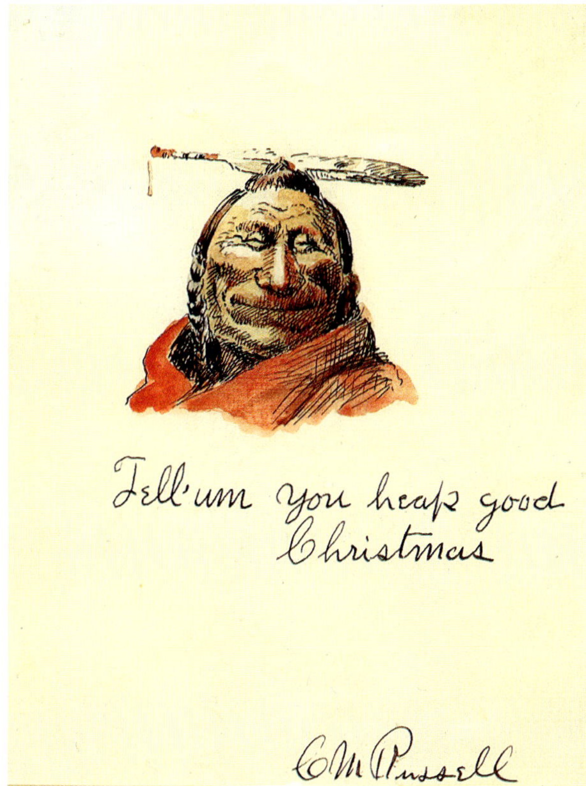
Tell'um you heap good
Christmas
CM Russell

83. New Years Eve Card
watercolor, ink on paper
4 x 11 inches

PROVENANCE: Private Collection, Oklahoma.

84. Happy New Year, 1923
watercolor, ink on paper
4 x 11 3/4 inches

PROVENANCE: Private Collection, Montana; Private Collection, New Mexico.

Early in Russell's career, he created individualized cards for his closest friends. By 1923, this practice became impossible as his number of friends grew over the years. One of Russell's favorite holiday illustrations was that of a lone cowboy bearing a bottle of whiskey, perhaps as a gift. The cowboy portrayed was often in Russell's likeness even though he no longer drank by the time they were produced.

If hosses were health my friend
And the gold of the Mountians
My poke
Id loosen the string and let the
bares down
Youd never be sick or broke

Happy New Year
to you and yours
from the Russells

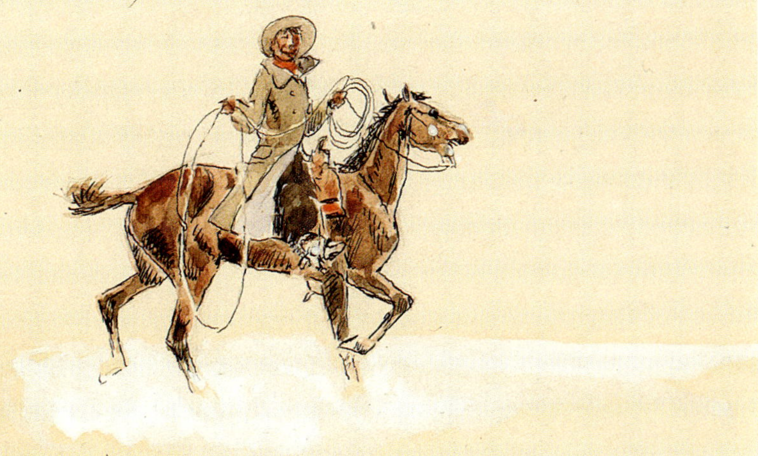

Hers hoping old sickness dont locate
your camp
and health rides herd on you
May Dad Time be slow a snuffing
your lamp
and your trail be smooth plum
through

Happy New Year
to you an yours
from the Russells

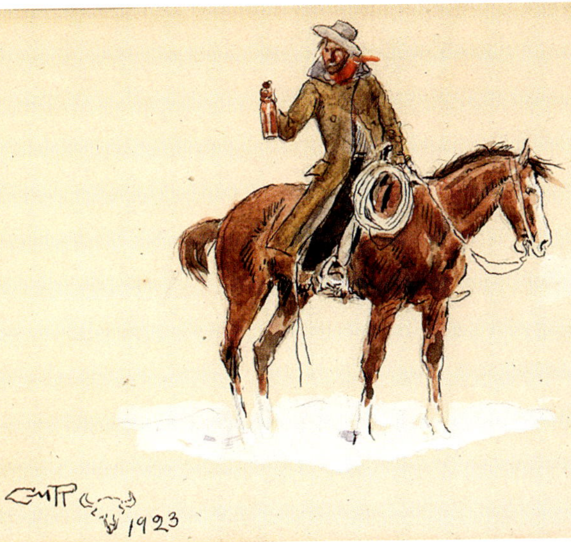

The Illustrations

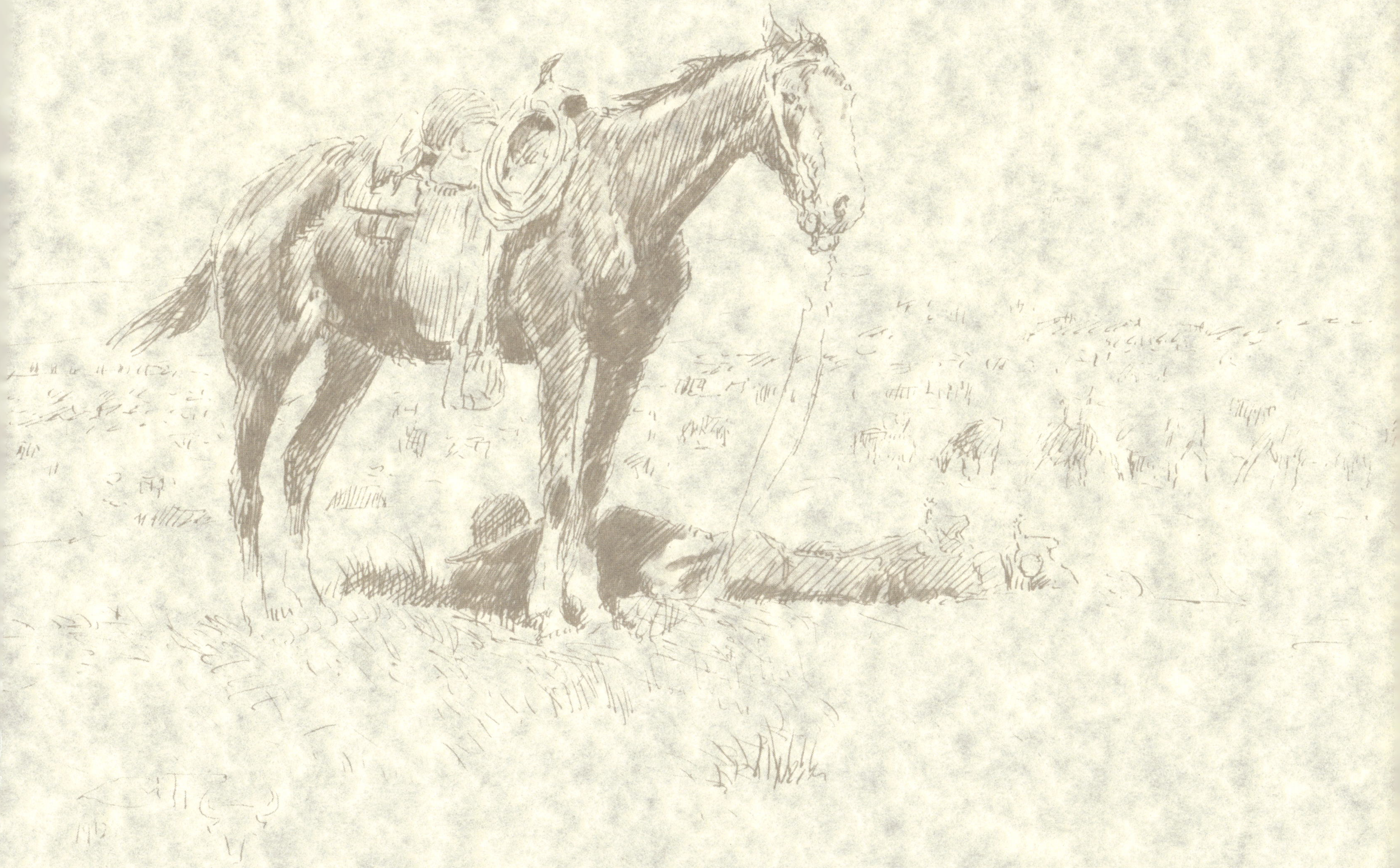

In the early part of the twentieth century, the country began to reminisce nostagically about the exciting era just past. In response, magazines clamored for more Western material and illustrators, especially since Frederic Remington eschewed the field to focus on the aesthetic merits of his painting alone. For Charlie Russell, "the cowboy artist," a career in illustration was a natural progression. His years on the range, sketching in his spare time, trained him in the swift notation of the moment which lay at the heart of Western life.

As a prolific illustrator, Russell published four of his own illustrated books, with two others appearing posthumously. His first book, Studies of Western Life, which appeared in 1890, was a portfolio reproducing twelve of his earliest oil paintings. His fourth book, More Rawhides, published the year before his death, was a collection of short stories illustrated with thirty-eight masterful line drawings like *Long George Bulldogging a Steer* (plate #91). Between these dates, Russell illustrated approximately fifty books by other authors and nearly twice that number of articles in many popular magazines such as The American, The Artist, Fine Arts Journal, Leslie's Weekly, McClure's, Scribner's and World's Work. Noted authors Bret Harte, Emerson Hough, and Theodore Roosevelt made use of Russell's illustratations and valued the candor and accuracy of his imagery. Ultimately, it was Russell's nationally distrubuted commercial art that accounted for his enormous popularity and success as the chronicler of the American west. While the following examples are by no means a comprehensive representation of the artist's illustrations, they form a select group of his work in the field.

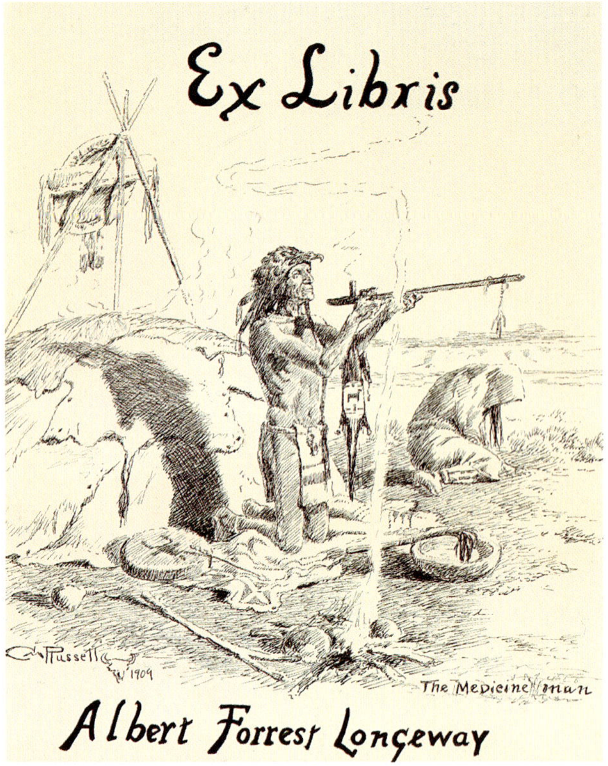

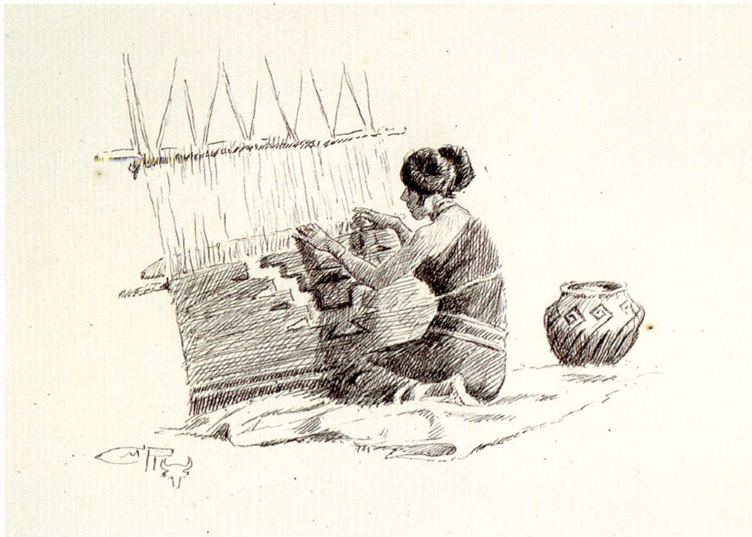

85. *Medicine Man #3*, 1909
pen and ink on paper
13 1/2 x 19 1/2 inches
signed and dated lower left: CM Russell/ skull cipher/1909
Bookplate for Albert Forrest Longeway

PROVENANCE: Albert Forrest Longeway, Great Falls, Montana; Robert Fry, Cincinnati, Ohio.

REFERENCES: Karl Yost and Frederic Renner, A Bibliography of Published Works by Charles M. Russell, University of Nebraska Press, Lincoln, Nebraska, 1971, p. 230.

86. *In the Land of the Navajos,* 1901
pen and ink on paper
signed lower left: CMR/skull cipher
Bookplate for Fifteen Thousand Miles By Stage by Carrie Adell Strahorn, G.P. Putnam's Sons, New York, Publishers. 1911.

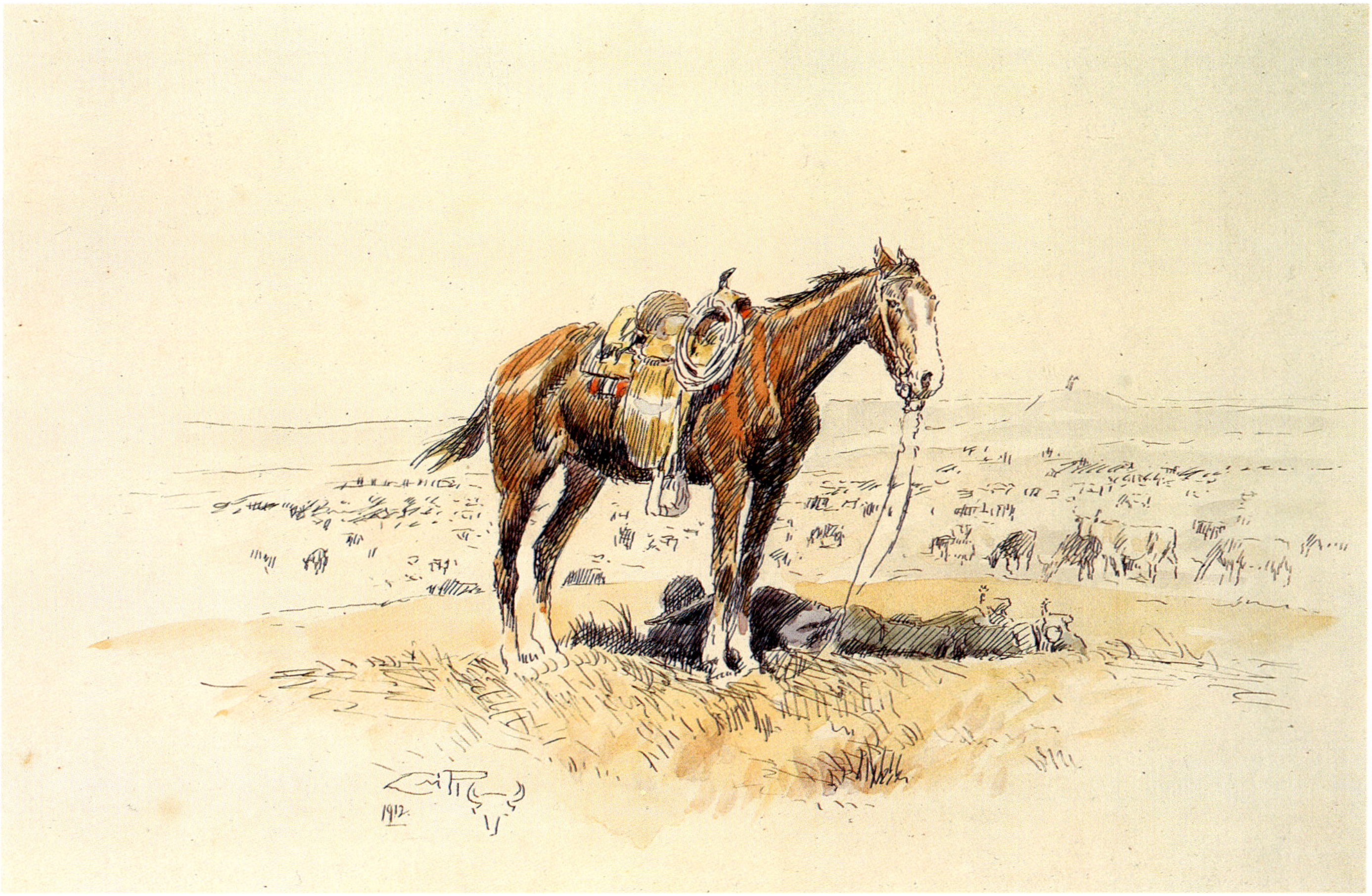

87. *On Day Herd*, 1912
watercolor, ink on paper
9 1/2 x 14 inches
Inscriptions: Chas M. Russell to E. I. Holland, Christmas 1912

PROVENANCE: The Artist; E. I. Holland, Los Angeles, California; to (his daughter) Virginia Holland Wilcox, California; {Gerald Peters Gallery, Santa Fe, New Mexico}; Private Collection, New Mexico.

REFERENCES: The Virginian, Owen Wistler, MacMillan Co., New York, 1911, special limited edition, p. 473.

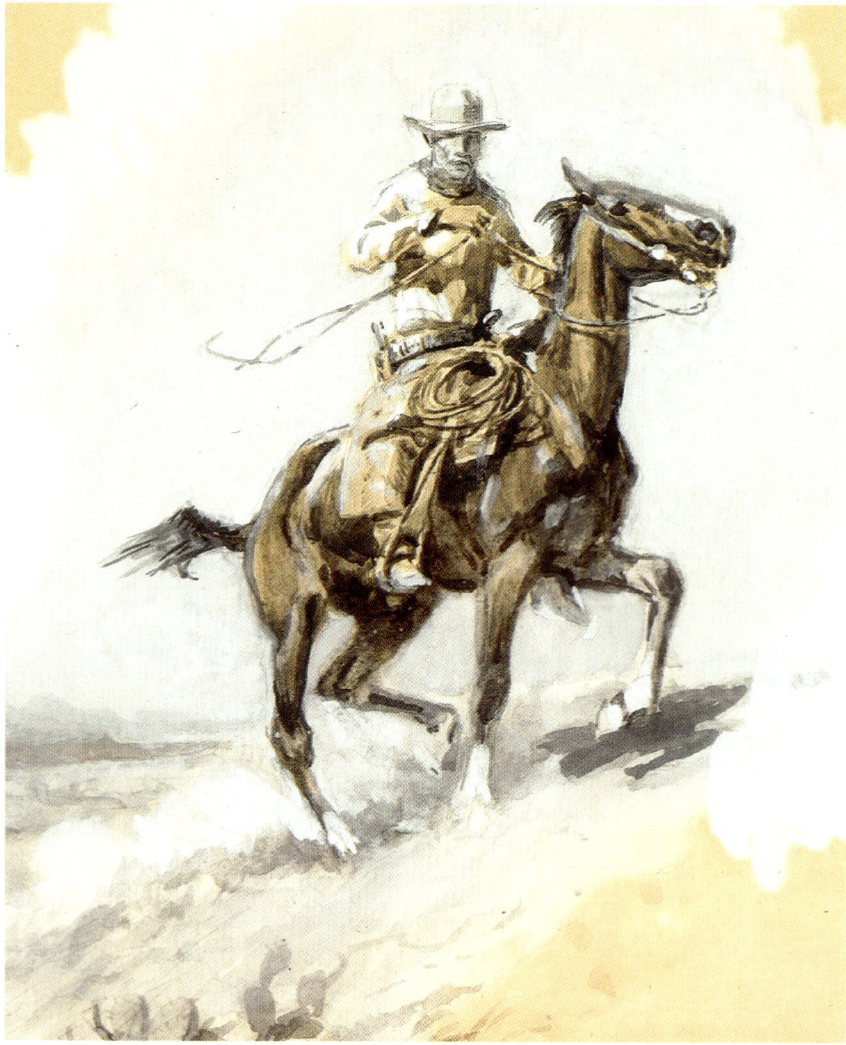

88. *Cowboy on Horse*, 1917
watercolor on paper
10 x 8 inches
signed lower right: CM Russell
dated upper right: July 12, 1917

PROVENANCE: The Artist to Will Rogers, Santa Monica, California; Jimmy Rogers (son of Will Rogers); Private Collection, Oklahoma.

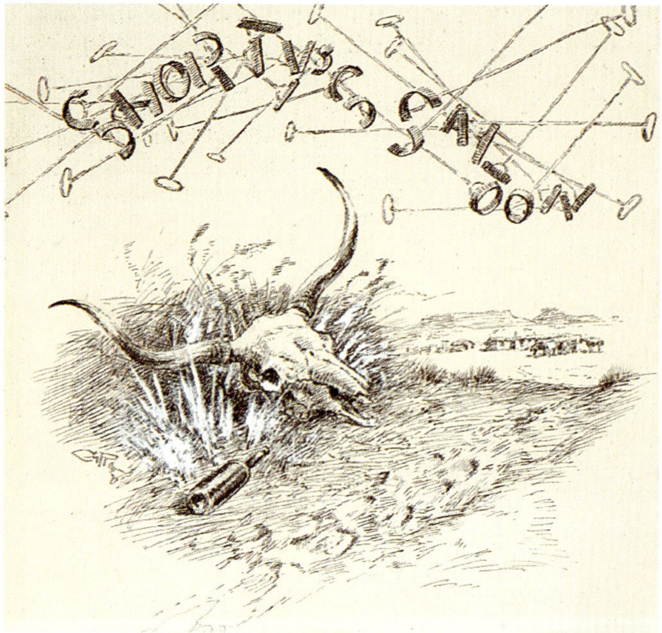

89. *Shorty's Saloon-Branding Irons*
ink on paper
7 1/2 x 7 1/2 inches
signed lower left: CMR

PROVENANCE: The Artist to Nancy Russell; Hammer Brothers, New York, New York; The Montana Historical Society, Helena, Montana; The Bruce H. Norris Estate; The Connie Jo Lockwood Collection, Cincinnati, Ohio.

REFERENCES: Horsefeathers by Johnny Ritch, Illustrated by Charles M. Russell, Helena, Montana, copyright 1940; Free Grass to Fences: The Montana Cattle Range Story, by Robert Fletcher, Karl Yost and Frederic Renner, Illusrtations by Charles M. Russell; A Bibliography of the Published Works of Charles M. Russell, University of Nebraska Press, Lincoln, Nebraska, 1971, pp. 26, 248, 255.

90. *Cowboy Wins*, c. 1918
ink on paper
5 1/2 x 7 inches
signed lower left: CMR/ skull cipher

PROVENANCE: Bartfield Galleries, New York; Harry and Connie Lockwood, Midestern Galleries, Cincinnatti, Ohio.

REFERENCES: Montana Newspaper Association inserts, "Historical Recollections by Rawhide Rawlins," written and illustrated by Charles M. Russell, March 4, 1918 issue; Karl Yost and Frederic Renner, A Bibliography of Published Works by Charles M. Russell, University of Nebraska Press, Lincoln, Nebraska, 1971, p.125.

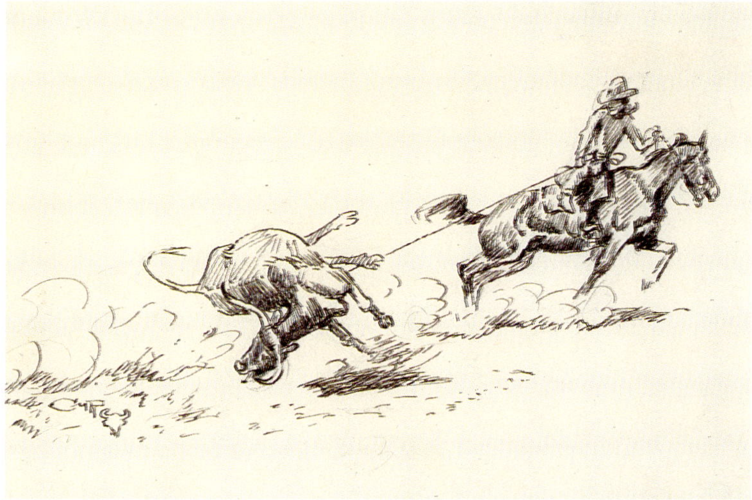

91. *Long George Bulldogging a Steer*, c. 1919
ink on paper
5 x 7 1/2 inches
signed lower left: CMR/ skull cipher

PROVENANCE: Bartfield Gallery, New York; Harry and Connie Lockwood's Midwestern Galleries, Cincinnatti, Ohio.

REFERENCES: The Butte Miner, November 23, 1919 issue; More Rawhides, by Charles M. Russell, 1925, pg 42; Karl Yost and Frederic Renner, A Bibliography of the Published Works of Charles M. Russell, University of Nebraska Press, Lincoln, Nebraska, 1971, pp. 20, 85, 112, 127.

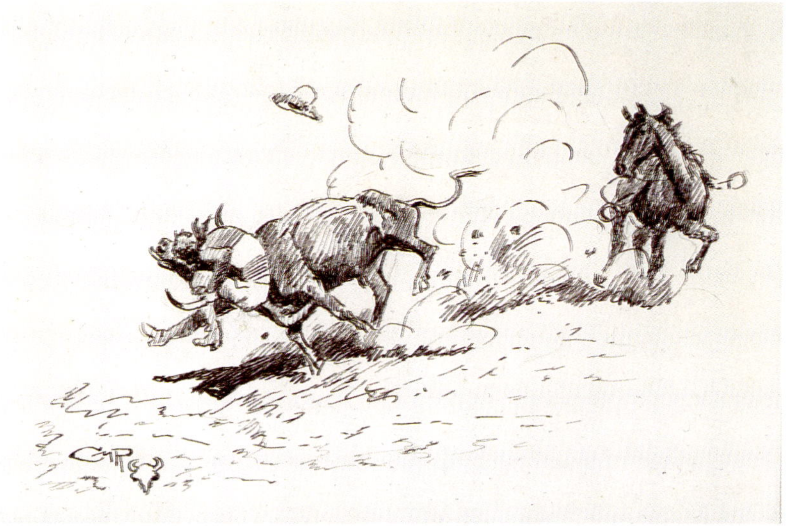

92. *The Oregon Trail* *Illustrations*
Parkman, Francis
Boston, 1923
Plates and text illustrations by Frederic Remington with 11 original watercolor drawings by Charles M. Russell at the begining and the end of some chapters.

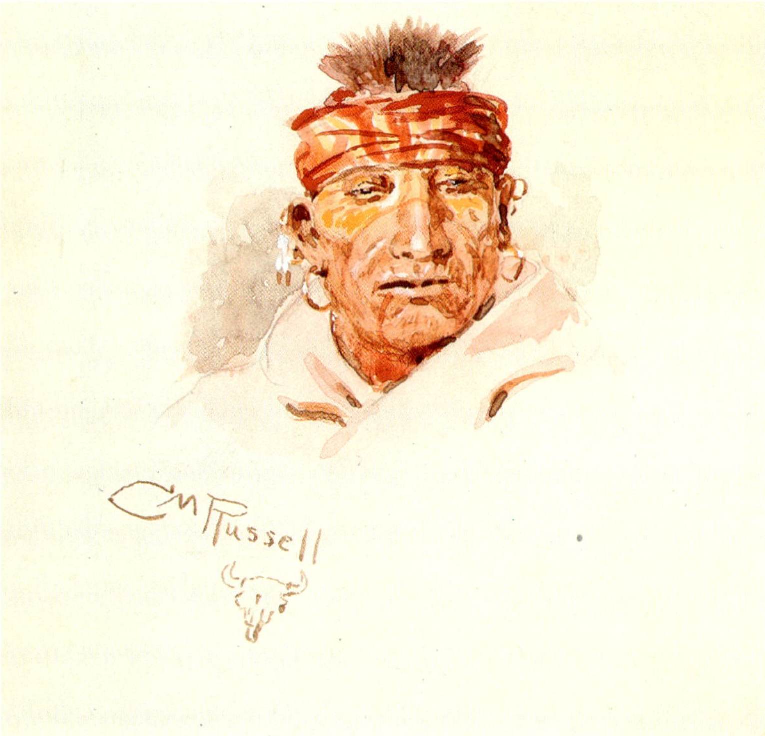

A. Indian Head With Yellow and Red Headband
watercolor
5 x 5 inches

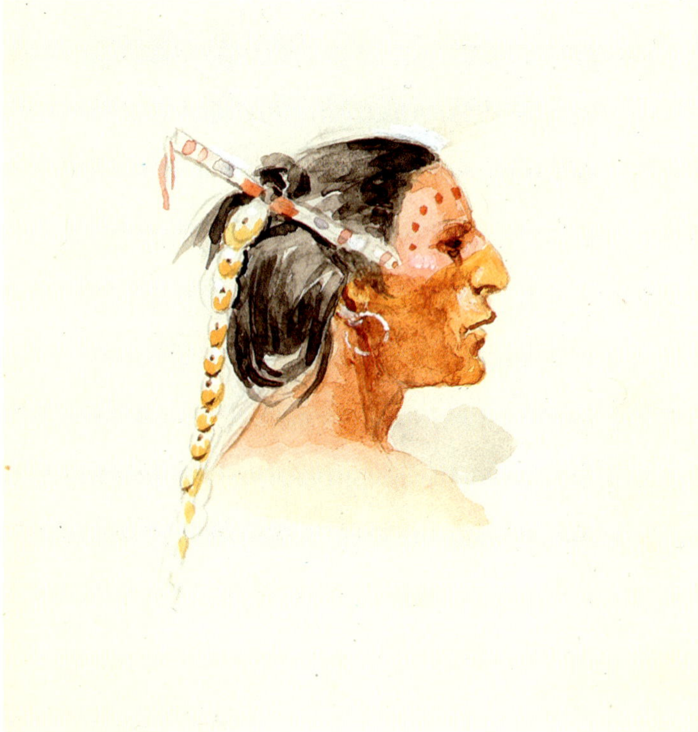

B. Indian Head, Profile
watercolor and gouache
6 x 5 inches

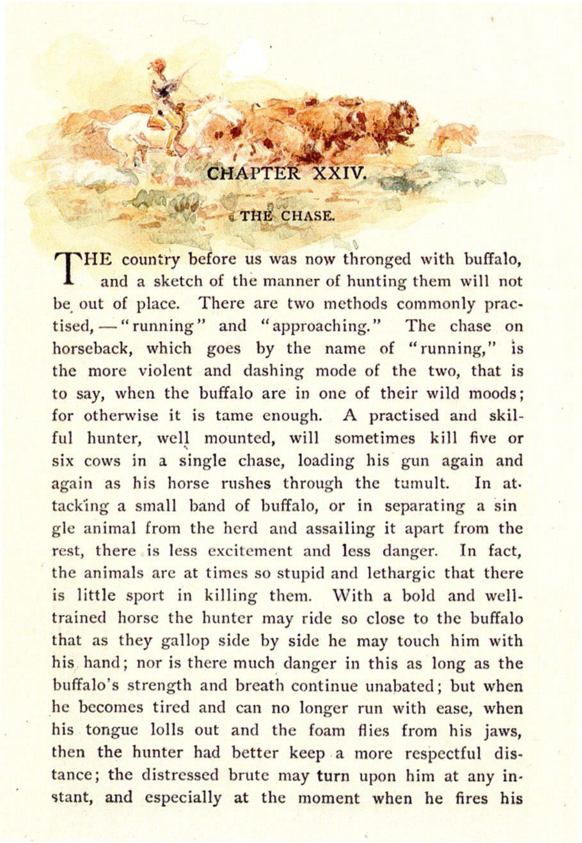

CHAPTER XXIV.

THE CHASE.

THE country before us was now thronged with buffalo, and a sketch of the manner of hunting them will not be out of place. There are two methods commonly practised, — "running" and "approaching." The chase on horseback, which goes by the name of "running," is the more violent and dashing mode of the two, that is to say, when the buffalo are in one of their wild moods; for otherwise it is tame enough. A practised and skilful hunter, well mounted, will sometimes kill five or six cows in a single chase, loading his gun again and again as his horse rushes through the tumult. In attacking a small band of buffalo, or in separating a single animal from the herd and assailing it apart from the rest, there is less excitement and less danger. In fact, the animals are at times so stupid and lethargic that there is little sport in killing them. With a bold and well-trained horse the hunter may ride so close to the buffalo that as they gallop side by side he may touch him with his hand; nor is there much danger in this as long as the buffalo's strength and breath continue unabated; but when he becomes tired and can no longer run with ease, when his tongue lolls out and the foam flies from his jaws, then the hunter had better keep a more respectful distance; the distressed brute may turn upon him at any instant, and especially at the moment when he fires his

C. The Chase, watercolor and gouache, 8 x 5 inches

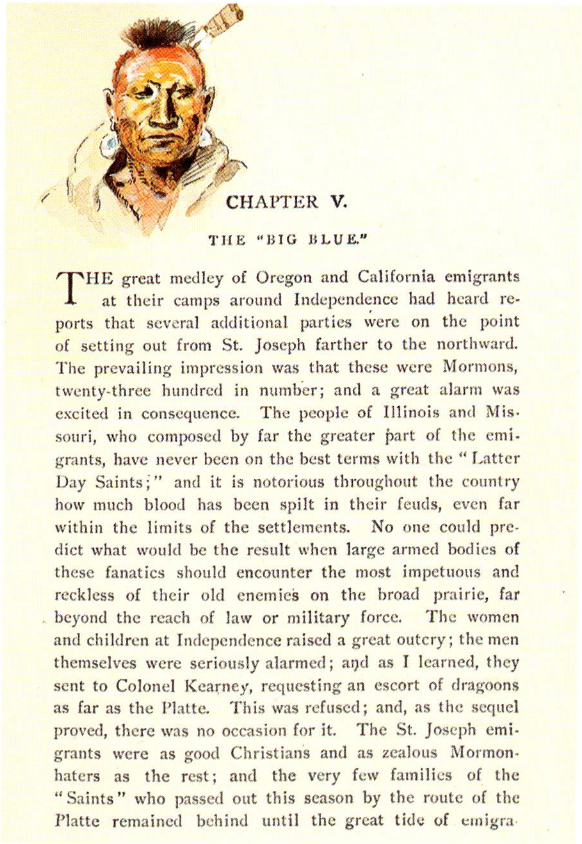

CHAPTER V.

THE "BIG BLUE."

THE great medley of Oregon and California emigrants at their camps around Independence had heard reports that several additional parties were on the point of setting out from St. Joseph farther to the northward. The prevailing impression was that these were Mormons, twenty-three hundred in number; and a great alarm was excited in consequence. The people of Illinois and Missouri, who composed by far the greater part of the emigrants, have never been on the best terms with the "Latter Day Saints;" and it is notorious throughout the country how much blood has been spilt in their feuds, even far within the limits of the settlements. No one could predict what would be the result when large armed bodies of these fanatics should encounter the most impetuous and reckless of their old enemies on the broad prairie, far beyond the reach of law or military force. The women and children at Independence raised a great outcry; the men themselves were seriously alarmed; and as I learned, they sent to Colonel Kearney, requesting an escort of dragoons as far as the Platte. This was refused; and, as the sequel proved, there was no occasion for it. The St. Joseph emigrants were as good Christians and as zealous Mormon-haters as the rest; and the very few families of the "Saints" who passed out this season by the route of the Platte remained behind until the great tide of emigra-

D. The Big Blue, watercolor and gouache, 8 x 5 inches

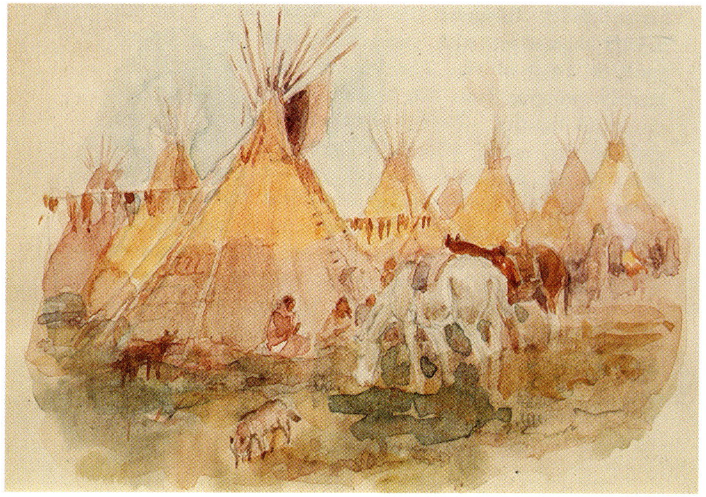

E. Plains Indian Camp, watercolor, 4 x 5 1/2 inches